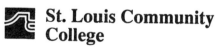

St. Louis Community College

Forest Park
Florissant Valley
Meramec

Instructional Resources
St. Louis, Missouri

HOPI DWELLINGS

Catherine M. Cameron

HOPI DWELLINGS

Architectural Change at Orayvi

The University of Arizona Press / Tucson

The University of Arizona Press
© 1999 The Arizona Board of Regents
First printing
All rights reserved
⊗ This book is printed on acid-free, archival-quality paper.
Manufactured in the United States of America

04 03 02 01 00 99   6 5 4 3 2 1

Library of Congress Cataloging-in-Publication Data
Cameron, Catherine M.
Hopi dwellings : architectural change at Orayvi / Catherine M. Cameron.
p. cm.
Includes bibliographical references and index.
ISBN 0-8165-1781-9 (cloth : alk. paper)
1. Hopi architecture—Arizona—Oraibi.   2. Hopi Indians—
Dwellings—Arizona—Oraibi.   3. Vernacular architecture—
Arizona—Oraibi.   4. Pueblos—Arizona—Oraibi.
5. Oraibi (Ariz.)—History.   6. Oraibi (Ariz.)—Social life
and customs.   I. Title.
E99.H7 C36   1999
720'.979135—dc21
98-40105
CIP

British Library Cataloguing-in-Publication Data
A catalogue record for this book is available from the British Library.

Publication of this book is made possible in part by the proceeds of a
permanent endowment created with the assistance of a Challenge
Grant from the National Endowment for the Humanities, a federal
agency.

For Mary Flynn Cameron

Contents

List of Figures   ix

List of Tables   xi

Acknowledgments   xiii

1 Archaeology and Pueblo Architecture   3

2 The Construction and Use-Life of Pueblo Structures   21

3 History, Data, and Methods   35

4 The Orayvi House and Household   47

5 Orayvi Architectural Dynamics, 1871–1901   57

6 Orayvi after the Split   82

7 Using Orayvi to Interpret the Past   103

Appendix 1. Summary of Household Information and Architectural Change   115

Appendix 2. List of Photographs Collected for the Orayvi Study   121

Appendix 3. Summary of Architectural Change to Rooms, 1871–1901   135

Appendix 4. Summary of Architectural Change to Rooms after 1906   138

Notes   143

References   145

Index   155

Figures

1.1   The northern Southwest.   5

1.2   The Hopi Mesas in northeastern Arizona.   6

1.3   A unit pueblo (Yellowjacket site, Colorado).   8

1.4   Pueblo Bonito, a Great House in Chaco Canyon.   9

1.5   Arroyo Hondo Pueblo, Component 1.   11

2.1   The Main Plaza at Orayvi, 1879.   22

2.2   Cross section of an Orayvi house.   23

2.3   Diagram of the use-life of vernacular buildings.   26

3.1   Mindeleff's 1887 map of Orayvi.   40

3.2   Titiev's map of Orayvi, 1900.   42

5.1   Room 551 in use, 1879; also terraces behind Roomblock 4.   59

5.2   Room 551 abandoned, 1901.   60

5.3   Room 398 intact.   61

5.4   Room 398 dismantled.   62

5.5   Building material stacked for future use.   63

5.6   Room 360 in 1896 before it was rebuilt.   64

5.7   Room 360 being rebuilt in 1901.   65

5.8   Women rebuilding a wall of Room 360.   66

5.9   Room 360 after it was rebuilt.   67

5.10   Roomblock E/F, constructed between 1887 and 1895.   68

5.11   Rooms 422 and 423 before they were combined into one room.   72

5.12   Rooms 422 and 423 after they were combined into one room.   73

5.13   An unknown roomblock at Orayvi in 1887.   78

5.14   A *tupu'bi*, a cooking and/or storage room.   80

6.1   Map of Orayvi showing the faction of the female head of household.   85

6.2   Aerial view of Orayvi, 1933.   91

6.3   Orayvi houses occupied, abandoned, or dismantled, 1902–1912.   93

6.4   Orayvi houses occupied, abandoned, or had been dismantled, 1913–1925.   94

6.5   Roomblock 12 showing occupied and abandoned houses.   96

6.6   Orayvi houses occupied, abandoned, or had been dismantled, 1926–1937.   97

6.7   Aerial view of Orayvi, 1948.   100

6.8   Orayvi houses occupied, abandoned, or had been dismantled 1938–1948.   101

7.1   Arroyo Hondo, Component 2.   108

7.2   The technique of "ladder construction."   110

7.3   Roomblocks 5 and 6 at Arroyo Hondo, showing uniformity of room sizes.   111

Tables

3.1   Time Periods Used in the Analysis   46

4.1   Size and Width of Houses at Orayvi, by Story   49

4.2   Size of Rooms, Houses, and Households at Orayvi   50

4.3   Rooms and Roofed Area of Pueblos of the Historic Period   51

4.4   Variation in House Size for Households of Different Types at Orayvi, 1900   54

5.1   Architectural Change at Orayvi, by Roomblock, Using Photograph Analysis   58

5.2   Doors Observed for Rooms in Photographs, 1871–1901   69

5.3   Architectural Change by Story, 1871–1901   70

5.4   Rooms Combined during Rebuilding, before 1901   71

5.5   Identification of New Rooms and New Houses Observed in Photographs, by Roomblock   74

5.6   Population Estimates for Orayvi, 1540–1900.   75

5.7   Architectural Change to *Tupu'bi*   81

6.1   Residence Location at Orayvi and Post-split Village Residence   86

6.2   Summary of Architectural Change for Rooms and Houses, 1902–1948   89

6.3   Abandoned and Dismantled Rooms in Occupied Houses, by Story, Based on Ground Photographs   90

6.4   Rooms Combined during Rebuilding, 1902–1937   92

Acknowledgments

My thanks go first to the Hopi people who have permitted anthropological study of their towns for more than a hundred years. The rest of the world has gained immeasurably because of their tolerance and assistance. Thanks especially to Leigh Jenkins of the Hopi Cultural Preservation Office who expressed an early interest in this study. Thanks also to Eugene Sekaquaptewa who facilitated my visits to Orayvi.

The study began almost a decade ago when I was a graduate student at the University of Arizona. In developing the study, I received wise counsel and guidance from a number of scholars in the large, friendly anthropological community in Tucson, especially E. Charles Adams, Richard Ahlstrom, Jeffrey S. Dean, Carol Kramer, Jerrold Levy, William Longacre, Barbara Pepper, J. Jefferson Reid, William Robinson, Michael B. Schiffer, and Emory Sekaquaptewa. Special thanks are due to Mike Schiffer, who chaired my dissertation committee and helped me form the study. Also to Jerrold Levy, who very generously offered me access to data from his study of Orayvi social structure, with many perceptive suggestions about their use that were critical to the study. Jeff Reid's early studies of the growth and development of settlements were also an inspiration.

Many reviewers helped improve the volume. Most recently Barbara Mills and an anonymous reviewer provided careful comments and suggestions that were extremely helpful in revising the manuscript for publication. Comments on early drafts were provided by Carol Cameron, Carol Gifford, Steve Lekson, Margaret Nelson, John Stein, Peter Whiteley, Richard Wilshusen, and other anonymous reviewers. The earliest chapters received meticulous attention from the University of Arizona's Department of Anthropology Writers Group (the DAWG): Kelley Hays, Laura Levi, Jonathan Mabry, Barbara Montgomery, Nieves Zedeño, Barbara Roth, James Skibo, Miriam Stark, Christine Szuter, Masa Tani, John Welch, and Lisa Young—a remarkable set of colleagues and friends. Dennis Marshall provided a final, skilled edit.

Archivists from numerous libraries, museums, and other institutions helped me gather photographs of Orayvi that were central to the study (these institutions are listed in appendix 1). Their aid is much appreciated. At the Smithsonian Institution, Karen Dohm procured copies of Victor Mindeleff's original field maps for me. Our parallel interests in Puebloan architecture have meant that Dohm's work is a continuing source of stimulation. Both Lee Horne and Carol Kramer shared important knowledge about the vernacular architecture of the Near East—similar in many ways to Puebloan construction—and were tremendously encouraging on this and related projects during the last decade. At the School of American Research in Santa Fe, Douglas Schwartz introduced me to the data from Arroyo Hondo pueblo and to the archeology of the northern Rio Grande. Skillful drafting expertise was provided by Barbara Montgomery, who produced figures 1.2, 2.3, 3.1, 3.2, 6.1, 6.4, 6.5, 6.7, and 6.9, and by Bill Semann, who produced figures 1.1, 2.2, 7.2, and 7.3.

Abundant thanks to Christine Szuter of the University of Arizona Press for her patience during the long process of revising the manuscript. It would certainly not have been completed without her cheerful and persistent encouragement.

The research was partly funded by the National Science Foundation (NSF #BNS-86-46597 and #BNS-88-13797), the Phillips Fund of the American Philosophical Society, and by the University of Arizona. A one-semester leave from teaching at the University of Colorado allowed me to make final revisions.

HOPI DWELLINGS

1 / Archaeology and Pueblo Architecture

By the late afternoon of September 7, 1906, the two sides found themselves facing each other on the level ground just outside the northwest corner of the pueblo. Yokioma shouted to his followers, and both sides paused to hear what he had to say. With his big toe trailing in the sand, the Hostile leader drew a line running east and west. To the north of it, facing south toward Oraibi, he grouped his own men, while the Friendlies clustered together south of the line with their backs toward the village. Then Yokioma announced the manner in which Oraibi's fate was finally to be settled.

"If your men," he said to Tawaqwaptiwa, "are strong enough to push us away from the village and to pass me over the line, it will be done. But if we pass you over the line, it will not be done, and we will have to live here." . . . *Forward and back went the opposing groups until at last Yokioma was conclusively forced well over the line, toward the north, away from the town. Oraibi's fate was decided.*

—Titiev 1944:86

The dramatic "split" of the Hopi village of Orayvi[1] is perhaps the best documented and most intensively studied incident of village factionalism known to anthropology. The tug-of-war was the climatic event of more than a decade of turmoil; the village was sundered. Volumes have been written about the causes of the split (Bernardini 1996; Bradfield 1971; Clemmer 1978; Levy 1992; Parsons 1922; Titiev 1944, 1972; Whiteley 1988), but that is not the focus of this book. The split had lasting consequences not only for the people of Third Mesa but also for their homes—the buildings around which they had centered their lives. It is the architectural effects of the split that are explored here.

This study began as an attempt to understand how prehistoric pueblos grew and declined. In the American Southwest, prior to Spanish entrada, Pueblo people moved frequently, even after A.D. 1200, when compact towns were home to several hundred people. Many of these large settlements were built and abandoned in little more than a generation. From a modern perspective, such frequent movement seems remarkable, although it is abundantly chronicled in Pueblo oral traditions. What would possess families to forsake their carefully constructed dwellings, their fields and shrines, to gather their children and their belongings and leave in search of a new home? Did they leave in large groups or did they scatter as families heading for pueblos where they knew relatives would take them in?

The well-documented Orayvi split offered an extraordinary opportunity to study the architectural effects of an event that must have happened many times in the past—the partial abandonment of a pueblo. In this volume, clues to how and why villages were abandoned and reestablished over and over in the prehistoric Southwest are discovered in a detailed study of houses at Orayvi across a period of almost eighty years—from 1871 to 1948. The transformation of these seemingly timeless structures also provides a unique window on the relationship between Pueblo houses and the active, dynamic people who occupied them. Projected into the past, architectural processes documented at Orayvi begin to reveal social behaviors and trends that shaped ancient Pueblo history.

Southwestern Pueblos and Archaeology

When the Spaniard Francisco Vásquez de Coronado first encountered the villages of the northern Southwest in 1540, he expected them to be built of gold and encrusted with turquoise (Winship 1896). Instead, he found stone or adobe *pueblos* (villages) much like those he had left in Spain. The lifestyle of the agricultural people who occupied these villages seemed more familiar than that of other Indians that the Spaniards had encountered on their travels north from New Spain (Mexico). Within fifty years, the Spanish had colonized the region (fig. 1.1), subjugating the Pueblo peoples, as they called these village Indians, who lived along the Rio Grande in what is now New Mexico (Simmons 1979).

Three hundred years later, the Southwest was taken from Mexico by the United States in the Mexican-American War of 1846–48. Expeditions were sent out at once by the U.S. government to explore the newly acquired territory. Reports of Pueblo people (Powell 1875), their exotic rituals, and especially the accounts of ancient ruined cities like those at Mesa Verde and Chaco Canyon, dazzled Americans in the eastern states.

Puebloan ruins became the focus of almost a century and a half of archaeological study that has made the Southwest one of the best-known archaeological regions in the world. In addition to containing abundant material remains left by ancient Pueblo people (tools, containers, ornaments, clothing), the buildings themselves have revealed, more than any other artifacts, prehistoric Pueblo lifeways—society, politics, and religion.

Generations of archaeologists, from the earliest Southwest scholars to the present, relied heavily on contemporary pueblos and their inhabitants for the interpretation of the archaeological remains. The Southwest is blessed (from an archaeological point of view) with an arid environment that affords remarkable preservation of ancient artifacts and buildings. Tree-ring dating and ceramic seriation—techniques that were developed and perfected in the Southwest—allow precise dating of archaeological sites and the materials they contain. But perhaps the most important reason for the immense success of archaeological studies in the Southwest is the obvious continuity between the ancient ruins found in the northern Southwest and the vital Native American cultures that still occupy the region. Modern and historic accounts of Puebloan lifestyles, economic practices, craft production, and religious customs are an enormous aid to archaeological interpretation.

Modern and historic pueblos have been especially valuable for the interpretation of prehistoric pueblo buildings because modern and ancient forms seemed remarkably similar in construction methods and materials, layout, and use. The intimate relationship that modern Pueblo people have with their homes (so different from the Western, utilitarian attitude toward dwellings) has helped archaeologists understand prehistoric interactions between ancient Pueblo people and their built environment (Saile 1977a,b). The pueblo, especially the central plaza where daily and ceremonial activities take place, is the center of their world. The rest of their world is defined by reference to that center place (Ortiz 1969; Swentzell 1988, 1990). The buildings are living things that come from the earth and return to the earth; they have a life cycle like any other living thing (Saile 1977a, 1990; Swentzell 1976, 1990, 1991).

Observations of modern pueblo buildings and historic accounts of how Pueblo people constructed and interacted with those buildings have been used by archaeologists to make a broad range of inferences about the past,

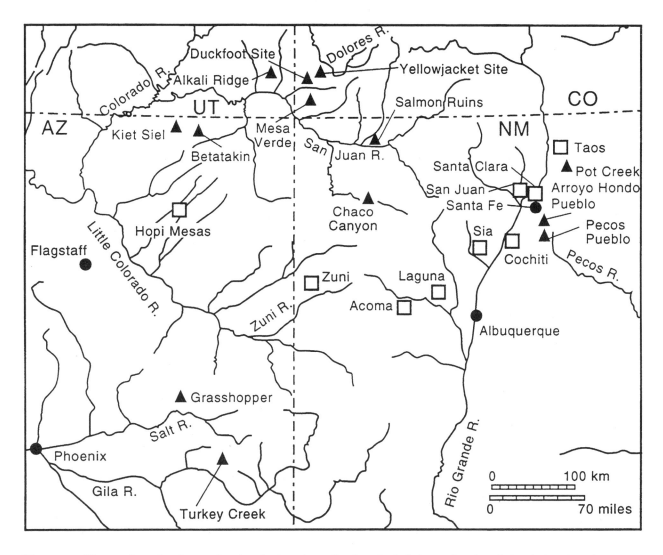

Figure 1.1 The northern Southwest, showing the locations of archaeological sites and regions (triangles) and modern pueblos (squares) mentioned in the text. Modern towns are indicated by disks.

from determinations of the function of puebloan rooms (Adams 1983; Ciolek-Torrello 1985; Hill 1970; Jorgensen 1975; Lipe and Hegmon 1989b; Lowell 1988) to studies of prehistoric social organization and levels of social complexity (Adams 1983; Dean 1970; Longacre 1968; Lekson 1986; Lipe and Hegmon 1989b). Archaeologists have become increasingly aware, however, that pueblos, ancient and timeless as they seemed, were the result of a lengthy architectural development that was part of a dynamic cultural evolution that continues to this day. Not only were the pueblo structures part of this evolution, but it is likely that the buildings themselves structured some of the changes that occurred (Cameron 1996; Lekson and

Cameron 1995). Modern pueblos, historic pueblos, and prehistoric pueblos each represent a different point on the continuum of architectural evolution that characterizes the pueblo form.

In spite of the recognition that modern and historic pueblos cannot be used as direct analogues for prehistoric pueblos, the present study demonstrates that they can make enormous contributions to our understanding of the form, function, and development of ancient pueblos and of the social groups that inhabited them. This is because there are certain dynamic social processes affecting architecture (and social responses to natural processes) that can be isolated and should remain constant through time.

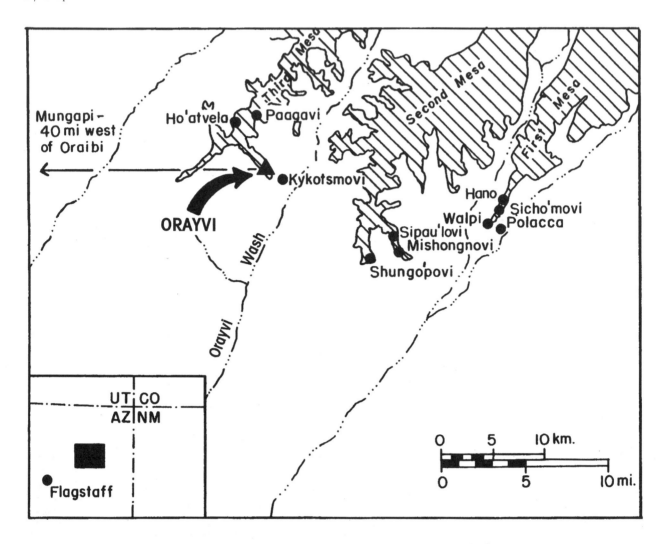

Figure 1.2 The Hopi mesas in northeastern Arizona, showing the location of Orayvi and other Hopi towns.

Historic photos and documents from Orayvi (fig. 1.2 shows its location), dating between 1871 and 1948, provide a unique database for documenting Puebloan architectural dynamics. This study investigates the social and natural factors, particularly village factionalism but also population growth and ordinary domestic cycles, that cause architectural change in pueblos in order to isolate those constant processes that will inform our interpretation of prehistoric pueblos. Specifically, the book examines two major aspects of Orayvi architecture: (1) the relationship between house (a set of rooms) and household (the group of people occupying those rooms), and (2) the processes of architectural change that occurred to houses and to the community both as a result of the normal domestic cycles and as the result of significant changes in the number of residents in the settlement (population growth and population decline).

Historic Orayvi represents Puebloan architectural canons at one point in time; the study, however, reveals a number of dynamic processes and principles that very likely shaped Puebloan architecture *through* time. These include continuity in household use of architectural space, evidence that architecture helped restrict the size of household groups, and factors conditioning settlement growth during periods of population increase. This short interval of Orayvi history illustrates the architectural consequences of abrupt population loss and suggests principles, such as continuity in the use of sacred space, that can help archaeologists discover similar events in the past.

The Orayvi study identifies processes and principles

that leave architectural evidence in the archaeological record; these factors, therefore, can be studied in prehistoric architecture. Although the data used in this analysis are from a historic pueblo, the study will show how they can be applied to the interpretation of prehistoric archaeological sites (chapter 7), focusing on the fourteenth-century pueblo of Arroyo Hondo, located in the northern Rio Grande region of New Mexico (Creamer et al. 1993).

The Development of Puebloan Architecture

Nineteenth-century Orayvi was the product of more than one thousand years of Puebloan architectural development. Before A.D. 700, native peoples in the northern Southwest lived in small hamlets of domed, subterranean pit structures, often clustered near a large subterranean structure—a Great Kiva—that was the locus of community ceremonies. The first fully aboveground structures were built during the Pueblo I period (A.D. 700–900), serving as storage structures for belowground pit houses. At first these aboveground rooms were ephemeral constructions made of interwoven sticks and twigs heavily coated with mud. Eventually, they had more sturdily constructed walls of stone mortared with mud. Strum (1990:19) has noted that surface dwellings maintained the Pueblo identification with the ground—they were intended to be extensions of the earth.

The typical Pueblo I settlement—called a *unit pueblo* by early archaeologists (Prudden 1918)—was assumed to be the home of an extended family.[2] These small structures follow a uniform pattern (i.e., Lightfoot 1994; fig. 1.3). They had five to ten aboveground rooms built into an arc that usually opened to the southeast for solar efficiency. In front (southeast) of these rooms were subterranean pit houses, one to three of them, and in front of the pit houses, a midden area where daily household debris was deposited. Great Kivas continued to be used for ceremonies by the residents of nearby unit pueblos.

Archaeological perceptions of the Pueblo I period have been that unit pueblos were isolated. Large Pueblo I sites—essentially, multiple adjacent unit pueblos—were

reported only rarely, the best-known example being the site of Alkali Ridge in southeastern Utah (Brew 1946). Wilshusen's (1991) study of the Pueblo I period in southwestern Colorado found, on the contrary, that many large Pueblo I sites in this area include clusters of unit pueblos with populations totaling several hundred people. These villages, however, tended to be short-lived and unstable.

The Pueblo I period is followed by the Pueblo II period (A.D. 900–1150). Archaeological understanding of the Pueblo II period has changed dramatically during the past two decades. Before 1975, the Pueblo II period was believed to have continued the Pueblo I pattern of scattered unit pueblos. In addition, a series of very large, remarkably well-constructed *Great Houses* were erected in Chaco Canyon, a remote valley in northwestern New Mexico. These Great Houses were known to exist in a few other places.

Great Houses had a form reminiscent of unit pueblos, but they were built much more massively, with costly labor input, and on a far larger scale than unit pueblos. The largest Great House in Chaco Canyon, Pueblo Bonito, had almost seven hundred rooms laid out in an arc that had been carefully designed and built in several construction episodes (fig. 1.4). Displaying perhaps the first multistoried construction in the Southwest, it eventually rose five stories tall. Round rooms were built into the tall roomblocks, continuing the older pit-house form. In the plaza were two Great Kivas, showing strong continuity with the religious forms of earlier centuries.

During the past two decades, a pattern called the Chaco Phenomenon has been recognized across most of the northern Southwest during the Pueblo II period (Lekson et al. 1988). Great Houses, like those in Chaco Canyon but smaller, have been found throughout the region. Interestingly, most of the Great Houses that have been excavated show little evidence of domestic use. Instead, Great Houses, even those in Chaco Canyon, are surrounded by communities of unit pueblos that apparently housed families who used the Great House (Lekson 1991). Great Houses and Great Kivas apparently functioned like local churches or town halls.[3] Most remarkable is the discovery of a series of prehistoric roads that seem to connect Great Houses throughout the northern South-

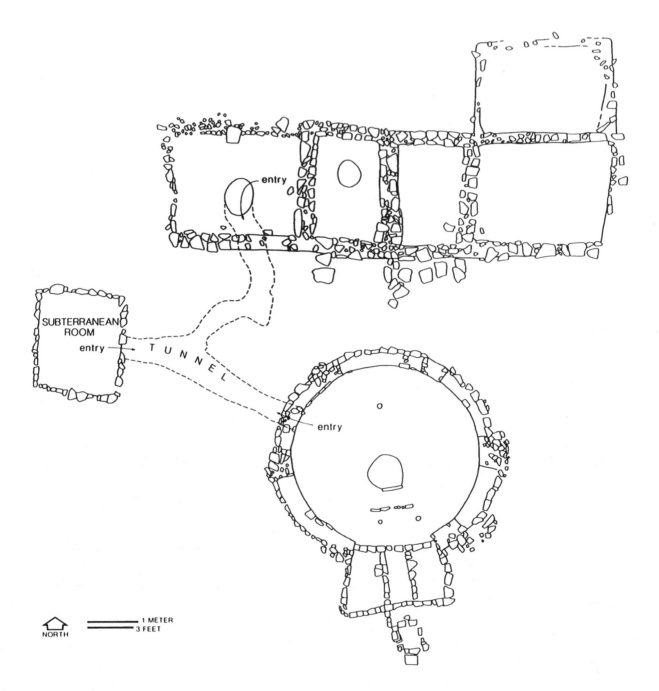

Figure 1.3 A unit pueblo, part of the Yellowjacket site in southwestern Colorado. (From Lange et al. 1986, fig. 27; reprinted with the permission of The Board of Regents of the University of Colorado)

west with Chaco Canyon (Lekson et al. 1988; but see Roney 1992).

The Chaco Phenomenon ended about A.D. 1150, and by the end of the following century (Pueblo III period, 1150–1300; Pueblo IV period, 1300–1540) most residents of the northern Southwest were living in large, multi-

storied pueblos much like those that the Spanish first encountered. By the 1300s, many of these pueblos housed communities of more than one thousand people. It is likely that the Pueblo II Great Houses served as models for the Pueblo III and Pueblo IV towns, and the first of these towns may actually have been Great Houses turned

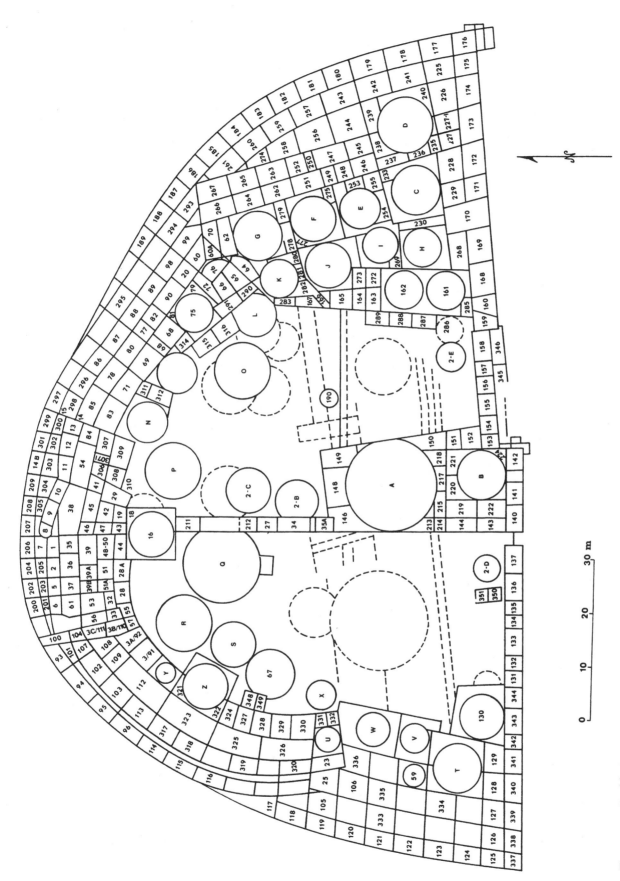

Figure 1.4 Pueblo Bonito, a Great House located in Chaco Canyon in New Mexico. Great Houses were an architectural form characteristic of the Pueblo II period across much of the northern Southwest. They usually served as a central focus for a surrounding community of unit pueblos. (From Stephen H. Lekson, *Great Pueblo Architecture of Chaco Canyon, New Mexico* [University of New Mexico Press, Albuquerque, 1986], fig. 4.17)

into residences (Lekson and Cameron 1995). The transition from living in scattered unit pueblos surrounding a Great House to living in closely built towns where families actually shared walls must have been difficult and almost certainly required new social mechanisms to integrate the large numbers of people these towns held.

The large, closely built pueblos of the Pueblo III and Pueblo IV periods contained hundreds to thousands of rooms that were usually oriented around an enclosed or partially enclosed plaza. Arroyo Hondo Pueblo, near Santa Fe, New Mexico, built about A.D. 1315, is a good example of this type of settlement (fig. 1.5). At its greatest extent, it contained one thousand rooms built around thirteen plazas. Several of the plazas contained kivas, and one very large kiva was found outside the pueblo. Arroyo Hondo—like many other large towns of the period—was built, occupied, and abandoned in little more than a generation. By A.D. 1335, it was apparently deserted. It was reoccupied in the late 1300s but by a much smaller population.

The development of the large towns of the fourteenth and fifteenth centuries was accompanied by enormous shifts in population and the abandonment of the entire part of the northern Southwest now known as the Four Corners region (Adler 1996; Cameron 1995). Some groups migrated southeast into the northern Rio Grande; others concentrated in a broad band between Acoma and Hopi. The cause of population aggregation into large towns during the thirteenth and fourteenth centuries and the associated population shifts and abandonments is a key research question for archaeologists today.

The pueblos that the early Spanish explorers found continued to change, from then on heavily influenced by European materials, construction methods, the introduction of domesticated animals, and colonial practices that restricted Native Americans in their movements and activities. These changes can be seen in historic photos and records of Orayvi discussed in the following chapters. A visit to Orayvi today shows that this ancient town continues to change as residents modify their homes and reorganize their settlement to suit current needs.

Archaeology and the Built Environment

When archaeologists or architects talk about the built environment, they include all aspects of human manipulation of space. Lawrence and Low define the built environment as "any physical alteration of the natural environment, from hearths to cities, through construction by humans" (1990:454). The concept of the "cultural landscape" current in contemporary archaeological usage embodies the same idea of vernacular architecture (where the designer, builder, and user are usually the same person) as part of a larger system of organization and manipulation of space (Rapoport 1990:12).

Although the built environment can include built forms such as fields, roads, or shrines, archaeologists have focused on buildings. Adams (1983:44) lists several reasons for the importance of buildings: architectural remains are relatively permanent and maintain their integrity longer than most artifactual material; they can be relatively or absolutely dated; they provide clues to prehistoric use of space; they often leave surface remains that provide information about settlement development, site use, and social organization without excavation; and they are more resistant to vandalism than other artifact types.

Requisite to the development of models for interpreting prehistoric buildings, however, is an understanding of the determinants of architectural form (McGuire and Schiffer 1983). This is a field of study encompassing both architecture and anthropology (see Ferguson 1996 and Lawrence and Low 1990 for reviews of this literature). The environmental determinist view expressed by scholars such as Fitch and Branch (1960) was challenged by Rapoport (1969), who proposed that the environment acts only as a major modifying factor in the design of vernacular structures. Nabokov and Easton (1989:16) list technology, climate, economics, social organization, religion, and history as the most important determinants of architectural form for Native American structures. If these factors determine architectural form, ancient buildings can be used to investigate each of these aspects of prehistoric society.

In 1881, anthropologist Lewis Henry Morgan suggested that architectural form reflected ancient social

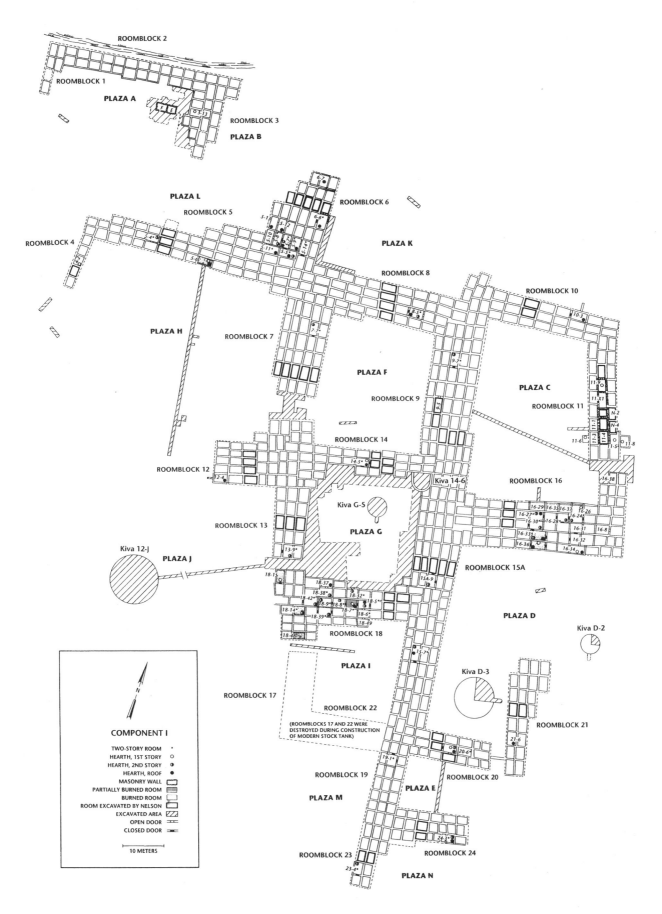

Figure 1.5 Arroyo Hondo Pueblo—a large, plaza-oriented settlement located near Santa Fe, New Mexico—was occupied twice during the fourteenth and early fifteenth centuries. This is a plan view of the extensive Component 1 occupation (A.D. 1315–1335). (From Creamer 1993; courtesy of the School of American Research)

organization. Throughout much of the early twentieth century, however, the archaeological emphasis on reconstructions of culture history resulted in the use of architecture primarily as an indication of cultural affiliation rather than as an interpretive tool. The form of prehistoric buildings was used to define and bound prehistoric cultures; in the Southwest, for example, regional cultural variation and change in cultures through time are defined to a large extent on changes in architecture. Yet, as Morgan recognized, prehistoric architecture is more than just a cultural marker. It is a relic of the organization and activities of past cultures. Architecture is also a system of nonverbal communication that represents "the world view writ small" (Rapoport 1969:2; see also Blanton 1994 and Hieb 1990). In other words, cultural ideals and values are encoded in vernacular buildings.

Prehistoric architecture in the Southwest was almost exclusively vernacular, meaning that the designer, builder, and user were the same individual or closely related individuals (but see Lekson 1986:39). Prehistoric southwestern architecture is also largely domestic; public or ceremonial structures form a very small proportion of pueblo constructions. Puebloan structures were relatively easily built and easily modified, and archaeologists have assumed a close fit between buildings and their residents. As a result, pueblo buildings are expected to reflect both the structure of Puebloan society and Puebloan views about how their society should be organized at both the household and community levels. Rapoport (1969) and others (e.g., Lawrence and Low 1990) have also observed that not only does the built environment reflect the culture that produces it, but it also helps shape that culture. The intimate involvement of people with their built environment is what makes it such an enormously useful tool for reconstructing the past.

Architecture and the Interpretation of Southwestern Pueblos

The Orayvi study builds on an extensive literature on the architecture of prehistoric pueblos. This section provides a brief overview of the major types of studies that have been applied to large, late (Pueblo III, Pueblo IV, or historic) pueblos that are architecturally similar to Orayvi (see fig. 1.1 for the location of sites discussed in this section). Four areas of archaeological interpretation to which the Orayvi study contributes are emphasized. These include the identification and interpretation of houses in clustered pueblos, the reconstruction of prehistoric population size, the reconstruction of settlement histories, and the interpretation of community-wide settlement patterns. These types of studies are, of course, closely interconnected. All rely heavily on ethnographic analogy for descriptions of social units, the interpretation of spatial units, and the articulation of social units with spatial units.

Finding Houses in the Southwestern Pueblos

Household archaeology, an alliance between settlement analysis and activity-area research (Steadman 1996), is a growing field of study. Household archaeology examines what has been described as the fundamental social unit in archaeological societies—the unit that articulates most directly with economic and ecological processes (Wilk and Rathje 1982:618). Netting and his colleagues (1984:xx) define the *household* as a task-oriented residence group. The prehistoric household is best identified and examined through studies of the remains of houses that are a focus for household activities and a container for the materials involved in those activities (Kent 1990a,b). In a recent review article, Steadman (1996) noted that household archaeology is moving from an emphasis on economic reconstructions to explorations of social structure, the development of social complexity, and other issues such as gender relations and wealth distribution.

In the Southwest, a great deal of effort has gone into defining the set of rooms within a pueblo that constitutes a house—the rooms belonging to a single family (Ciolek-Torrello 1978, 1985; Hill 1970; Lightfoot 1994; Lowell 1991). House boundaries are not obvious because pueblos, especially the large late pueblos, are clustered dwellings, where houses share walls. Archaeologists attempt to identify room function, often based on analogy with modern or historic pueblos rooms, and then assign rooms to houses based on the assumption that each house contains a set of rooms of different functions.

Even early southwestern archaeologists used architecture to identify houses and made attempts to define the group that used them. Prudden's "unit pueblo" was an early description of the architectural manifestation of a household (1914:34). At Pecos, Kidder (1958:124) was less specific, describing a four-story suite of seven rooms as "the standard space allotment for a group of some sort, I presume of kindred." Archaeological examination of the household, including household developmental cycles, has been approached systematically only in the last two decades (see Lowell 1991 for an overview of archaeological approaches to the household in the Southwest). For example, at the Grasshopper site, a fourteenth-century pueblo in east-central Arizona, a number of studies in the early 1970s used architecture to identify and examine prehistoric households (Ciolek-Torrello and Reid 1974; Rock 1974; Sullivan 1974); other studies followed.

A number of methods have been developed for locating the architectural boundaries of houses in large, clustered pueblos (Adams 1983; Reynolds 1981:110–15; Rohn 1965; Wilcox 1975, 1982). These include (1) evidence of construction sequences, such as wall bond/abutment studies and dendrochronological analyses that would indicate contemporaneous construction of several rooms (Reid and Shimada 1982; Wilcox 1975); (2) assignment of room function and connections (via doorways) so that "sets" of rooms can be identified (Ciolek-Torrello 1978; Creamer et al. 1993; Dean 1969, 1970; Jorgensen 1975; Lightfoot 1994; Lowell 1988; Reid and Whittlesey 1982; Rohn 1965; Sullivan 1974); and (3) the location of wall openings that indicate access between sets of rooms (Adams 1983:58; Wilcox 1975:144).

There are problems with the application of each of these methods. Wall bond/abutment studies are plagued by ambiguities in identifying and interpreting wall relationships. Dendrochronological analyses are only useful where an extensive tree-ring record exists, which is not the case for most prehistoric sites (discussed below). The identification of room function relies on floor artifacts and features that may change over time (Lowell 1991; Sulli-

van 1974; although Ciolek-Torrello [1985] found floor artifacts a better indicator of room function than architecture). Assumptions about the numbers and functions of rooms that make up a "typical" pueblo household vary widely and are often based on scanty, recent ethnographic sources.

Even the interpretation of wall openings is not unambiguous. For example, Mindeleff (1891:182) observed that the Hopi opened temporary doors in rooms for use during construction and subsequently blocked them when construction was completed. This practice would complicate room-set analysis based on interconnecting doorways. While temporary doors would not be expected to connect at the time of construction with rooms owned by another household, subsequent adjoining construction by adjacent households could place temporary doors in an interior "interconnecting" position. Archaeologists might easily interpret these blocked doors as evidence of a change in the relationship between two adjacent households (e.g., Wilcox 1975). Furthermore, many pueblo rooms were entered through ceiling hatchways. Rooms belonging to the same household would not necessarily show any connection.

Recent studies have tried to avoid the difficulties inherent in each of these methods by using multiple approaches to identifying and studying prehistoric pueblo households. Lowell (1991) used room features, room size, interconnecting doors, and other architectural features to create a typology of room functions at Turkey Creek Pueblo in east-central Arizona. She then identified a typical dwelling as consisting of a standard set of rooms of different types. Lowell found significant variability in the size of dwellings that she related to variability in the size and structure of households and also to, possibly, differences in wealth (Lowell 1991:60).

In a detailed study of houses and households at the Duckfoot site, a Pueblo I site in southwestern Colorado, Lightfoot (1994) identified "architectural suites" consisting of rooms and associated pit structures that sheltered a household. A nested hierarchy model allowed him also to recognize structures associated with lower- and higher-order social groups (the dwelling group, roomblock group, hamlet group, and village group). Once households were identified architecturally, Lightfoot used artifacts, features, and network analysis to examine household size, the activities undertaken by households, the distribution of these activities at Duckfoot, and the role of the household within larger social groupings, such as the hamlet or village.

At Pot Creek Pueblo, a late-thirteenth-/early-fourteenth-century pueblo in the Taos region in northern New Mexico, Crown and Kohler (1994) observed an increase in residence-unit size that they attributed to a shift from nuclear to extended families. They identified residence units through bond/abut relationships, contemporaneously dated rooms, wall and feature construction styles, and the presence of interconnecting doorways. Kulisheck and others (1994), however, while not questioning the suggested change in family organization, observed that Crown and Kohler's residence units were based largely on contemporaneity of construction. Kulisheck and his colleagues question the assumption that contemporaneous construction necessarily implies that rooms were built and occupied by a single family. In other words, they see a change in the organization of construction—a switch from the accretional construction of a few rooms at a time to the simultaneous construction of a number of rooms—instead of (or in addition to) a change in social organization at Pot Creek.

The identification of residential units is important not only for examining the organization and activities of households, they also form the building blocks of reconstructions of population size, social organization at the community level, and community population dynamics. Ethnographic and ethnohistoric data, such as that provided by the Orayvi study, are essential to reconstructions at each of these levels.

Architecture and the Measurement of Prehistoric Population Size

It is hard to overestimate the importance of accurate reconstructions of prehistoric population to all sorts of archaeological interpretations, ranging from studies of environmental carrying capacity to the development of social complexity. Where architecture is visible, as is the case at excavated southwestern pueblos, population size is typically determined by multiplying the number of structures (rooms) by an ethnographically derived population constant (Hill, 1970:75; Longacre 1975, 1976; Plog 1974:77, 88; Rohn 1977:267). These calculations involve either dividing the number of rooms in a settlement by the estimated number of rooms that make up a "house" or simply assuming one "living room" per family (Schlanger 1987). To reach the final settlement population, the resulting figure is multiplied by the estimated number of persons per household. Estimates of house and household size are typically derived from ethnographic data (Hayes 1981:49; Hill 1970:75; Lightfoot 1994; Schlanger 1987; see also Hassan 1978:55–58; Plog 1974:94).

Hassan (1978:56; also 1981:72–77) discusses problems with the use of structures in estimating population for "multichambered houses," an architectural category that includes southwestern pueblos. He lists six types of information required for accurate population estimates: (1) number of rooms, (2) number of rooms per household, (3) number of habitation rooms, (4) household size, (5) number of rooms occupied contemporaneously, and (6) duration of occupation. Assembling each of these types of information poses problems for the archaeologist. For example, typically only the ground-floor rooms in multistory pueblos are archaeologically visible, limiting calculations of the total number of rooms per settlement (Adams 1983:52).

Determining room contemporaneity is especially problematic. In an occupied settlement at one point in time, many rooms may be abandoned. This is especially true as length of settlement occupation increases. The number of contemporaneously occupied structures in settlements is dependent also upon structure use-life and fluctuations in population within the settlement (see below). During periods when population is growing, the proportion of abandoned rooms will be low; when population is declining, the proportion of abandoned rooms will be greater (Cameron 1991a).

Archaeologists have used a number of methods to

assess the numbers of contemporaneously occupied rooms at southwestern pueblos for purposes of population estimation. The simplest is to assume that all rooms were occupied at the same time, although most archaeologists acknowledge that this assumption is erroneous (Cully et al. 1982:161; Rohn 1971:262). Another approach is to assume that a constant proportion of rooms in all sites is abandoned (Bernardini 1996; Hill 1970:75; Longacre 1975, 1976; Plog 1974:91). In most cases, the proportion of abandoned rooms is derived from ethnographic data. The variety of assumptions involved in each of these types of calculations makes their use in estimating prehistoric population sizes unreliable.

Archaeologists, especially in the last two decades, have recognized the importance (and difficulty) of refining population estimates and have produced carefully considered reconstructions of momentary population for specific regions (e.g., Schlanger 1987). A few studies have looked more broadly at the use of ethnographic data in population estimates, evaluating ethnographically derived estimates of house and household size, room function, and other variables (Cameron 1996, Lightfoot 1994, Schlanger 1985). The Orayvi study builds on, but goes beyond, such evaluations, contributing detailed ethnographic evidence that will help refine a number of the parameters that comprise population estimates.

Settlement History

The reconstruction of patterns of settlement growth and abandonment is possible only where sites have been extensively excavated and, as a result, such studies are not common. One of the most detailed models of growth and abandonment was produced by Reid (1973) based on his analysis of Grasshopper Pueblo, a fourteenth-century site in northeastern Arizona. He proposed a four-stage model of the developmental cycle of a pueblo settlement: (1) The establishment phase begins with the first occupation and construction episodes. (2) The expansion phase consists of additions to the original construction as the result of either expansion of the founding group or immigration of new groups. (3) The dispersion phase in-

volves gradual movement away from the site of origin and establishment of a new site. (4) During the abandonment phase, normal domestic activity ceases and remaining residents depart (Reid 1973:123).

Reid's model is an ideal sequence, and departures from this model may be as important as the model itself. For example, some briefly occupied sites may never expand, and some sites may be rapidly abandoned, bypassing the dispersion phase. Each of these variations may have important implications for understanding the size and organization of prehistoric communities.

Techniques used by archaeologists to define settlement developmental sequences are based, to a large extent, on determinations of structure contemporaneity. Reid and Shimada (1982:12) define growth as an increase in units resulting in an increase in community size (see also Carneiro 1967:240, cited in Reid 1973:101). They identify growth at Grasshopper Pueblo through the addition of rooms and describe a number of techniques for determining construction sequences. These include dendrochronology, bond/abutment studies, and wall-face analysis (Reid and Shimada 1982:14–15; see also Reynolds 1981:103–10).

Dendrochronology may provide the most accurate method of determining settlement construction sequences, but sites with large enough numbers of tree-ring dates for detailed studies of construction sequence are rare (e.g., Ahlstrom 1985:598–601), and dating construction episodes through tree-ring dates is not always unambiguous (Dean 1978). Dean's (1969, 1970) classic study of two thirteenth-century pueblos located in northeastern Arizona, Kiet Siel and Betatakin, relied on dendrochronology to identify building sequences. Through a detailed analysis of patterns of construction, Dean not only linked clusters of rooms to household groups but also suggested that Betatakin was settled by a group of people who had constituted a functioning community elsewhere (1970:159). Kiet Siel, on the other hand, grew through the immigration of small groups of people from a number of different places. At Pot Creek Pueblo, Crown (1991) used more than two hundred tree-ring dates to reconstruct settlement history. She demonstrated population aggregation in the A.D. 1260s, a steady population size until the 1310s, then a slight population increase. Pot Creek was abandoned shortly after A.D. 1320. Kulisheck and others (1994) suggest a short-term abandonment of Pot Creek during the late 1200s, based both on stratigraphy and a different interpretation of the tree-ring dates.

Wall bond/abutment studies have been used to identify contemporaneously constructed structures since the early days of southwestern archaeology (Wilcox 1975) and are used by many archaeologists to determine patterns of site growth (Creamer et al. 1993; Morris 1986). Assumptions associated with bond/abutment studies are (1) continuously bonded walls were constructed during a single building episode (Reid 1973:106; Wilcox 1982:21) and (2) the abutment of one wall onto another indicates contemporaneous or later construction (Reynolds 1981: 17). At Arroyo Hondo Pueblo, Creamer et al. (1993) used bond/abutment patterns and other architectural indicators to reconstruct the growth of this large settlement. Although more than three hundred tree-ring dates were obtained at Arroyo Hondo, few were cutting dates. As a result, tree-ring dates could be used only to establish periods of occupation at the site. Bond/abutment study, on the other hand, suggested that the first occupation of the site (Component I) was built in four stages.

Wall bond/abutment patterns are not always easily discerned, however. Reid and Shimada (1982:14) note that deterioration processes affecting wall relationships and remodeling can make determinations of original wall relationships unclear, and they suggest wall-face analysis as a supplement to bond/abutment relationships. They assumed (see also Scarborough and Shimada 1974) that smooth-faced walls at Grasshopper Pueblo were once exterior walls. They found patterns of smooth and rough walls to be a better indicator of construction sequence than bond/abutment studies, presumably because such analysis avoided deterioration and remodeling ambiguities.

Patterns of trash deposition can also help determine patterns of settlement growth. At Turkey Creek Pueblo, Lowell (1991:32) was able to differentiate rooms that were built on sterile ground from those built on trash. Rooms built on sterile soil are most likely to have been built early in the construction sequence of the settlement, while those built later are more likely to have been underlain with trash. Although Lowell cautions that trash could be removed before a room was built during preparation for construction, this "sterile-trash dichotomy" worked well at Turkey Creek to determine a relative construction sequence for the pueblo.

The types of analyses just discussed aim to identify construction sequences. Equally important, but perhaps more difficult to address, is the sequence of settlement abandonment. Chronometric techniques include dendro-chronology and archaeomagnetism. Dendrochronology typically identifies only cessation of construction (except in cases where firewood can be dated) and is most applicable for determining complete site abandonment rather than staged abandonment (Ahlstrom 1985:653). Archaeomagnetism may provide dates for the last use of some features (primarily hearths), but archaeomagnetic dates are rarely ubiquitous enough at a single site to use as a reliable indicator of abandonment sequence.

The most commonly used methods of determining sequences of abandonment are superpositioning of rooms and patterns of trash disposal. Superpositioning of rooms is straightforward: a room or series of rooms built on top of other rooms indicates an early abandonment of that room or part of the settlement.

Trash deposition is more complex. Many archaeologists simply note that trash deposits in rooms indicate that some rooms were abandoned while the settlement was still occupied (Rohn 1971:262). At Grasshopper Pueblo, the Room Abandonment Measure was developed to establish temporally equivalent sets of artifacts (Reid 1973:114; Reid and Shimada 1982:14). As Reid and Shimada note, there is no necessary relationship between initial room construction and its subsequent use-history because of reoccupation, rebuilding, and other processes. They assumed (1) that rooms abandoned while the site was still occupied contain little or no de facto refuse (cultural material left behind when an activity area is abandoned, Schiffer 1987:89) on the last utilized floor but have a high density of secondary refuse, and (2) that rooms abandoned at or near the time of site abandonment should have a high density of de facto refuse on the last utilized floor and a low density of secondary refuse in the fill (Reid 1973:114; Reid and Shimada 1982:14–15). (See Montgomery 1993 for use of the Room Abandonment Measure as a method for identifying site-abandonment processes.)

In spite of the difficulties of reconstructing settlement histories, they are critical for most interpretations of social and spatial relations at prehistoric sites, especially community organization and use of space (discussed below). Southwest archaeologists have found the use of multiple indicators of site growth and abandonment to be most productive in constructing settlement histories. Reid's developmental model for Grasshopper Pueblo, based on patterns of both gradual population increase and abandonment, provides a useful point of departure for such studies. The Orayvi case, presented in the following chapters, shows that dramatic population fluctuations may produce slightly different patterns and require different interpretive methods.

Community Organization and Use of Space

Until the 1960s, suprahousehold social organization was assumed to be beyond the reach of archaeological investigation (Adams 1983:45). With the theoretical switch to the New Archaeology, there began a search for larger social groupings (see Lipe and Hegmon 1989b for a summary of these studies), as well as patterns in the use of extramural and ritual space. In two groundbreaking but heavily criticized studies from this era, Longacre (1970) and Hill (1970) used the distributions of ceramics within architectural units to distinguish localized descent groups. Much of the criticism surrounding their work pointed to their failure to recognize the processes that led to the deposition of ceramic artifacts within structures and their use of inaccurate models of social organization and ceramic production derived from ethnographic pueblos (Schiffer 1989).

Two contemporary studies were more successful. Dean (1969, 1970) used architecture and tree-ring dates only to identify household units associated with "room clusters" at Kiet Siel and Betatakin (1970:155–56), yet his careful reconstruction of building sequences allowed him to suggest that the matrilocal extended family was the only localized subvillage social unit at these two sites (1970:169). At Mesa Verde, Rohn (1965) was able to identify three levels of social integration at Mug House, using a number of architectural characteristics such as room functions and associations, building and remodeling sequences, and doorway locations. He was able to identify not only the space used by individual households but also a larger grouping called a "habitation unit," which involved the association of several rooms with a pit house or kiva. At the level of the community, Rohn believed he could identify a dual social division at Mug House based on doorless walls that divided Mug House into two parts. More recently, at Turkey Creek Pueblo, Lowell (1991) found that groups of rooms separated by long walls were the result of a suprahousehold level of social organization. She was also able to identify a dual division at Turkey Creek Pueblo based on the use of space around a Great Kiva.

In 1989, Lipe and Hegmon (1989a) produced a collection of papers that examine social integration in prehistoric pueblos using architecture, particularly kivas. Even the earliest southwestern archaeologists interpreted kivas as gathering places for multiple households and, as such, indicators of a suprahousehold level of social organization (Hegmon and Lipe 1989:1). Lekson has questioned this now well-established assumption for small ("clan") kivas (1988, 1989),[4] but most other contributors to Lipe and Hegmon's volume continue to see kivas as indicators of the existence of social groups above the level of the household, at least after—or perhaps during—the Pueblo I period (Varien and Lightfoot 1989; Wilshusen 1989).

Some of the contributors to Lipe and Hegmon's volume also identify other types of space, such as plazas, as the locus of activities of community-wide social groups (see Adler 1989 for a cross-cultural examination of integrative facilities). Such community-wide ceremonial activities still take place on plazas in modern pueblos. Adams (1989, 1991) has suggested that the enclosed-plaza settlement form was adopted with the development of the kachina religion during the late thirteenth and early fourteenth centuries in the Little Colorado area of east central Arizona. Immigrants from the north strained social relations in this area, and the kachina religion, with its elaborate public rituals performed in enclosed plazas, served to integrate unrelated groups in large settlements.

Although archaeologists recognize that many (perhaps most) activities, domestic or otherwise, took place outside the pueblo house, studies of the use of extramural space are not as common as those of the use of space within architectural boundaries. Both ethnographic and archaeological evidence shows that rooftops were used for many domestic tasks, from food processing and cooking to toolmaking and storage (Creamer et al. 1993, Dohm 1996). The plaza space adjacent to each house was also used for domestic activities. For example, at Arroyo Hondo Pueblo, ramadas, hearths, mealing areas, and the remains of turkey pens were found in plazas (Creamer et al. 1993).

Some archaeologists have attempted to look more broadly at patterns in the use of both domestic and ritual space across pueblo communities. Morenon (1972, 1977 cited in Ciolek-Torrello 1978:105, 170, 218) found functionally distinct zones at Salmon Ruins, an eleventh-/twelfth-century pueblo in northwestern New Mexico. He suggests that ceremonial areas, as well other spatial units such as plazas, form focal points for community growth and activities. Ciolek-Torrello (1978) found a similar pattern of functional differentiation at the settlement level at Grasshopper Pueblo. Central zones at Grasshopper Pueblo contained most abandoned and special-function manufacturing and storage rooms, while habitation rooms and ordinary storage rooms were located in peripheral zones.

Some of the most recent work on community-level social organization has applied the concepts of space-syntax analysis to prehistoric or historic pueblos. Using Hillier and Hanson's (1984) premise that culturally constructed space has a social logic, Ferguson (1996) demonstrates a change in the degree of social integration at historic settlements among the Zuni, a Puebloan people located in west-central New Mexico. In the northern Rio Grande, Shapiro (1997) employed space-syntax analysis to compare the arrangement of space at Arroyo Hondo

Pueblo during early and late occupations. He found that the arrangement of space at the pueblo changed over time from relatively more integrated to relatively more segregated settlement and that plazas become increasingly important for community integration. Shapiro ties these changes to an increase in sociopolitical complexity between the two occupations (1997:259).

At Pot Creek Pueblo, in addition to changes in household size, Crown and Kohler (1994) used changes in site layout to examine the effects of population aggregation on site structure and community dynamics. They found increasing spatial differentiation through time, including a change from an open, amorphous plaza to an enclosed plaza that would have structured and channeled movement along specific paths. They relate some of these changes to population increase at the site.

Studies of social organization and use of space at the community level hold great promise for increasing understanding of major transitions in Pueblo prehistory, such as the emergence of aggregated settlements and regional abandonments. For example, in a volume that examines population aggregation during the Pueblo III period, Cordell (1996:236) urges southwestern archaeologists to explore site layouts as a means of making broad comparisons of social organization. Interpretation of settlement layout, of course, requires an understanding of settlement histories—not only of how settlements grow but also of their configuration at one point in time. Without these, questions of room contemporaneity and associations of rooms into houses cannot be resolved, and the definition of intracommunity patterns of interaction and use of space are impossible.

Archaeology and the Identification of Factional Competition and Archaeological Explanation

An emerging field of study in archaeology focuses on the identification of instances of factional competition in the past, and this has become a useful concept for exploring the development of complex social systems and other social transformations (Brumfiel and Fox 1994). Because the Orayvi study focuses on the effects of a factional split on the built environment, it offers a remarkable opportunity to link factionalism and its effects on material culture.

Factions are "structurally and functionally similar groups which, by virtue of their similarity, compete for resources and positions of power and prestige" (Brumfiel 1994:4). Factions compete within kin groups, villages, ethnic groups, or other large social units. Factional competition does not refer to the class struggle that Marxist archaeologists see as the source of social change; it refers to competition between members of the same class or group. Factional competition looks for the source of social transformation within social systems, not in the interaction between system and environment. Transformations occur because of the self-aggrandizing activities of individuals who seek power and goods. Although the Orayvi split has been attributed to a number of different causes, it clearly involved the formation of two factions that were in competition for goods or power—deciding which of the two it was depends on which cause one believes was at the root of the split.[5]

Factions have only recently been sought in the archaeological record, but this concept clearly has the potential to advance the understanding of prehistoric social change. Based on the studies presented in a volume edited by Brumfiel and Fox (1994), most of which are drawn from Latin American cases, the built environment is an important source of data for the identification of prehistoric factions. These studies use house size, settlement size, agricultural constructions that suggested communal labor, fortifications, and monumental architecture to identify the presence and effects of factional competition. As demonstrated in the following chapters, the Orayvi case provides an important model of the effects of factional competition on the puebloan built environment that can be applied to prehistoric southwestern cases.

The Orayvi Study

Orayvi was selected for study because the split provided a perfect opportunity to explore the effects of sudden population decline on puebloan architecture. The first goal of the project was to gain an understanding of the puebloan architectural form and the varied social and environmental processes that influence the life-cycle of these structures. In this portion of the study, presented in chapter 2, both southwestern and cross-cultural examples are used to explore the life-cycle of stone or mud vernacular structures, showing the effects that processes as varied as domestic needs, wall or roof decay, and access to external resources have on the use-life of a structure.

Data for the Orayvi study were collected from a number of sources—described in detail in chapter 3. Historic photographs are the foundation upon which a large part of the study rests. The Hopi Pueblos were relatively isolated from Euroamerican contact until the late nineteenth century. Exploratory expeditions sponsored by the U.S. government during the 1870s and 1880s often included photographers, and they captured early images of Hopi. After the transcontinental railroad was completed in 1882, running just sixty miles south of Hopi, the region was inundated with tourists, missionaries, teachers, and proto-anthropologists. Many took photographs of their experiences in Hopi country, and their photos provide a unique record of change to the stone and earth structures at Orayvi. Copies of these photos were collected from photo archives at museums, universities, and government repositories throughout the United States for use in this study. The study used the concept of "casual repeat photography," which involves analysis of sequential views of the same scene taken at different points in time (Ahlstrom 1992; and see chapter 3).

The effectiveness of the study was greatly enhanced by several additional sources of data. In 1887, Victor Mindeleff, an employee of the Smithsonian Institution's Bureau of American Ethnology, produced a richly detailed map of Orayvi as part of a study of southwestern Pueblo architecture. All structures were shown, multiple stories were indicated, and even the locations of doors, windows, and ladders were recorded on the map.

At the time that the present research was under development, Dr. Jerrold Levy of the University of Arizona was undertaking a study of Orayvi social stratification, and he had developed a detailed transcription of notes taken during the 1930s by cultural anthropologist Mischa Titiev. Titiev interviewed residents of Orayvi and produced a reconstructed "census" that documented all individuals living in Orayvi in 1900, just before the village split. Most important for the present project, Titiev recorded, on a copy of Mindeleff's map, the rooms where each family lived. Levy not only used Titiev's census to characterize the size and composition of Orayvi families but also incorporated data on these same families from the 1900 U.S. census, generating an extremely useful set of data on the composition of Orayvi households at a single point in time (Levy 1990, 1992). Levy generously offered the use of his census material for this study, permitting me to explore the relationship between the Orayvi house and household. The results of this portion of the study are presented in chapter 4 (and in Cameron 1996), including data on house size and household configuration that are strongly grounded in careful observations of architecture and reliable census data.

The collection and analysis of the historic photos was challenging but tremendously rewarding. With the combination of the photographs and the maps, it was possible to examine how Orayvi buildings changed over a period of almost eighty years (1871 to 1948). The photos show how the dynamics of short-term architectural change are related to the needs and choices of individual families, as well as the influences on indigenous architecture of Euroamerican building materials and technology (chapter 5). The photos documented a previously unknown population increase at Orayvi during the last decades of the nineteenth century. Photographs taken after the 1906

split show the dramatic effects of factional competition on Orayvi architecture (chapter 6). As the photos show, the settlement was gradually reshaped by the people who remained there, demonstrating continuities in the use of ceremonial space and the processes by which abandoned houses were reused or reclaimed.

Architectural processes and principles identified in the Orayvi study are reviewed in chapter 7, and their utility in archaeological interpretation is evaluated. Then, using insights derived from Orayvi, population aggregation and abandonment at the fourteenth-century site of Arroyo Hondo are explored. Processes of architectural change observable over a short span of time are shown to be similar at these two pueblos, even though they are separated by more than five hundred years. Such similarities among prehistoric, historic, and modern pueblos result from similarities in construction, the common exigencies of maintenance techniques, a constancy in household processes, and, perhaps, similarities in prehistoric and modern attitudes toward architecture.

The results of the diachronic architectural study of Orayvi should also have implications for prehistoric architecture beyond the Southwest. In villages of vernacular structures in arid areas, such as northern Africa and the Middle East, compact structures of stone or earth are similar to southwestern pueblos. Patterns of architectural change found at Orayvi may also be recognized in these distant sites.

2 / The Construction and Use-Life of Pueblo Structures

Pueblo architecture is essentially a product of the plateau country, and its bounds are, in fact, practically coincident with those of that peculiar region popularly known as the mesa country. . . . [T]hrough a great abundance of excellent building material, the product of the mesas, and through peculiar social conditions, the product of the peculiar environment, whereby a frequent use of such materials was compelled, pueblo architecture developed.

—C. Mindeleff 1900:640

Cosmos Mindeleff appreciated the unique and dynamic nature of Puebloan architecture (1900:647), as did many nineteenth-century visitors to the Southwest. Pueblo structures were made of local materials and in forms that reproduced local topography. Like Pueblo people themselves, the buildings reflected and celebrated the starkly beautiful southwestern environment from which they grew (Scully 1972). In fact, Puebloan architecture seemed so much a part of the Southwest that Euroamericans who moved to the region adopted many of the forms and architectural details that distinguish Puebloan architecture, creating the *Pueblo style* that can be found today in public buildings and residences in cities like Santa Fe and Albuquerque (Markovich et al. 1990).

This chapter creates a context for the Orayvi study by describing key characteristics of Puebloan architecture and highlighting those factors that cause structures in pueblos to change in form or function. Like vernacular architecture worldwide, puebloan structures were subject to constant modification and rebuilding. Construction techniques were relatively simple, involved locally available materials, and did not require the assistance of specialists. Reuse of materials was common, and building or rebuilding, as in other cultures, was a response to structural deterioration and changing social needs.

In the first part of the chapter, the layout and construction of modern and historic puebloan masonry structures is described, using ethnographic and historic data. This section describes recent pueblos, but many aspects of design and methods of construction are applicable to prehistoric structures, especially those built after A.D. 1250. Important differences between historic and prehistoric structures are emphasized. Much of the discussion is based on Victor Mindeleff's (1891) monograph on the architecture of Zuni and the Hopi villages, which remains the most comprehensive study of Puebloan building techniques available. Mindeleff's descriptions are especially valuable because the observations were made before these villages experienced extensive Euroamerican contact. The discussion focuses on masonry structures like those at Orayvi, but many of the observations, especially in the construction of roofs and the use of doors and windows, also apply to adobe structures.

The second half of the chapter examines factors

Figure 2.1 This 1879 photograph by J. Hillers shows the Main Plaza at Orayvi, bordered by the front (southeast face) of Roomblock 4 (right) and the rear of Roomblock 7 (left). Note the "terrace" of collapsed rooms along the rear of Roomblock 7. These rear rooms were abandoned and filled in as new rooms were added to the front of the roomblock. Similar terraces are located at the rear of Roomblock 4 (see figure 5.1). Roomblocks 4 and 7 may be the oldest buildings at Orayvi. (Courtesy of the Smithsonian Institution, National Anthropological Archives; photo no. 56394)

affecting the use-life of pueblo structures. Both cultural and natural processes affecting use-life are discussed, using cross-cultural data for comparison where possible. Structures of masonry or mud in other areas of the world are comparable to southwestern pueblos in settlement form and approaches to construction. Hence, they are useful analogues for examining variables conditioning structure use-life among southwestern pueblos. Again, the emphasis is on masonry structures, but factors affecting mud-walled structures are also discussed.

Puebloan Architecture

Puebloan architecture, from at least A.D. 1250 through the historic period, consisted of blocks of contiguous, clustered dwellings with shared walls—a roomblock—and the internal and external spaces those structures create (fig. 2.1). Historic pueblos and many prehistoric pueblos were multistoried, some containing as many as four or five terraced levels (fig. 2.2). Both historic and prehistoric pueblos show a variety of settlement forms, but almost all pueblos exhibit open plaza space that served as a daily work area and as a space for ceremonial activities. In fact, Scully suggests that "the major environmental function

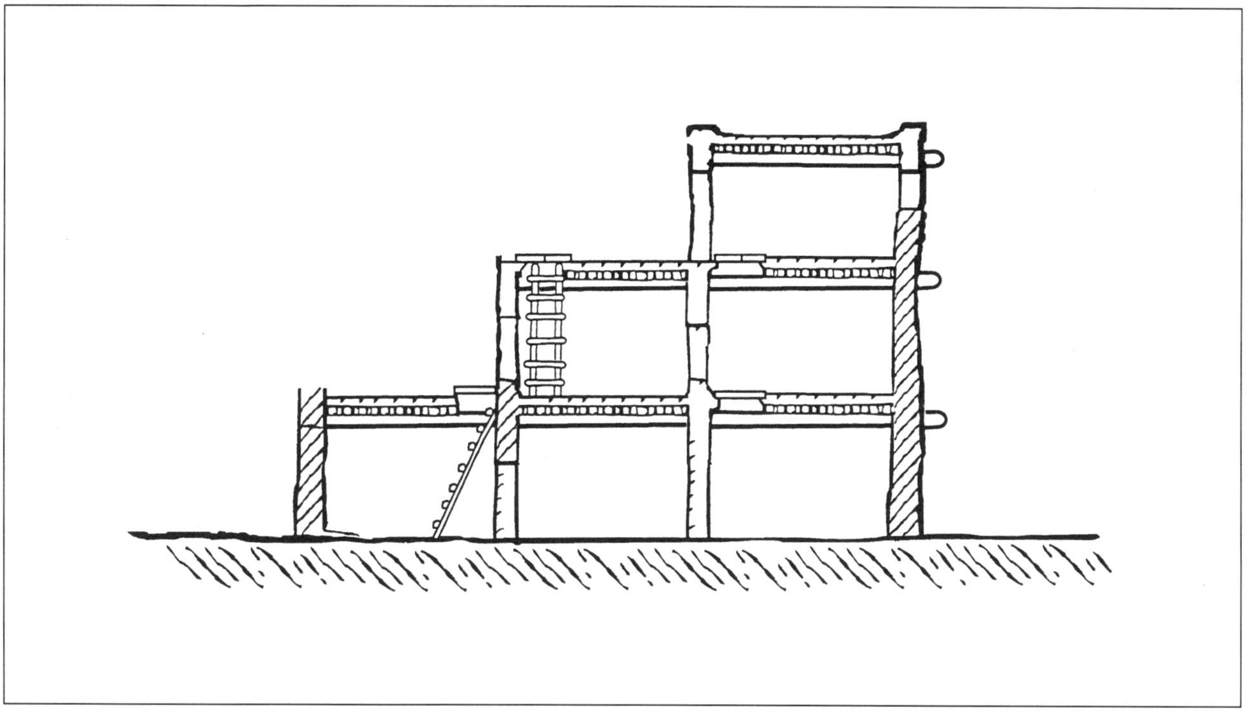

Figure 2.2 A cross section of an Orayvi house. Most houses at Orayvi were only one room wide (table 4.1). Rear lower-story rooms may have been little used except as dead storage or an architectural platform. (Modified from Adams 1982:77)

of Hopi . . . is not to provide complex interior spaces or a variety of individually expressive buildings but instead to use buildings to frame a plaza in which ritual dances can be performed and from which they can be watched" (1972:10, 14).

Kivas, semisubterranean religious structures, either round or rectangular (as at Hopi), are located in plazas or in the "streets" between roomblocks. Prior to A.D. 1300, kivas were, at times, built into roomblocks. The use of a formal plaza may have begun with the development of the Chacoan Great House after A.D. 900 (Lekson 1986: 64; but see Adams 1991), but even in earlier unit pueblos, the area between the roomblock and trash midden may have served as an important activity area—a protoplaza.

Most modern pueblos have several plazas, but, typically, one of the plazas is ceremonially most important. To modern Pueblo people, this special plaza is not only a useful work space—it defines the center of the community. Alfonso Ortiz (1969:18–21), an anthropologist from San Juan Pueblo, has described the Tewa world as a series of concentric circles with a single point in the plaza as

the sacred center of the village. Rina Swentzell (1988), an architectural scholar and Santa Clara Pueblo Indian, describes the plaza as the physical, spiritual, and symbolic center of the Pueblo world. The plaza area, where much of the daily life of the pueblo is enacted, is defined by high, terraced, human-made structures that replicate the distant, enclosing mountains. The rooftop work area extends the plaza space.

Mindeleff (1891) refers frequently to the "symmetry" of the "ancient" pueblos, and the lack of planning in the nineteenth-century pueblos he visited. Chacoan Great Houses, to which Mindeleff may have been alluding, were certainly the first and perhaps the only Puebloan structures that were planned and constructed on a very large scale (but see Cameron in prep.). After A.D. 1250, two different types of layouts seem to characterize much Pueblo construction. Adams (1991:101–3) notes that the "enclosed plaza" layout developed in the thirteenth century and was common throughout the northern Southwest by A.D. 1300 (e.g., Arroyo Hondo, fig. 1.5). As discussed in chapter 7, this settlement plan does require some planning and coordination in order to build roomblocks that define plaza space of a generally uniform size. By A.D. 1400, the "street-oriented" layout begins to replace the enclosed plaza (Adams 1991:103; Lekson in press). The street-oriented layout is characteristic of many modern pueblos, including Orayvi. In pueblos showing a street-oriented layout, roomblocks tend to face southeast, making them solar efficient (Fewkes 1906; Knowles 1974).

The primary building unit of the pueblo house is a rectangular room. A single room can be a complete house but more often is the nucleus of a larger structure; rooms are added as the domestic group expands (Mindeleff 1891: 102). Most households have several rooms with different functions (fig. 2.2). Adams (1983:48) has defined six categories of room use at the Hopi pueblo of Walpi: storage, religious storage, granary, habitation, piki house (a small structure with a hearth for cooking thin piki bread), and nonkiva religious.

Saile (1977b), using ethnographic and historic sources, describes rituals that accompany Pueblo house and kiva construction. Rituals involved in construction all show a concern for the cardinal directions and recognize that the built structure is a "living" being. Prayers are offered for the health and well-being of both the house and its inhabitants. At Hopi, the construction of a pueblo room began with the builder pacing out the dimensions of the room and marking each corner with a stone. There seemed to be little preparation of the ground surface, and in most cases buildings were modified to suit existing ground conditions (Mindeleff 1891:101–2, 143). Rituals were performed before the construction of ground-level rooms, but upper stories required no rituals, perhaps because they were considered extensions of the already existing structure (Mindeleff 1891:102).

Mindeleff emphasizes the lack of planning in Hopi and Zuni construction, noting no preplanning for either multistoried structures or contiguous structures (1891: 100). "The pueblo plan of to-day readily admits of additions at any time and almost at any point of the basal construction" (1891:148). Some historic southwestern pueblos—for example, Acoma (Earls 1988; Robinson 1990)—have a "planned" core (a large group of structures that were built contemporaneously). Contemporaneous

construction of a large number of rooms also characterizes some prehistoric pueblos, especially the Eastern Pueblos, and may reflect a greater degree of social integration in these villages (Cameron in prep.)

Walls

Walls at both Zuni and Hopi were of stone masonry mortared with mud, although adobe brick was used at Zuni after Spanish contact, especially in construction outside the main village (Kroeber 1917:199; Mindeleff 1891:138). There is little information on the source of construction stone in either area. The nearest outcrop of suitable building stone is located at some distance from Zuni (Mindeleff 1891:139). Donaldson (1893:6) states, "when the Moquis and Pueblos build of stone . . . they do not use cut or hammered stone, but waterwashed or disintegrated stone, picked up in the beds of arroyos or from along the streams, frequently washed from a long distance." Unfortunately, Donaldson's report was based on little ethnographic information. Stone quarrying was practiced prehistorically (Lekson 1986:10; Scarborough and Shimada 1974), and extensive masonry preparation has been documented at many archaeological sites in the northern Southwest (e.g., Lekson 1986). Building stone was frequently recycled at both Hopi and Zuni (Adams 1976; Ferguson and Mills 1987:253; Ferguson et al. 1990: 110; Kroeber 1917:195), and recycling was perhaps the most common source of this material in long-lived historic pueblos. Evidence of recycled stone has also been noted at prehistoric pueblos (Rohn 1971:44; Scarborough and Shimada 1974:61; Vivian and Mathews 1965:36).

Mindeleff (1891:137, 140) noted a more liberal use of mud mortar at Zuni than at Hopi. Occasionally, Hopi walls were laid without mortar during the dry season, and later, when the rains came, these walls would be chinked with mud mortar and small stones. Bunting (1976:12–13) reports that this practice produces a more stable wall because the dry-laid stones do not settle later when mud mortar in the joints begins to wash out. Roys (1936) found that various methods were used to provide stability to prehistoric stone walls in the Four Corners area, involving mud mortar, chinking stones, or combinations of the two (see also Rinaldo 1964:19–23). Roys (1936:119–23) noted the use of both Chacoan masonry (see Lekson 1986:15–24) and "block-like" masonry at Lowry Ruin in southwestern Colorado, masonry types that may be more carefully executed than those at historic Hopi pueblos.

In general, Mindeleff (1891:140) believed that masonry walls at Hopi and especially at Zuni were thin and subject to deterioration. At Zuni, Mindeleff attributed this to sparing use of stone because usable outcrops were not close by (1891:139). (The Hopi said men were masons, but although men apparently hauled the building materials [E. Charles Adams, personal communication, 1990], women, in Mindeleff's observation, did much of the masonry work [Mindeleff 1891:101].)

Mindeleff (1891:114) found that kiva walls at both Zuni and Hopi tended to be more poorly constructed than other types of rooms. When kivas were built in depressions, an interior masonry wall was often added. Although structurally unnecessary, these walls may have served as better foundations for interior plaster or may simply have been part of traditional construction practices.

Doors and Windows

In early historic pueblo buildings, ground-level rooms were entered through the roof, while upper-story rooms had doors. Windows were found primarily in upper stories, although exterior walls tended to have small windows placed high in the wall face. At both Hopi and Zuni, as the need for defense decreased, doors and windows began to be added to first-floor rooms (Adams 1976; Ferguson and Mills 1987; Ferguson et al. 1990). Before the use of wooden doors, doors and windows were often closed with masonry during temporary absences of the owner (i.e., during absences for agricultural activities) or during cold weather, when all but the most necessary apertures were often sealed (Mindeleff 1891:183–88). Although these masonry seals were intended to be temporary, they were often very nicely constructed and well finished.

Door and window locations were changed as the needs of the inhabitants changed. For example, if a new room was added to an existing room, a window in the existing room might become superfluous and be converted to a niche. Rooms in the interior part of a room-block tended to be very dark, with the only light coming from a roof entry hole. In many of these rooms, a hole was added at the juncture of the roof and wall and angled obliquely to admit light (Mindeleff 1891:207).

At Hopi, when a ground-floor room was under construction, a doorway was usually left in one wall so that the builders could enter and exit easily. This doorway was generally sealed when construction was completed and a roof entry provided (Mindeleff 1891:182).

Roofs

Roofs were of very sturdy construction, not only because they protected the entire structure from the elements but also because the roof of one room frequently formed the floor for the room above. Roofs typically consisted of primary beams socketed into the walls, smaller secondary beams laid perpendicular to the primary beams, a layer of brush and twig closing material, and a thick cap of earth (Ahlstrom, Dean, and Robinson 1978:19–20; Mindeleff 1891:148–51). At the Hopi village of Walpi, primary beams are of pine, fir, or cottonwood; secondary beams are of juniper; closing material is generally willow or reed (Adams 1982:51). When a roof forms the floor of an upper-story room, it is occasionally paved with thin stone slabs; with external roofs, flat stones cover only the coping (Mindeleff 1891:149). Most roofs were constructed with a slight slope to allow for drainage (Kroeber 1917:193; Mindeleff 1891:151).

Timber for roof construction may have been especially difficult to obtain at Hopi. Near Orayvi, local sources of preferred timber, such as pine and Douglas fir, were apparently exhausted by the late 1700s (Douglass 1929:754). The size of available timber affected the size of rooms. With the advent of draft animals and wagons, larger beams from greater distances could be procured and the size of rooms increased (see chapter 3).

Use-Life of Pueblo Structures

Puebloan structures seem timeless, but like vernacular architecture everywhere, they are in a constant state of

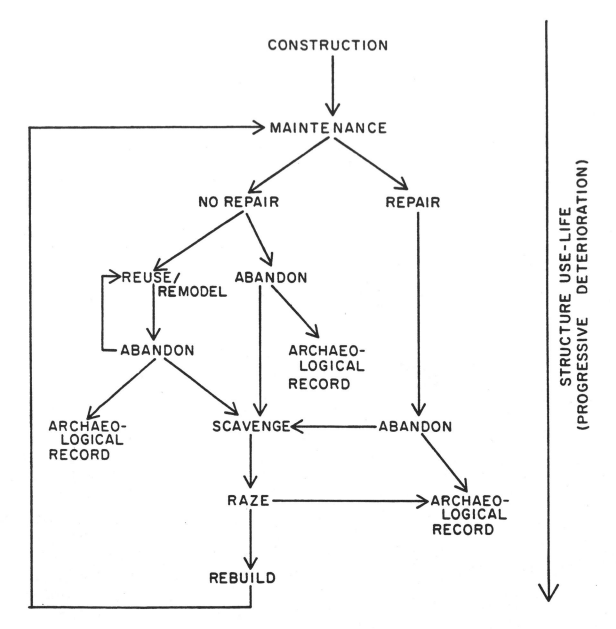

Figure 2.3 The use-life of vernacular buildings. As buildings progress from initial construction to final abandonment, owners make decisions about maintenance, repair, and reuse of the structure or its building materials.

change due both to natural deterioration processes and changing social needs (Cameron 1991a). During the use-life of the structure, as it deteriorates, the homeowner faces a series of decisions: it may be maintained and re-paired, temporarily abandoned, remodeled to fit changing social needs, reused for secondary purposes, or perma-nently abandoned (fig. 2.3). After abandonment, the structure may be reused, scavenged for usable material,

partially or completely razed, or rebuilt. Identifying those factors that cause structure deterioration and architectural change will help archaeologists reconstruct the causes of prehistoric architectural change. This section examines factors affecting architectural change in both the South-west and other parts of the world where architectural and environmental variables are similar.

Structure use-life is the period from initial construction to final abandonment (Cameron 1991a). Although technological and social causes of structure modification and abandonment interact in their effects on structures, they are examined separately here. Technological factors affecting the length of structure use-life include original siting of the structure, construction techniques, weather, natural catastrophes (earthquake, fire, and flood), human wear and tear, levels of maintenance applied to the structure, and changes in structure function resulting from deterioration. Social factors include architectural adjustments to accommodate the developmental cycle of the domestic group, the degree of coherence among residents of a settlement, and external social interactions.

With proper maintenance, pueblo structures can last a very long time. Some of the modern pueblos have rooms that were constructed almost three hundred years ago (Adams 1979; Ahlstrom, Dean, and Robinson 1978; Robinson 1990). Even though sturdily made, however, few rooms in active or abandoned settlements have such lengthy use-lives. The factors that cause architectural change and structural abandonment in modern southwestern pueblos and vernacular structures in arid areas elsewhere should be similar to those affecting prehistoric pueblos.

Causes of Structural Decay

The rate at which structures deteriorate depends on a number of technological and environmental conditions. Although these conditions affect the maximum *possible* use-life of a structure, social factors, such as willingness to repair and maintain structures, and changing social needs, may be far more crucial in determining the *actual* structure use-life.

Siting and Construction. The longevity of a masonry structure is affected by the location selected for the structure and the materials and construction techniques used (Firor 1988:1). Masonry walls that are located in well-drained areas, that are footed on bedrock, and that are attached to other walls can be expected to stand for a long time. A single room located in a swale and footed on

dirt can be expected to deteriorate more rapidly because of uneven subsidence of the ground surface and lack of support from other walls or structures (Jeffrey S. Dean, personal communication, 1987).

Well-constructed walls in which little or no mortar is used (dry-laid) with stones that are shaped to fit together well (such as those at some Chacoan and Mesa Verde sites) are more resistant to deterioration because weight is transmitted from stone to stone and no load is carried by mortar (Firor 1988:5); these types of walls are also very resistant to the effects of rainwater (Bunting 1976:12–13). Stone used in construction may be soft and easily eroded, however, while mortar may have little clay content or be high in organic content, either of which will form a less adequate seal between stones. Especially with poor-quality construction material, the weight of stone upon stone may cause stones in lower courses to crack, resulting in instability in the walls (Firor 1988:5; Seeden 1982).

Walls in puebloan roomblocks are often not well tied where they bond or abut (Adams 1976). Back walls, often built first as a single continuous unit, tend to be thicker and sturdier than interior walls. When these back walls deteriorate, they may fall as a unit, especially if they are north-facing. North-facing walls suffer greater deterioration from moisture because snow accumulations remain there longer (see below). When exterior walls fall, thinner and less sturdy interior walls are exposed and then used as outside walls. These new exterior walls are subject to rapid decay (Adams 1976).

Inherent construction flaws may be less important in occupied structures because points of deterioration can be repaired as soon as they are observed. In abandoned structures, the effects of such flaws can cause rapid disintegration of the structure (Firor 1988:1).

A number of techniques were used in pueblo construction to protect walls from the eroding effects of rain. The tops of walls were capped with thin, flat stones set very close together to prevent erosion (Mindeleff 1891: 151). At Zuni and at Hopi, after about 1880, projecting cornices were constructed that protected the face of the walls from rain (Ahlstrom, Dean, and Robinson 1978). Large sherds were often placed, convex side out, at the base of walls and at the base of rooftop chimneys to prevent undercutting (Mindeleff 1891:139). Roof drains with projecting members were used to direct rain off the roof and away from the wall. If the drain dumped water onto a lower roof, stones (sometimes discarded metates) were placed beneath it to protect the lower roof and wall (Mindeleff 1891:153–56).

Abandoned lower-story rooms were sometimes filled in to provide a firm foundation for the construction of rooms above them. Ferguson and Mills (1987:253; Ferguson et al. 1990:110) note that dismantling a single room within the dense cluster of rooms at Zuni would cause problems for the stability of nearby rooms. Filling lower rooms alleviated this problem and was accomplished by cutting around the roof, allowing it to fall into the room, and filling the remainder of the room with trash or sand. This process was also observed at archaeological sites in the Hopi area by Mindeleff (1891:86), at prehistoric sites in Chaco Canyon (Lekson 1986:10), and at the Hopi village of Walpi (Adams 1976, 1979, 1982).

Environmental Causes of Decay. A variety of environmental factors affect the integrity of mud or masonry structures, including rain, snow, wind, the percolation of groundwater and salts into walls, and the decay of wooden members through the actions of weathering, bacteria, fungi, and insects (Carter and Pagliero 1966; Crosby 1983; Firor 1988:5; Guillini 1968; Hayden 1945; McIntosh 1974; Schiffer 1987; Schiffer et al. 1987).

Mud walls are especially subject to deterioration if a protective coat of mud plaster is not applied regularly. Cracks can allow moisture to become trapped between the wall and the plaster layer and cause erosion of the wall surface. Cracks and bulges in the wall itself will also hasten collapse (Crosby 1983). The use of stone footings for mud walls can deter problems with undercutting of walls from rain splashing and percolation of groundwater. Stone footings are commonly used in adobe structures in the American Southwest today and were also used at some sites in the prehistoric Southwest (Creamer et al. 1993; Stubbs and Stallings 1953).

For either masonry or mud structures, if a roof begins to leak where it joins the wall, rainwater will be concentrated at this point and will hasten the deterioration of that portion of the wall. Leaks most often occur at corners, where the seal between the walls and roof is least secure. Wall bases can be undermined by surface runoff or by the action of an arroyo where structures are located near water courses (Firor 1988:5). Accumulation of snow along north-facing walls increases the absorption of water into the wall and the surrounding soil; freeze-thaw cycles cause mortar to deteriorate (Adams 1976; Firor 1988:11). Water drawn into walls through capillary action from the ground surface can cause deterioration of lower courses of stone. Salts in soil are also drawn into walls from surrounding soils, hastening stone deterioration (Firor 1988:11; Hayden 1945).

Rainwater can have serious effects on masonry structures, tending to wash away mud mortar and sometimes leaving behind an unstable collection of stones that are prone to collapse. Yearly applications of mud plaster help prevent this sort of deterioration (see maintenance, below). Seeden's study (1982) of Syrian villages constructed of stone liberally mortared with mud shows that these structures begin to disintegrate after about a year if left unrepaired. She presents a remarkable series of photographs illustrating the amount of wall reduction that can occur in only a few seasons.

Torrential rains occur infrequently in the Southwest, but when they do occur, they may cause wall collapse. A very bad rainstorm in 1947 created a lake behind the excavated prehistoric site of Chetro Ketl in Chaco Canyon (Lekson 1983:6). Water from the lake percolated into the masonry walls of the ruin, dissolved the mud mortar, and caused the collapse of walls that had stood for nine hundred years. Heavy rainstorms in 1973 caused the deterioration of many masonry walls at the modern Hopi village of Walpi and forced major renovation of the pueblo (Jeffrey S. Dean, personal communication, 1987).

Other factors causing deterioration of masonry walls are organisms such as bacteria, lichen, algae, and fungi that attack surfaces of stone and break them down through chemical action (Firor 1988:16–21). Such weathering is especially severe on north-facing walls that have better conditions for the growth of vegetation (E. Charles Adams, personal communication, 1990).

Plant roots may widen small cracks in stone and cause them to break. Rodents may burrow beneath walls and weaken foundations (Firor 1988:16–21).

In some situations, roofs are less subject to deterioration than are walls. They require some maintenance to prevent leaks, but even when totally unmaintained, beams will remain in good condition because they are not in contact with the ground and hence dry quickly and are not subject to rot (Jeffrey S. Dean, personal communication, 1987). Insects may occasionally consume wood beams and other perishable construction material, however (Firor 1988:21), especially in the southern part of the Southwest. Top-floor roofs are most subject to decay because they are most exposed to rainfall. First- and second-floor roofs may last for centuries.

Natural Catastrophe. Catastrophic events such as earthquakes or fires can cause serious damage and shorten structure use-life. Earthquakes are relatively rare in the Southwest, but even minor tremors can cause shifting, cracking, and instability in walls. Pueblos constructed in caves or rockshelters are often damaged by rock spalling from the cave or shelter ceiling. A large section of the rear rooms at Pueblo Bonito in Chaco Canyon was destroyed in 1941 when a huge rock separated from the main part of the adjacent mesa and tumbled onto the site (Schumm and Chorley 1964). This rock had apparently been threatening the site even during the prehistoric period; there is evidence that the inhabitants of Pueblo Bonito had attempted to shore it up (Judd 1959).

Human-Induced Deterioration. Occupied pueblos suffer from normal processes of wear and tear entailed in daily living. For example, roof beams were frequently used as storage areas, causing additional wear not directly related to their function as roof supports (Jeffrey S. Dean, personal communication, 1987). Other human activities in occupied or abandoned structures also hastened deterioration. Abandoned rooms were often used as trash dumps by prehistoric inhabitants or were otherwise artificially filled (Ferguson and Mills 1987:253; Ferguson et al. 1990:110). Open, partially filled rooms can introduce water into walls through capillary action, causing deterioration

(Adams 1976). Furthermore, empty rooms adjacent to trash-filled rooms are subject to decay because the fill presses on the wall between the two rooms, causing it to bulge and become unstable—a process that can be observed at partially excavated archaeological sites. Such "dead load" pressure also causes collapse of subterranean structures as surrounding soil presses against interior walls (Firor 1988:5).

The fact that roof beams are often well preserved makes them valuable to scavengers. There is considerable evidence that roof beams were scavenged and reused within occupied pueblos and that used beams were transported from abandoned sites to construct new settlements nearby (Ahlstrom 1985; Ahlstrom, Dean, and Robinson 1978). The removal of roof beams leaves walls unprotected and therefore more subject to deterioration. If roof beams remain in place, even though the roof no longer functions to repel water, the interlocking structure of beams will tend to prevent walls from collapsing. Removal and reuse of architectural wood is a common occurrence in villages elsewhere in the world (Kramer 1982:94; Park 1988:66; Serageldin 1982). Research at modern pueblos indicates that individual beams may become worn-out and be replaced without replacing the entire roof (Ahlstrom, Dean, and Robinson 1978:20).

Maintenance and Remodeling

Regular maintenance is one of the most important factors affecting the rate at which buildings decay. Structure use-life can be greatly increased with regular, careful repair and maintenance. In spite of maintenance, structures do decay, and they then may be used for secondary purposes. Decisions to repair, rebuild, or raze structures may be based in part on the availability and cost of land and construction materials.

Maintenance and Repair. When structures become damaged, decisions must be made to repair, to reuse for secondary or tertiary functions, to abandon and rebuild, or to raze and rebuild. These decisions will be based on the cost/benefits of repair versus abandonment/reuse but also in part on idiosyncratic factors. Studies have shown that some homeowners are more willing than others to make the constant repairs that maximize the use-life of structures (McIntosh 1974). For example, elderly homeowners may be less likely to make necessary repairs than younger ones (Horne 1983:20; Seeden 1985). Mindeleff (1891:140) noted that during the rainy season, violent storms caused frequent damage to puebloan structures and a need for immediate repair. But he pointed out that "in most villages, little care is taken to repair the houses until the owner feels that to postpone such action longer would endanger its stability" (1891:73).

In the Southwest, the most consistent and effective form of maintenance for pueblo structures was frequent renewal of exterior mud plaster. Mud plaster applied to masonry walls prevents erosion of mortar, which can cause serious structural damage (Lekson 1986:29). However, such precautions were not always taken. A thick coat of mud plaster was usually applied to the interior walls of pueblo structures but not consistently to exterior walls, where protection was most important. Exterior walls tended to be plastered more consistently at Zuni than at Hopi, possibly because Zuni walls needed more protection than Hopi walls. Mindeleff believed that because the stone from which Zuni was built was very thin and tabular, Zuni walls required more protection from the eroding effects of rain (Mindeleff 1891:139). Furthermore, parts of Zuni were of poorly made adobe brick that was especially subject to deterioration (1891:140). At Hopi, ground-floor storage rooms were plastered less frequently than upper-story habitation rooms. Mindeleff even noticed a difference among the Hopi villages in the frequency of plastering: First Mesa villages were plastered more freely than Second Mesa villages, and Orayvi, on Third Mesa, used plaster only rarely (1891:143–44). Photographs of Orayvi, discussed in chapters 3, 5, and 6, tend to support Mindeleff's observations.

Roofs, too, must receive frequent attention to prevent leaks and deterioration that will cause further structural damage. Winter snow accumulations must be removed rapidly, and damage to the roof must be repaired immediately to avoid deterioration of both roof and walls, a problem both in the Southwest (Adams 1976) and some parts of the Near East (Seeden 1985).

Changing Structure Function Resulting from Deterioration. As they deteriorate, structures in houses constructed for one purpose, such as habitation, may be reused subsequently for other purposes, such as storage or animal containment. David (1971), in his study of the villages of the Fulani of Africa, calls this process the "devolutionary cycle" (1971:119). He found that structures are successively used for different purposes depending upon their state of decay but noted that most structures are demolished before the cycle is complete because of rapid decay or differing social needs. This same cycle, which was found in other parts of Africa (McIntosh 1974, 1976, 1977) and in the Near East (Horne 1983), certainly occurred in southwestern pueblos. These changes in function are affected by social needs and desires as well as deterioration processes. For example, a homeowner's need for a storage room may be greater than his or her need for a habitation room, influencing decisions relating to a deteriorating structure. For abandoned structures, the common practice of removing wooden structural members hastens deterioration (see above) and decreases potential for later reuse.

Availability and Cost of Land and Construction Materials. Decisions to repair, rebuild, abandon, or dismantle structures may be partly based on the availability and cost of land and construction materials. More durable materials are often more costly, making economics a factor in structure use-life. For example, in the village of Hassanabad in western Iran, Watson (1979) found that wood was expensive; hence, upper-story rooms and porches could be built only by the most affluent residents. Furthermore, when the grain crop was meager, poorer residents had no chaff (and no ability to purchase any) for use in repairing house and courtyard walls. This caused significant deterioration of these structures.

In some villages, material may be scavenged from abandoned structures, and new structures be rebuilt in the same location by the reuse of old foundations or a partial wall. Alternatively, if land and materials are readily available and construction is relatively easy, it may be simpler to build a new structure in a new location and allow the old structure to fall into ruins (cf. David 1971:

115). This often results in lateral movement of villages, with new structures being built at one end of a village while old structures are abandoned at the other end (Ascher 1968; McIntosh 1976). Lateral movement of villages might be expected to occur most often where extensive land-clearing before construction is unnecessary. Where land ownership is formalized, however, new land may not be available, and it may be more economical to repair or reuse rather than to raze and rebuild. In an Iranian village, Jacobs (1979) found that extended families tended to split up when new land for housing became available, but she predicted that they would develop again as the new housing area became filled.

Social Causes of Architectural Change

Before structures in occupied villages become structurally unsound, they may be abandoned, reused, razed, or remodeled for a variety of social reasons. Houses may be adjusted as families gain or lose members. The movement of families into and out of a village will determine the frequency with which structures are constructed or abandoned, although the location of ceremonial space may be a major determinant of structure treatment. Finally, external social conditions and the location of important resources will condition the construction, remodeling, and abandonment of structures.

The Developmental Cycle of the Domestic Group. The composition of the household unit and the developmental cycle of the domestic group (Goody 1958) affect construction, remodeling, reuse, and abandonment. A household may add structures to accommodate either additional children, adult children who return home with spouses, or in polygamous households, additional wives. Alternatively, interconnected structures may lose internal connections if household relationships change through the death or departure of some residents or if relationships between residents change (see David 1971:117 and Prussin 1969 for African examples of these practices).

Structures with shorter maximum use-lives are more likely to reflect the composition of the social unit occupying them than are structures with longer use-lives (David

1971:115; Kramer 1982:119; Schwerdtfeger 1982). Where structure use-life is long, houses built for one household may be inherited by a household with a different social composition. Modifications may occur to bring the house into line with the composition of the household, but if building costs are high or household composition is variable, houses may be used unaltered.

The Degree of Social Integration. Frequency and type of structure modification may be related to the degree of social integration among residents of a settlement. For example, at Hopi and Zuni, individual structures are built or razed based on the needs of owners. There is little concern for the coordination of construction efforts with neighbors. At the Pueblo of Acoma, in contrast, most remodeling has consisted of internal modifications that seem to reflect the division of extended families. Suites of rooms are broken up, and rooms may change function (e.g., the creation of a new kitchen to serve a newly independent suite of rooms). In general, there has been far less major structural modification at Acoma than at Zuni and Hopi, and this may be partly attributed to greater coherence among members of the Acoma community (see chapter 7). Another factor, however, may be a greater decline in full-time residents of Acoma than at either Zuni or Hopi (William J. Robinson, personal communication, 1990).

Changes in Population. Changes in population levels can have a dramatic impact on structures and intrasite settlement patterns. In conditions of declining population, many structures may be abandoned and allowed to decay. Where population is rising, these structures, or at least their construction materials, will probably be reused. As Deal (1985:267) has noted in reference to the Maya highlands, "abandoned structures were relatively rare in growing communities, and if they were left erect for any length of time they often served as refuse dumps, animal shelters, play areas for children or a convenient covered activity area."

Stanislawski's (1973) study of Hopi settlement formation and abandonment indicates that populations in Hopi villages vary in response to clan extinction or factionalism between clans. He suggests that variable population size has a major effect on the construction, abandonment, and reuse of structures. For example, during times of economic hardship, lower-status clans are sometimes forced to leave a village and reside elsewhere (Stanislawski 1973:384; see also Levy 1992). Furthermore, through the natural operation of demographic processes, clans occasionally become extinct or nearly extinct. Hopi property (including structures) is held by clans, and the demise of a clan may cause the abandonment of some structures that it owned, although structures may also be traded, sold, or reused by others (Stanislawski 1973:386).

An architectural study of the Turkish settlement of Asvan (Hall, McBride, and Riddell 1973) provides a dramatic example of the effect of population fluctuation on village structures. This village of stone and mud houses was almost entirely abandoned in the early twentieth century. The few remaining inhabitants immediately moved into the larger and better-built structures. Over the next seventeen years, people from the surrounding area gradually moved into the village and almost entirely dismantled the older buildings, reusing materials and often the walls and foundations for new construction. Settlement during this period was mostly in the east section of the village and consisted of a random and dispersed pattern of structures. In the 1930s, a large population influx occurred. The government organized resettlement, and the ruined west section of the village was gridded; individual building plots were assigned. The new layout did not follow in any way the layout of the old village, the earlier buildings having been almost completely dismantled. This new village configuration was maintained with minor modifications until people began to leave in 1969 in advance of a dam that soon caused the area to be inundated. At Asvan, population fluctuation changed the layout of the village almost entirely over a twenty-year period.

Continuity in the Use of Ceremonial Space. It is apparent that ceremonial areas may retain their location and functions in spite of dramatic growth or abandonment of communities. Schiffer (1987:89) reports that in the abandoned Cypriot village of Kividhes, a church is still maintained. In northern Ghana, an abandoned village has become a dump, yet shrines there continue to be maintained by residents of the new village nearby (Agorsah 1985:107). As residents have moved to Polacca, the Hopi village of Walpi has now become largely a ceremonial center, used seasonally, and full-time occupants are only those individuals with religious responsibilities. It is interesting to note that many structures in Walpi have recently been restored (Adams 1979), presumably because Walpi is still an important ceremonial place to First Mesa Hopi, and also because Euroamericans see it as a historically important settlement. Laguna Pueblo, near Albuquerque, is another that has become largely a ceremonial center for individuals who live in nearby farming villages (Eggan 1950:253–54; Parsons 1923:145). Many houses at Laguna are used as storerooms or temporary living quarters during ceremonial activities.

In spite of almost total reconstruction and great expansion at Zuni Pueblo in the last one hundred years, the basic spatial orientation of the pueblo remains the same, and continuities in the function of religious space are apparent (Ferguson 1996; Ferguson and Mills 1987; Ferguson et al. 1990; Kroeber 1917). Ceremonially used plazas have maintained their locations, and kivas (religious structures) have some of the oldest masonry styles in the pueblo. Furthermore, kivas continue to have roof entry, a construction feature no longer used in domestic structures. At Acoma Pueblo, in western New Mexico, the change from multistory construction to single-story large rooms was common throughout the village, except in ceremonial areas where the older "stairstep" design prevailed (Robinson 1990:103). The importance of ceremonial areas in conditioning patterns of village growth and abandonment for Orayvi is discussed in chapter 6.

External and Internal Social Factors. At times, external social factors may affect the availability of land and cause structure abandonment or modification. Lee Horne (1980:20) found that agricultural villages in northern Iran, which were once tightly nucleated for defensive reasons, are now growing accretionally because social tensions have been removed. They tend to grow laterally, with new structure placement based on kin ties, the location of water, and other resources. With respect to the Maya highlands example discussed above (Deal 1985), Margaret Nelson (personal communication 1992) has noted that federal land controls and usurpation of land rights has caused more intensive use of available structures even where communities are not growing.

The rebuilding of Zuni Pueblo was the result of changing needs for defense and increasing contact with Euroamerican culture (Ferguson and Mills 1987; Ferguson et al. 1990). Before 1881, the pueblo was massively constructed, with three- and four-story roomblocks (clusters of rooms) facing onto interior plazas. When the threat of Apache and Navajo raids decreased in the late 1800s (a result of increased U.S. military presence), and with greater access to European tools and construction materials, the Zuni began to open up ground-floor storage rooms with doors and windows, and these rooms became preferred living rooms. Upper-story rooms were torn down or allowed to disintegrate. Open space was created in the pueblo because it was often easier to raze whole sections of the village and rebuild outside the original pueblo boundaries. Building materials were frequently reused in repair or new construction. At Orayvi, these same types of architectural changes are observed in relation to increasing Euroamerican contact (see chapters 3 and 5).

Some of the constant architectural change at Zuni Pueblo is also the result of religious practices. Kroeber (1917) estimated that the exterior walls of every home in Zuni were rebuilt every thirty to forty years, partly because of the winter Shalako ceremony. In preparation for Shalako, six to eight houses must be totally rebuilt or newly constructed to hold ceremonial figures. Ferguson and Mills (1987:256; Ferguson et al. 1990:105) estimated that between six hundred and eight hundred houses would be constructed or remodeled in the space of a hundred years as a result of Shalako ceremonial requirements.

Access to Resources and Social Services. Sometimes patterns of settlement growth, as well as fluctuations in population levels, may be directly linked to the location of important resources or social services. In Iranian cities, Bonine (1979) has shown that houses are built along water channels, giving most of these cities an orthogonal network of streets rather than the maze of twisting lanes that is the ideal Islamic pattern.

Social services may also determine patterns of settlement growth. During the past century, the Hopi village of Walpi atop First Mesa has been slowly abandoned as residents moved to the settlement of Polacca at the base of the mesa. The establishment of schools, trading posts, and other Euroamerican services below the mesa has been the primary cause of abandonment, and it has resulted in major changes in household and community patterns (Adams 1989a). In Northern Iran, villagers have recently made decisions about which village to live in based on the location of schools and other social resources (Horne 1994:76). As at Hopi, this has caused some areas, especially those in outlying regions, to be abandoned (Horne 1980:17; see Agorsah 1983, 1985 for an African example).

Summary

Puebloan buildings are relatively sturdy when properly maintained. Initial construction flaws can be overcome by vigilant repair, but they may become critical when buildings are abandoned. Environmental agents of decay, most importantly water, can cause serious damage, but rapid repair and preventive maintenance lessen their impact. Normal wear and tear on occupied buildings and scavenging and reuse of structural elements constitute an important source of decay in occupied and abandoned buildings.

A variety of social factors insures that most buildings never reach their maximum potential use-life. The developmental cycle of the domestic group requires periodic architectural change, and population fluctuations and the availability of land in villages will result in the modification and abandonment of structures. If population is declining, abandoned structures will probably be allowed to decay, although they may be used as sources of construction material for repair in other parts of the settlement. If population is increasing, abandoned structures may be remodeled or razed and rebuilt for use by the new occupants.

The spatial growth or decline of a settlement is affected by the cost of land and building materials and by the location of important resources and social services. If topographic or social conditions restrict the spatial growth of villages, razing and rebuilding may be the only option. The location of ceremonial spaces and structures conditions the location of new construction, the location of abandoned structures, and the nature of structure remodeling. Structures and spaces used for ceremonial purposes retain their function far longer than structures and spaces used for other purposes.

Social and technological processes cause architectural change in modern southwestern pueblos, and therefore architectural change identified in prehistoric pueblos can be used to identify these processes in the past. Data from Orayvi presented in chapters 5 and 6 link detailed architectural changes to a number of these social and technological processes, providing a key to the identification of these processes in prehistoric contexts. The reconstruction of prehistoric architectural change is complex, however. The longer a village is occupied, the more structural remodeling, rebuilding, and razing will occur, erasing some architectural patterns entirely. For example, the number of abandoned rooms in an occupied settlement should increase as the span of occupation lengthens, an important fact for archaeologists attempting to ascertain the number of contemporaneously occupied rooms in an archaeological site or trying to determine patterns of population movement in a region. But whether the spatial extent of the settlement grows horizontally or vertically (or both, or neither) will be determined by the factors discussed in this chapter: fluctuations in population levels, the degree of social coherence, the location of important resources, the availability and cost of land and building materials, and so on.

3 / History, Data, and Methods

Orayvi is located in northeastern Arizona on Third Mesa, the westernmost of the three Hopi Mesas (fig. 1.2). It may be the oldest continuously occupied village in the United States, having been founded as early as the twelfth century (Hargrave 1932). It was once the largest of the Hopi pueblos, with almost nine hundred residents, and it has been described as one of the most conservative (Titiev 1944:72; Whiteley 1988:5, 28–29). Subsistence, prior to this century, consisted mainly of farming in the adjacent Orayvi valley (Beaglehole 1937; Bradfield 1971). Orayvi has been the subject of intensive study in part because of the dramatic 1906 factional split. The split has been examined in three major books (Levy 1992; Titiev 1944; Whiteley 1988) and several articles (Bernardini 1996; Bradfield 1971; Clemmer 1978; Parsons 1922).

The first part of this chapter provides a general history of the Hopi since European contact, with emphasis on Orayvi, highlighting European influences on traditional Hopi architecture. The events leading up to the split are described, and varying interpretations of the split are presented because they provide an important framework for interpreting the effect of the split on structures at Orayvi. The remaining sections of the chapter discuss sources of data and methods used in the analyses presented in chapters 4, 5, and 6.

The Spanish Period

The Spanish first visited Hopi in 1540 (Winship 1896), but early contact between the two cultures was sporadic (Adams and Hull 1981:17; Brew 1979:519; Montgomery, Smith, and Brew 1949). About 1630, missions were estab-lished at Orayvi and at two other Hopi pueblos (Brew 1979, 519–20; Ellis 1974:1–2; Montgomery, Smith, and Brew 1949:12). For the next fifty years, the Hopi were subjected to a program of directed culture change as the Spanish attempted to impose European social, political, and religious ideas (Adams and Hull 1981:17). The geographic isolation of the Hopi and internal problems within Spanish colonial society ameliorated Spanish impact on Hopi social and political organization, but the introduction of Euroamerican domesticated plants and animals had long-lasting economic effects. For example, by the middle of the eighteenth century, cotton had been almost completely replaced by wool, and sheep and goats had become primary meat sources (Adams and Hull 1981: 18). Blacksmithing and new types of farming implements were also introduced (Adams 1981:325).

Spanish missionaries were expelled during the Pueblo Revolt of 1680, and Spain ultimately failed to resubjugate the Hopi after the reconquest of 1692 (Whiteley 1988: 19). Spanish reconquest in New Mexico resulted in the migration of a large number of Rio Grande Puebloans to Hopi (Ellis 1974:3). The immigrants had a noticeable impact on the material culture of the Hopi, which is especially apparent in ceramic designs (Adams and Hull 1981: 18; Wyckoff 1985:75). The immigrants began to return home during the 1740s, although some never left. Their descendants now occupy the First Mesa village of Hano (Dozier 1954).

Drought and a smallpox epidemic between 1777 and 1781 forced many Hopi to move to Zuni and other pueblos for several years (Adams and Hull 1981:18; Dockstader 1954:155, cited in Whiteley 1988:27; Ellis 1974:3). After the Hopi returned to their villages, the impact of

Spanish-influenced Rio Grande pueblos was again apparent in Hopi ceramic designs and ceremonies (Adams and Hull 1981:18). About this time, Navajo raids began to pose a significant problem for the Hopi, and they continued into the middle of the nineteenth century, when they were ended by the U.S. Army.

The Spanish period had a lasting effect on a number of details of Hopi architecture. For example, chimneys, including the use of chimney pots, and corner fireplaces were a Spanish introduction; before contact, hearths were simply open firepits in the center of a room, with smoke vented through door and window openings (Mindeleff 1891:168–69, 180). Mindeleff notes that corner placement of the fireplace provided structural support for the chimney (1891:169). Wood-paneled doors were introduced by the Spanish (Mindeleff 1891:183–84), and Spanish influence is also evident in a change in the shape and placement of windows and the use of sawn-wood lintels, sills, and jambs around windows (Mindeleff 1891: 195–96). Domed ovens, more common in Zuni than in Hopi, were used only after Spanish contact (Mindeleff 1891:164).

American Influences

By 1850, the United States governed the Southwest, and an official Indian agent was assigned to deal with Native American tribes in the area. Occasional contact with the new Americans in the first years of the decade resulted in a disastrous smallpox epidemic in 1853, followed by a drought that significantly decreased population (Dockstader 1979:524). The epidemic was especially severe on First Mesa and resulted in the movement of many people to Zuni and Acoma (Adams and Hull 1981:19). During this period, some First Mesa Hopi may have moved to Orayvi and become permanent residents (Levy 1992, and this volume chapter 5).

During the American Civil War, troops were withdrawn from the Southwest, and Navajo raids on the Hopi became more frequent (Dockstader 1979:525). A drought between 1864 and 1868 again caused many Hopi to relocate to Zuni for a number of years (Adams 1981:327), and resulted in strong Zuni influences on Hopi pottery

(Wyckoff 1985:77) and other aspects of Hopi culture (Dockstader 1979:525). Another smallpox epidemic, in 1866–67, was most severe on Second Mesa, especially at Songòopavi, and may have caused immigration of Second Mesa residents to Orayvi (Bradfield 1971:62; Levy 1992; see chapter 5).

In 1874, the U.S. Indian Agency established a school and Hopi agency near First Mesa; the following year, Thomas Keam established the first trading post in Keam's Canyon, east of First Mesa; and between 1870 and 1875, Morovians, Mormons, and Baptists all established missions at Hopi (Dockstader 1979:525–26). These events effectively ended the protohistoric period at Hopi (Adams 1981:327). In 1882, the completion of the transcontinental railroad just sixty miles south of Hopi started a new era in Hopi-Euroamerican relations (Whiteley 1988:71–72). With more convenient access, Hopi began to attract numerous tourists, scholars, and other travelers, especially during the last decade of the nineteenth century.

American influence on Hopi architecture was far more extensive than Spanish influence had been, in part due to the railroad, which provided access to new tools and materials, but also because of the U.S. military presence. As at Zuni (chapter 2), the decreasing need for defense at Hopi resulted in the dismantling of upper stories and the conversion of lower-story storage rooms to habitation (Ahlstrom et al. 1978:58). The conversion of storage rooms to habitation rooms may also have been encouraged by the adoption of wage labor, which reduced the need for storage.

Several technological introductions allowed the Hopi to build larger living rooms. First, wood stoves were much more effective than small, poorly ventilated hearths in heating large interior spaces. Second, wagons allowed the Hopi access to larger roof beams, available at a considerable distance from Hopi (Ahlstrom, Dean, and Robinson 1978:25). Wagons were also used to haul inexpensive and readily available coal supplies from nearby Black Mesa for heating (Adams 1979:44). The earliest construction of separate piki houses (an architectural form that may not have been in use at Orayvi) may have coincided with the adoption of the wood stove (Adams 1982:72). Milled lumber and glass windows, introduced after 1880 (Adams

1989a:175; Ferguson and Mills 1987:251), also changed Hopi architectural styles.

U.S. government policy in the late nineteenth century was aimed at assimilating Indian populations into mainstream Euroamerican culture. One way of trying to achieve this goal was to educate Indian children in Euroamerican schools. Not surprisingly, many Hopi people were violently opposed to the education and Americanization of their children. In 1890, several Hopi chiefs, including Loololma of Orayvi, were taken to Washington, D.C., where they met President Benjamin Harrison. Loololma returned to Hopi apparently convinced that the Hopi must accommodate the requests of the U.S. government, and he agreed to persuade the people of Orayvi to send their children to school (but see Levy 1992:91–92 for evidence that Loololma was not sincere). His evident change of heart was greeted with great opposition by many people at Orayvi. Two factions developed, one that sided with Loololma and his support of White ways, and another that opposed him. Americans termed the first group the Friendlies, the second group the Hostiles (Titiev 1944:72–82; Whiteley 1988:74–83).

The Orayvi Split

The 1906 Orayvi split is the best-known example of village factionalism in the Southwest. Both Titiev (1944) and Whiteley (1988) have provided lengthy descriptions of the split, but they offer very different interpretations of the event. Other interpretations have also been suggested (Bernardini 1996; Bradfield 1971; Clemmer 1978; Hargrave 1932; Levy 1992; and Parsons 1922). Most authors, however, agree on the sequence of events leading up to and following the split. The following brief description of these events draws on both Titiev (1944:69–95) and Whiteley (1988:71–118). Contrasting interpretations of the split are then presented.

Conflicts between Hostiles and Friendlies increased in intensity during the 1890s and the early years of the twentieth century. Then, on September 7, 1906, the dispute climaxed. After the dramatic tug-of-war recounted in chapter 1, the Hostile faction, which included almost half the population of Orayvi, was forced out of the village.

The Hostiles camped the first night at springs seven kilometers north of Orayvi, at a place called Ho'atvela. They eventually founded a new village there. In November, after further disagreement among the Hostiles, many returned to Orayvi, but the returnees stayed for only three years (Whiteley 1988:6; Titiev [1944:212] erroneously reported the stay as one year), leaving again to found the village of Paaqavi near Ho'atvela. Economic problems and further discord at Orayvi (Bradfield 1971:30) caused subsequent, gradual migration of many Friendlies to Kiqotsmovi (New Orayvi), at the foot of Third Mesa, and to Munqapi, a farming village twenty miles west (Titiev 1944:94). The factionalism that climaxed with the split continues to be a major sociological force on Third Mesa today (Clemmer 1978; Wyckoff 1985).

The causes of the factional split have been variously described as the result of social or economic factors. Orayvi's large population is often considered a catalyst. Clemmer (1978:58, 76) and others (Hargrave 1932:7; Parsons 1922:283) suggest that the split was caused by tensions resulting from acculturative pressure on the Hopi by the U.S. government. Although battle lines between Hostiles and Friendlies were defined in terms of U.S.–Hopi conflict, others see underlying causes for the split. Titiev (1944:69, 99) suggests that the matrilineal clans that compose Hopi society were only loosely combined into villages and that large pueblos, like Orayvi, were operating with social systems better adapted to much smaller communities. Under these circumstances, the potential for division was ever-present (see Nagata 1977 for another example of factionalism at a Hopi village). Titiev (1944:99) believes the dispute between Hostiles and Friendlies over the education of Hopi children and the adoption of American culture was symptomatic of a division that was in some ways inevitable. Bernardini's (1996) study makes essentially the same argument, applying the term "scalar stress" to the problems of information flow at the large pueblo. Bernardini suggests that population increase at Orayvi during the late nineteenth century multiplied problems of information flow (1996:380).

In a study of Hopi agriculture, Bradfield (1971) observed that in the years just prior to 1906, the main wash in the Orayvi Valley began a period of severe entrenchment that destroyed one-third of the farmland available to Orayvi farmers. He suggests that the split occurred because the large Orayvi population could no longer be supported by the available agricultural land (Bradfield 1971:23). The division of the village alleviated this problem. In a postscript to his manuscript, Bradfield quotes informants who date the erosion of the Orayvi wash to after the split (Bradfield 1971:45; see also Hack 1942:47). Bradfield still maintains, however, that poor climate between 1892 and 1904 put an economic strain on Orayvi residents that resulted in the split.

Whiteley (1988) has offered a third explanation for the split: that it was the result of a deliberate plot by leaders of Orayvi (see Clemmer 1978 and Levy 1992 for different interpretations of this theory). The split had been foretold in prophecies and was necessary for the overturn of the politico-religious order, which, in the eyes of some Orayvi leaders, had become corrupt. Whiteley offers this "ethnosociological" analysis as the primary explanation for the Orayvi split but suggests that other social and economic factors may also have been important.

In a major reanalysis of the Orayvi split, Levy (1992) proposes that because of an uncertain environment, Hopi had evolved a stratified social system based on unequal access to agricultural land by clans. During times of scarcity, low-status clans were cast off (for critiques of the argument see Bernardini 1996:380 and Whiteley 1994). Levy presents evidence for population increase at Orayvi and discusses the encroachment of Navajos and Anglos on available agricultural land. He demonstrates that the Hostiles were primarily drawn from low-status clans, and he ties their departure to the economic distress caused by a large population facing drought and other environmental problems that occurred during the late 1800s and early 1900s. He calls the split a "flight of the landless" (1992: 95). Levy also believes that the strong and unbending personalities of some of the Orayvi leaders caused the intensity and anguish of the split (1992:153–54). Without these individuals, many people might still have left Orayvi but in a more orderly fashion, as was already happening with the settlement of the farming village of Munqapi.

As a result of the 1906 split, the population of Orayvi was almost halved; 298 of the 622 adults left the village

(Titiev 1944:87). Using Bradfield's (1971:43) formula of nine children for every twenty adults, a total of 432 individuals left; these individuals represented forty-eight entire households and parts of other households (Titiev 1944:89). In subsequent years, households continued to leave, drifting off to Kiqotsmovi, Munqapi, or elsewhere. Titiev (1944:95) reports only 112 people in Orayvi in 1933; Stubbs (1950:117) estimates 87 people in 1932.

The split and subsequent population decline had a dramatic impact on architecture in the village. Many structures at Orayvi were abandoned and began to disintegrate rapidly. Within a few decades, many of the original roomblocks had been completely dismantled, and large parts of many others were in ruins. By 1948, aerial photographs show that only twelve of the original twenty-five roomblocks remained, although several small groups of rooms had been added. These transformations are discussed in chapter 6.

The History of Research at Orayvi

During the last two decades of the nineteenth century and throughout the twentieth century, Orayvi has been visited by numerous artists, writers, photographers, anthropologists, museum curators, and other scholars. A fairly large literature on Orayvi exists, dealing especially with the Snake Dance and the 1906 factional split (Laird 1977), and numerous photographs are available in archives. In this section, five projects will be described in some detail, as they produced materials (including maps and census data) used in the present study. These are (1) the Bureau of American Ethnology's 1887 mapping project under Victor Mindeleff; (2) the 1900 United States Census; (3) the Carnegie Institution and National Geographic Society's Second Beam Expedition; (4) Mischa Titiev's anthropological study of Orayvi in 1932–34; and (5) Jerrold Levy's (1990, 1992) study of Orayvi social stratification.

The Bureau of American Ethnology Mapping Project

In 1881, Victor and Cosmos Mindeleff, brothers aged twenty-one and nineteen, were part of a Bureau of American Ethnology expedition to the Southwest (Nabokov 1989). Their task was to produce architectural drawings of Zuni Pueblo so that an accurate scale model of the pueblo could be produced. This project launched them on a study of southwestern pueblo architecture that continued into the next decade. They spent nine seasons in the Southwest mapping contemporary and prehistoric pueblos. In 1891, Victor published "A Study of Pueblo Architecture: Tusayan and Cibola," which is, even today, the most comprehensive study of the subject. The Mindeleffs first planned to map Orayvi in 1882, but residents of the village objected. It was not until 1887 that Victor gained access to Orayvi (Nabokov 1989:xxiii). (Although Mindeleff implies that all modern Tusayan pueblos were surveyed during the 1882–83 season [1891:14], this apparently did not include Orayvi.)

The map of Orayvi that Mindeleff produced in the field was extremely detailed (fig. 3.1). Each major roomblock was given a numerical designation, then small groups of rooms were given the number of the nearest major roomblock, with the addition of a superscript. The map showed the location and size of doors, windows, hatch openings, ladders, and chimneys. It was color-coded to indicate multiple stories (Mindeleff 1891:44–45). This level of detail was not reproduced in the published version (Mindeleff 1891:plate 36); nor is it in figure 3.1 of this volume. But fortunately the original field maps were archived at the Smithsonian Institution (V. Mindeleff n.d.). Less fortunate is the loss of a notebook in which Mindeleff recorded detailed descriptions and measurements of architectural details. In the present study, Mindeleff's original field map provides an initial baseline for the description of architectural change at Orayvi.

The 1900 and 1910 U.S. Censuses

The United States Census for 1900 (U.S. Census of Population 1900) is an extremely valuable supplement to Titiev's census, described below. Census takers reported the name, age, and relationship of each household member. They reported how long couples had been married, the number of children born to each woman, and the number surviving. It is apparent that some men hid dur-

ing the census and that occasionally individuals were counted as residents in households in which they were only visitors (Levy personal communication 1990; also Levy 1992:6). In general, however, there is a good degree of correspondence between the 1900 U.S. census and Titiev's reconstructed census (Levy 1992:6). The 1900 census is used in the present study to calculate the number of persons in each household and their ages and relationships. These data are used in chapter 4 to examine the fit between Orayvi houses and their households.

The 1910 census was consulted to determine who was present in the village four years after the split (chapter 6). This census could not be used to associate individuals with houses because it was too far removed in time from Titiev's census and because patterns of residence had obviously been greatly changed by the split. It did, however, largely confirm Titiev's list of houseowners who stayed in Orayvi after the split.

The Second Beam Expedition

The Second Beam Expedition, funded by the Carnegie Institution and the National Geographic Society, visited the Hopi pueblos in 1928 in an attempt to collect tree-ring samples that would bridge the gap between the established modern dendrochronological sequence and a "floating" prehistoric sequence. Orayvi, reported to have been occupied since before the Spanish conquest, was a major focus of the expedition (Douglass 1929; Douglass n.d.).

Andrew E. Douglass, who had developed the process of dendrochronological dating at the University of Arizona, had hired Lyndon Hargrave to collect samples at Orayvi and other villages during the spring and summer of 1928. Douglass apparently visited Orayvi several times during this period, and he helped Hargrave with the project (Douglass 1929). As an aid to the collection of samples, Hargrave or Douglass apparently traced Mindeleff's map of Orayvi (Mindeleff 1891:plate 36) and numbered each room so that the provenience of collected samples could be easily recorded. The map was annotated to show roomblocks that had been abandoned or dismantled, and rooms constructed since 1887. This map

FIRST STORY
SECOND STORY
THIRD STORY
FOURTH STORY

Figure 3.1 Map of Orayvi produced by Victor Mindeleff in 1887. This version of the map has been redrawn from Mindeleff's original field maps, although not all the rich detail recorded on those maps is reproduced here. The named structures are kivas. (Courtesy of the Smithsonian Institution, National Anthropological Archives)

was subsequently used by Titiev in his study of Orayvi households (see below). The map remains on file at the University of Arizona's Laboratory of Tree-Ring Research and is used in this study to identify individual rooms (Laboratory of Tree-Ring Research n.d.).

The Second Beam Expedition obtained more than one hundred dated samples from Orayvi. Combined with the dated samples taken during the First Beam Expedition and later samples collected by Gila Pueblo, a total of 161 dates were obtained from fifty-four structures in Orayvi (Bannister, Robinson, and Warren 1967). Unfortunately, only three of the dates are "cutting dates"—dates that indicate the year the tree was cut, and presumably the year the structure containing the dated wood was built. The three cutting dates range from A.D. 1691 to 1759. Another nineteen dates were given the symbol *v* by the Laboratory of Tree-Ring Research, indicating that they were subjectively determined to be within a few years of the cutting date. The *v* dates range from A.D. 1619 to 1760. A.D. 1760 was the latest date of any kind from Orayvi (Bannister, Robinson, and Warren 1967:20–24), although, obviously, construction continued after 1760.

Douglass reported that many of the beams at Orayvi were of cottonwood or juniper, two types of wood that are very difficult to date. The use of pine and Douglas fir, types with the greatest dating potential, apparently ceased about A.D. 1770, probably because Hopi woodcutting had eliminated nearby stands of these species (Douglass 1929: 753). Douglass notes that the samples obtained at Orayvi were therefore predestined to be early.

Bannister and his colleagues (1967:24) state that "the long series of dates from houses and kivas suggest the reuse of many beams, and there seem to be no clearly dated construction clusters." However, they also note that "these factors may be overemphasized because the collections were aimed at crossing the gap [in the tree-ring sequence] and not at dating the structures." Reuse of construction wood is a very common practice among the Hopi because wood is so scarce in the immediate area (Ahlstrom, Dean, and Robinson 1978; see also Ahlstrom 1985:629–31; Dean 1969:76–77). For example, one of the three cutting dates at Orayvi, A.D. 1759, is from a structure labeled Quincy Jame's House (Bannister, Robinson, and Warren 1967:23). Evidence presented below indicates that this structure (located in Roomblock W[1]—see fig. 3.2) was built after 1887, probably in the late 1890s.

Titiev's Orayvi Census

In 1932, Mischa Titiev was part of a University of Michigan field party in ethnology that visited Orayvi. He returned to the village for the fall and winter of 1933–34 for a more detailed study of social and ceremonial organiza-

tion. The published results of these two periods of field study focused on the relationship of Orayvi social organization to the 1906 factional split (Titiev 1944), which, as discussed above, Titiev believed was the natural result of the loosely knit Hopi clan system. Working primarily with two informants, the Orayvi chief, Tawaqwaptiwa, and Don Talayesva (the Sun Chief of Simmons 1942), Titiev conducted a "house to house" census of Orayvi, reconstructed for the period 1900 to 1905.

Titiev used the same map of Orayvi to locate the residence of each household that Hargrave had used in 1928 during the Second Beam Expedition: the tracing of Mindeleff's map with room numbers assigned (Laboratory of Tree-Ring Research n.d.). Titiev reports (1944:51) that this map was furnished to him by Harold S. Colton of the Museum of Northern Arizona, where Hargrave worked for many years (fig. 3.2). Titiev identified, by room number, the structures occupied by each household and listed the female head. Details about her husband(s) and children were recorded, including migration patterns during the 1906 split. These data are used in chapter 6 to explore the effect of population decrease on structures.

Based on informant interviews, Titiev recorded a number of new structures on the Orayvi map that were built after Mindeleff's visit but before 1906. Some of these structures were recorded by Hargrave on his version of the map, but Hargrave's map shows Orayvi in 1928, and his annotations are very sketchy. Titiev apparently attempted to record the location of every new structure in existence between 1887 and 1900. These new structures are given letter designations in figure 3.2. (Titiev did not use Mindeleff's numerical roomblock designations but labeled all roomblocks with letters. In the version of Titiev's map presented here, Mindeleff's roomblock numbers are used for consistency [fig. 3.2], while Titiev's letters are used for the new roomblocks he identified). Although Titiev's map does not indicate multiple stories for new structures and probably does not present their exact location or shape, it does provide the total number of households occupying these new structures. Titiev's map is fundamental to the arguments for population increase presented in chapter 5.

Figure 3.2 Mindeleff's 1887 map of Orayvi annotated by Mischa Titiev for the period around 1900. Room numbers were assigned by the Laboratory of Tree-Ring Research during the Second Beam Expedition. The map shows new rooms and new roomblocks built after 1887.

Levy's Analysis of Orayvi Social Stratification

The most important aspect of Levy's project for this study is his merging of data from the 1900 U.S. census with Titiev's census (Levy 1990, 1992). Levy transcribed Titiev's original census field notes, numbered each indi-

vidual mentioned by Titiev, and prepared a computerized database that lists, for each household, the female head and her clan and society affiliations; the name, sex, and society affiliations of her children; and the name, clan, society affiliations, and economic activities of her husband. The female head, her husband, and often her children were reported as affiliating with the Hostile or

Friendly faction at Orayvi or as being deceased in 1906. Additional information, including multiple marriages or unusual qualities or activities of individuals, were reported in narrative form.

The names of individuals recorded in the 1900 census were then matched with individuals recorded in Titiev's census. The task was undertaken by Barbara Pepper (University of Arizona), aided by Emory Sekaquaptewa (University of Arizona), a former resident of Ho'atvela with personal knowledge of Orayvi families. Names recorded in the 1900 census were often phonetic renderings of names reported by Orayvi residents to the census taker. Fortunately, a majority of the 1900 census was recorded by Herman Kampmeier, a local schoolteacher who knew most of the Orayvi residents quite well (Jerrold Levy, personal communication, 1990). For the present study of Orayvi architecture, the most important items provided by the combination of the two censuses are the age and relationship of individuals *resident in each house at a single point in time* (this information is summarized in appendix 1). Household structure could not be determined from Titiev's census alone. While he aimed at the period around 1900, Titiev often included in households the deceased, the unborn, and the absent. The 1900 U.S. census, of course, did not report the locations of the houses of the households they recorded.

In the 1900 U.S. census, the name of each individual was followed by that individual's relationship to a male head of the household; census takers failed to acknowledge the matrilineal nature of Hopi society and recorded the senior male as household head. Following his name were the names of his wife, children, and other relatives residing in "his" household. The structure of each household was apparent. For example, a matrilineal extended family would be recorded as having a household head, wife, daughter, son-in-law, and perhaps mother-in-law. In this study, individuals are presumed to reside in the rooms in the village where Titiev placed them. In a few cases, a senior woman discussed by Titiev had died before 1900, but her daughter and daughter's family were recorded on the 1900 census. The daughter was presumed to have remained in the mother's house; often additional notes by Titiev confirmed that this was the case.

In summary, Titiev's map and census and Levy's database were used to associate groups of rooms that made up houses and to identify individuals living within houses by age, sex, and relationship (chapter 4 and appendix 1). In chapter 6, these data are used to plot post-1906 migration patterns for the female household head of each house, and architectural change to the house is examined, where possible, using either ground or aerial photographs.

Photographic Data

More than three hundred photographs of Orayvi taken over a period of almost one hundred years, between the early 1870s and the 1960s, form the foundation of this study (appendix 2). Some were taken by well-known photographers such as A. C. Vroman (Webb 1973), but many others were taken by tourists, missionaries, students, and other travelers (e.g., Dewar 1989). The photographs were obtained from archives in museums, libraries, and universities throughout the United States. Some photographs are well dated and described; others have virtually no dates or locations. In many cases, the location and date of photographs used in this study were obtained through comparison with attested photographs (see "Methods of Photographic Analysis" below).

The photographs used in this study are a representative sample of the photographs of Orayvi taken within the past one hundred years. All museums and libraries in the United States that had major collections of southwestern photographs were contacted, and many were visited to ensure that unidentified photographs of Orayvi were examined. Copies were not obtained for all available photographs. Many views were redundant or showed little useful architectural detail. Some of the photographs that were obtained were not used in the analysis because the structures they showed could not be identified or could be located only generally; this was especially true for structures in the northeast end of the village.

The greatest number of photographs dated between 1895 and 1901 (appendix 2). During this six-year period, a number of professional photographers visited Orayvi. It was also the climax of photography at Hopi ceremonials, especially the Snake Dance. Photographers became so disruptive at these events that the Hopi eventually banned photography at most pueblos (Lyon 1988). The ban on photography was especially well enforced at Orayvi immediately after the split: very few photographs are available between 1906 and about 1912. Photographs taken after 1912 are almost exclusively of buildings. They show very few people and almost no ceremonial activity.

The same areas of the village were photographed at Orayvi over and over because they provided long, unobstructed views and were often the location of ceremonial activities. These were the area around the Main Plaza, the area around the Snake Dance Plaza, and the areas in front of Kwan Kiva and in front of Is Kiva and Hawiwvi Kiva (fig. 3.1). The continuity represented by photographs in the same area is important for the sorts of analysis used in the present study. Some parts of the village, unfortunately, lack photographic coverage, at least by ground photos. Aerial photographs, taken between 1933 and 1948, provide much more extensive views of the village and permit detailed description of the effects of the split on structures not seen in ground-level photos.

Ground photographs were typically taken from the east, to show the fronts of the houses and places where most daily activity took place. The few photographs of back walls typically do not show enough detail to permit accurate identification of individual rooms (but see Cameron 1991b: appendix 1, Roomblock 7, west side). Most distant views of the village do not show enough detail to aid descriptions of architectural change, although a few such photographs are useful for examining architectural change to one of the easternmost roomblocks, Roomblock 12 (appendices 2 and 3).

Photographs by John Hillers are apparently the earliest extensive photographic record of Orayvi, although they are not precisely dated. Fleming and Luskey (1986) report that Hillers photographed Orayvi in 1871, 1872, 1875, and 1876, when he was a photographer for John Wesley Powell's expeditions through the Southwest. Powell favored Hillers over other photographers who had been in his employ, and he gave Hillers credit for many photographs that had actually been taken by E. O. Beaman or James Fennemore (Fleming and Luskey 1986: 108–10). Hillers also visited Orayvi in 1879 and possibly

in 1881 as a photographer for the Bureau of American Ethnology (Fowler 1989:82, 106).

The photographs by Hillers used in this study were obtained from the Smithsonian Institution archives. All are dated 1879, although one is the basis for a drawing in an article published by Powell in 1875 (Smithsonian photo no. 1844) and is presumed to have been taken in 1871. The other photographs are assumed to have been taken in 1879.

A large collection of photographs by Charles Carpenter essentially marks the end of the pre-split photographic record of Orayvi. Carpenter was a photographer for the Field Museum of Natural History in Chicago at the turn of the century. In 1901, he apparently spent an entire day photographing Orayvi from almost every angle. His photographs provide the most detailed photographic record of Orayvi available. They are especially valuable because they are so comprehensive.

Aerial photographs are the best source of information on architectural change at Orayvi for the period after the split. A 1933 aerial photograph, probably taken by A. E. Douglass, is the first such photograph of Orayvi available. Subsequent aerials were taken during the 1930s, in 1940, and in 1948 (appendix 2). All show progressive deterioration of roomblocks and construction of new structures. Other ground photographs of individual roomblocks taken between 1906 and 1961 show detailed change to structures during this period.

Methods of Photographic Analysis

Photographs of Orayvi collected for this study represent "casual repeat photography" (Ahlstrom 1992). Repeat photography is commonly used to document change in landscapes. The process involves taking successive photographs of the same scene at different points in time, from the same camera position. Ahlstrom notes that historic photographs, such as those taken at Hopi, do not meet the strict requirements of repeat photography (matching successive photographs exactly, even to the season and time of day), but do form temporal sequences of views. He suggests the term *casual repeat photography* for "the unintentional and uneven repetition of views in sequences of historical photos" (1992:174) and shows the value of casual repeat photography for documenting architectural change at the Hopi pueblo of Walpi.

Ahlstrom (1992) notes that casual repeat photography can reflect several biases in the location and timing of photographs. One of the major limitations of the photographic data used in this study is that architectural change can be examined only for exterior rooms. Rooms in roomblock interiors—the "back rooms" of a house—are not visible. It is assumed, especially when the village was fully occupied, that more architectural change would have occurred to exterior rooms in which most daily living was taking place. This assumption cannot be tested with the available photographic record, however. Furthermore, photographs in this study do not show room interiors, where many architectural modifications may also have taken place. Extensive examination of photographic archives suggests that interior views are rare and cannot be consistently used to examine interior architectural change (for example, Kroeber 1917:189–90 notes that the Zuni consider their homes to be very private and refused to let him enter to conduct a survey).

Some of the photos collected for this study were well dated and described, whereas others had incorrect information or no information about where and when the photo had been taken. The initial task, then, was to order the photos in time and space so that particular buildings at Orayvi could be identified; change over time could then be observed (Cameron 1993). While collecting photographs for the study, it became obvious that the most useful views were oblique shots that showed long rows of houses with enough clarity that modifications to individual structures could be observed. Overlapping views taken at the same time were especially revealing because they provided a "panorama" with a great deal of detail and resolution.

Mindeleff's 1887 map was the key for ordering the photographs. In 1887, Orayvi had about eleven hundred rooms arranged in twenty-five linear roomblocks (fig. 3.1). I began the process of photographic analysis by matching photos, looking for similarities in buildings, and grouping those that showed the same set of buildings. Mindeleff's map was essential for clues to the location

of buildings in the photos, and the positioning of kivas was the most helpful clue. In the late nineteenth century, Orayvi had thirteen named kivas, all of which had been photographed at one time or another.

The Main Plaza was the most easily recognized location at Orayvi. Most views of the Main Plaza showed the front of Roomblock 4, which provided an anchor from which other areas could be identified. A second frequently photographed area was the Snake Dance Plaza, where the Snake Dance was performed. Mindeleff's map showed five kivas located in the Snake Dance Plaza, the only place at Orayvi with so many kivas. Two kivas located in the center of the settlement helped identify photos of Roomblock 9. A kiva with a distinctive bent ladder pole allowed photos of Roomblock 12 to be grouped together and eventually identified. Photos of other areas of the pueblo were more difficult to identify. Several photos might clearly show the same buildings, but there were no clues to where in the site they were located—therefore, no way to tie them to Mindeleff's map. Careful examination of structures in the background and at the edges of the photos identified the locations of some of these sets of photos.

Every area of the site had at least a few well-dated photographs, and these were used to put photographs in temporal order. Undated or poorly dated photos could be placed in approximate sequence by reference to the dated architectural changes observed. For example, if a room appeared to be occupied in a well-dated 1890 photograph but is shown abandoned in another photograph, the other photograph was most likely taken later.

Most of the photographs (N = 268) could be associated with specific map locations, although some photographs remain unidentified (appendix 2). Of the twenty-five roomblocks at Orayvi, rooms from ten roomblocks were identified in ground photographs. In addition, at least a portion of every roomblock could be seen in one or more aerial photographs after 1933.

After the photos had been ordered temporally, I began experimenting with methods of recording the abundant evidence of architectural change evident in the photos. I tried isometric drawings and a computer-mapping program (AutoCAD) to record the addition or removal of individual rooms observed in photos, but both processes were time-consuming, and neither could handle the rich detail that the photos provided. I eventually developed a standard written description of architectural change to each individual identifiable room. For each room, I recorded new construction, the addition of doors and windows, repair to roofs, rebuilding episodes, and the addition and removal of specialized cooking shelters. During the latest time periods, after the split, when aerial photographs became the primary source of data on architectural change at Orayvi, the unit of analysis changed from the *room* to the *house* (the set of rooms defined by Titiev as containing an independent household). Descriptions of architectural change to rooms and houses form the basic data used in chapters 5 and 6 and can be found in appendices 1 and 2 of Cameron (1991b) (for summaries of architectural change, see appendices 3 and 4 of this volume).

Documenting Architectural Change at Orayvi

Once the written descriptions were completed, the analysis of architectural change at Orayvi could begin. The seventy-seven-year span of the study was grouped into six time periods for analysis, two before the split and four after the split (table 3.1). There were some differences in the methods of photographic analysis used in the pre- and post-split periods (especially because of the change in analytic unit from room to house); these are discussed in chapters 5 and 6.

Before the split (chapter 5), I hoped to identify and document the types of architectural change that characterized typical Hopi construction, maintenance, and

Table 3.1   Time Periods Used in the Analysis

Period 1	1871–1887
Period 2	1887–1901
Period 3	1902–1912
Period 4	1913–1925
Period 5	1926–1937
Period 6	1938–1948

remodeling. Because the pre-split period was a time when many Euroamerican tools and building techniques were being introduced, I wanted to document the effect of an intrusive culture on indigenous southwestern architecture. Photographic analysis also showed a significant population growth at Orayvi before 1900, a demographic trend that had only been suggested in other documentary sources.

Photographs taken after 1906 allowed me to examine the effects of factional competition on Orayvi houses (chapter 6). I wanted to explore the effects of a sudden population decline on individual houses, and the architectural expression of partial abandonment on the entire settlement. Architectural change could then be related to longer-term population trends in the village, such as the slow emigration of remaining Friendlies to Kyqotsmovi or Munqapi.

The sources described above—photographs, archival data (especially Mindeleff's and Titiev's maps), and Levy's incorporation of Titiev's census and the 1900 U.S. census—form a rich and exceptional set of data for the study of both buildings and people at Orayvi. Most exciting is the potential of this data for the interpretation of prehistoric pueblos (chapter 7).

4 / The Orayvi House and Household

The combination of Titiev's census and the 1900 U.S. census provide a unique opportunity to examine the relationship between the pueblo house and the residents who used it. Such precise linking of houses and households is not available, as far as I know, for any other southwestern pueblo. These data (summarized in appendix 1) permit the examination of two population constants—house size and household size—that are critical to reconstructions of prehistoric population size and social organization (as discussed in chapter 1). This chapter begins with an examination of varying views of Hopi social organization, especially as they relate to the house and household. Then house and household parameters at Orayvi—derived from the combination of Titiev's census, the 1900 U.S. census, and Mindeleff's map—are compared with data from other historic pueblos.

Hopi Social Organization

The following section examines traditional descriptions of Hopi social organization as well as recent critiques of those accounts. It focuses on those aspects of Hopi social organization that should have architectural consequences, especially the structure of the household. The concept of the household is difficult to define (Lowell 1986:3–6; Wilk and Rathje 1982:620), but Netting and his colleagues (1984:xx) clearly distinguish the *family* (a group of kin) from the *household* (a task-oriented residence group). The Orayvi household, as used here and in chapters 5 and 6, is the group that occupies the set of structures defined by Titiev (n.d.) as an individual house. In the following discussion, the term family refers only to a related group of individuals, such as an extended family.

Social organization at Hopi, and especially at Orayvi, has been examined in a number of studies (Connelly 1979; Eggan 1950; Levy 1992; Titiev 1944; Whiteley 1985, 1986, 1988). According to the traditional anthropological view, the village as a whole is divided into a series of matrilineal, totemically named clans composed of one or more matrilineal lineages. The clans are grouped into exogamous, unnamed phratries (Eggan 1950:18–19). The lineage is not a named group, and scholars have viewed its importance differently. For Eggan (1950:109) it is the most basic unit of Hopi society because rights, duties, land, houses, and ceremonial knowledge are passed through the lineage. Titiev (1944:69), however, stressed the role of the clan as the owner of rights, duties, land, and so on. He calls the lineage a "nascent clan" (1944:49).

Connelly found (1979:545), during fieldwork among the Hopi, that the household was the smallest distinct unit of Hopi society; therefore, it should, I believe, be the unit reflected most clearly in structures. Eggan (1950:29), based on his fieldwork among the Hopi, reports that the basic household unit was the matrilineal extended family: a matrilocal residential and economic unit that consisted of a woman, her husband, their married daughters, the daughters' husbands, unmarried sons, and children of the daughters. This group occupied an adjoining set of rooms. Eggan notes (1950:30) that division of this "household" may occur as a result of increased numbers, conflicts among sisters, and modern conditions, but he emphasized that, conceptually at least, the unity of the household group remains.

The ideal-typical view of Hopi social organization is complicated by the overlap between household, lineage, and clan. As Whiteley (1988:49) points out, in some cases only two or three people constitute the total membership of a clan, a lineage, *and* a household. He believes that clan and lineage are not always clearly distinguishable and suggests, like Titiev, that the clan, not the lineage, is the most important social group recognized by the Hopi (1988:49–51). Furthermore, Whiteley (1985, 1986) demonstrated, using data from Orayvi, that Hopi clans are not corporate groups either economically, ritually, or jurally as defined by classical descent theory. He believes that the classic view of Hopi clans is simply a useful means of describing some elements of Hopi social organization (Whiteley 1986:78).

Levy (1992), on the other hand, did find the lineage very useful for understanding Hopi social organization. Using the census data described in chapter 3, he found that clans had prime, alternate, and marginal lineages and that the highest status was accorded to prime lineages. The importance of these lineage categories was that they defined the order of succession to clan property, especially agricultural land. For low-status clans with little or no land, lineage status was not nearly as important as it was among the high-status clans with a great deal of land to assign. Levy (1992) found that it was families with little or no access to land that left Orayvi during the split: low-status, marginal, or alternate lineages.

Pueblo House Size

A comparison of house size at Orayvi and at other modern and historic pueblos shows that the number of rooms per house is larger at multistoried pueblos like Orayvi than it is at pueblos that have few upper-story rooms. Multistoried construction has apparently decreased with increases in Euroamerican contact, resulting in a decrease in the number of rooms per house and an increase in room area. However, evidence is presented that shows that even at houses in multistoried pueblos that included many rooms, only a few of the rooms may have been in active use at any one time, resulting in an active house size of two or three rooms.

Ethnographic Accounts of Numbers of Rooms in Pueblo Houses

Early Spanish accounts of the pueblos reported large villages with multistoried buildings, and at Zuni houses were reported to have eight rooms or more (Gallegos Relation of the Chamuscado-Rodriguez Expedition, 1581; Hammond and Rey 1966:108). In the 1880s, Mindeleff (1891:101) noted that at Hopi a single room is regarded as a complete house, yet in an idealized cross section, he shows a typical Hopi house of four stories with a total of ten rooms, each with a Hopi name (1891:223, fig. 114). At the Hopi village of Walpi for the period around 1900, Adams (1983:54) illustrates a typical house with eight rooms in three stories (excluding the detached piki house, a postcontact form). The cross sections presented by Mindeleff and Adams suggest that Hopi houses were one room wide. Mindeleff's idealized Hopi house has four ground-floor rooms, while Adams's has three.

At Acoma, a Western Pueblo, diagrams of two typical houses drawn in the 1930s had six and eleven rooms in three stories, each one room wide (Nabokov 1986:120, 128). One house has three ground-floor rooms, and the other has five. Knowles reports six rooms in the three-tiered sections of Acoma (Knowles 1974:28–29). At Zuni in the nineteenth century, Ferguson and Mills (1987) report that the home of an extended family encompassed four to six contiguous rooms, "sometimes on several different levels within a room block" (1987:250). Parts of nineteenth-century Zuni were five stories high, but upper stories began to be dismantled after 1880 (chapter 2).

Among pueblos along the Rio Grande in New Mexico (Eastern Pueblos), ethnographic data indicates that the number of rooms per house was smaller than in Western Pueblos, and multistoried construction was uncommon. At Santa Clara, Hill (1982:74) reports that houses at the turn of the century typically had two rooms, and most buildings were one story high, but multistoried structures may once have been common. Pictures taken in the late nineteenth and early twentieth centuries show two-story structures. Hill also notes that "three- and four-room houses resulted from a father either enlarging his

Table 4.1 Size and Width of Houses at Orayvi, by Story

House Size

	No. of Houses in Sample	Mean No. of Rooms Per House	s.d.
All rooms	160	6.35	3.28
With first-story rooms	141	3.62	2.19
With second-story rooms	136	2.22	1.02
With third-story rooms	82	1.48	0.67
With fourth-story rooms	7	—	—

House Width

	N	Percent of Sample	s.d.
One room wide	111	79	16.5
Two rooms wide	28	20	16
Three rooms wide	2	1	1

house upon the marriage of his sons, or allocating them a section of his home" (1982:74). At Jemez in the early part of this century, houses had between two and four rooms, and only the older houses were two stories (Parsons 1925:12). The typical house at Sia in the first part of this century had three rooms on one story (White 1962: 47). Even in the 1880s, only a single house at Sia was reported to be two stories high (Bloom 1938:223; cited in White 1962:47).

The Size of Houses at Orayvi

Titiev's census recorded 188 households—a group of individuals occupying an adjoining set of rooms—in Orayvi in 1900. More than half of these households could be identified in the 1900 U.S. census. By counting the number of stories for each room number on Mindeleff's map[1] and accounting for architectural change observed in photographs, the number of rooms for most households can be determined for the period around 1900 (see appendix 1).[2] Households in new houses recorded by Titiev (houses not on Mindeleff's original map) were only included when they could be seen in photographs and the

number of stories could be counted. Titiev did not provide information on the number of stories for these new houses.

The number of rooms per house at Orayvi could be determined for 160 houses (table 4.1). Houses had between one and eighteen rooms, with an average of more than six rooms. Houses averaged almost four ground-floor rooms, more than two second-story rooms, and one third-story room. Only seven houses had fourth-story rooms. As with the idealized Hopi house, most houses were only one room wide (table 4.1). Fewer than 20 percent of houses were two rooms wide, and only two houses were three rooms wide. These figures suggest that a typical Orayvi house had between three and four ground-floor rooms, two second-story rooms, and sometimes a third-story room—a total of five to six rooms, and occasionally a seventh room (fig. 2.2).

Mindeleff's map was used to calculate floor area for rooms and houses at Orayvi. Measurements were taken from photographs of Mindeleff's five original field maps, each reduced to 8″ by 10″.[3] Measurements were obtained for 1,002 upper- and lower-story rooms in 154 houses.[4] Average room size at Orayvi varied from less than 2 sq. m.

Table 4.2   Size of Rooms, Houses, and Households at Orayvi

	Mean	Minimum	Maximum	s.d.	Number
Room size (sq. m.)	15.6	1.2	59.0	9.4	1,001
House size (area sq. m.)	103.1	5.7	306.4	59.0	154
House size (no. of rooms)	6.5	18	1	3.4	160
Household size (no. of individuals)	5.5	1	12	2.2	110

to almost 60 sq. m., with a mean of almost 16 sq. m. (table 4.2). Average house size (the combined area of each room—all stories—associated with one of Titiev's households) varied from about 6 sq. m. to more than 300 sq. m., with a mean of more than 100 sq. m. (table 4.2). As demonstrated below, average room size at Orayvi is similar to that found at other nineteenth-century Hopi pueblos but smaller than that found at twentieth-century Eastern Pueblos.

House Size and Multistoried Construction

A comparison of house size at Orayvi with that at other historic pueblos establishes that houses at Orayvi and other Hopi pueblos have far more rooms than other, especially Eastern, pueblos. This apparent geographic difference in house size results from a difference between Eastern and Western Pueblos in the use of multistoried construction. The near absence of multistoried construction in the Eastern Pueblos is a result of early contact with Euroamericans. Even in multistoried pueblos, however, not all rooms may be in active use, a conclusion that has important implications for archaeologists reconstructing house or household size at prehistoric pueblos.

Data on house size from Eastern and Western Pueblos, other than Orayvi, are taken from Dohm's (1990) intriguing study of Pueblo house size. She suggests that the number of rooms per house is dependent not only on numbers of residents and economic and environmental factors but also on the physical proximity of houses to one another, or *nucleation*. Although not an intended aspect of her study, a reanalysis of Dohm's data suggests that the decrease in vertical nucleation (multistoried construction) may be separated out as a key determi-

nant of pueblo house size as determined by room counts (Cameron 1996).

Table 4.3 shows a ratio of first-floor area to roofed area for eighteen Eastern Pueblos and seven Western Pueblos, including most of the Hopi pueblos (except Orayvi). Lower ratios indicate more multistoried construction; pueblos with ratios of 1.0 are all single-storied. Ratios for the Rio Grande pueblos, including Taos, ranged from 0.81 to 1.0, while the figure for Acoma was 0.75. The Hopi pueblos had ratios ranging from 0.53 to 0.63, indicating far more multistoried construction than at the Rio Grande pueblos. While Dohm (1990:229) finds only weak correlations between this particular measure of aggregation and room counts, there is clearly far more multistoried construction at the Hopi pueblos than at other pueblos.

Examination of Dohm's data (presented here in table 4.3) shows that, in addition to having more upper stories, Hopi pueblos also had more rooms per house (per family in table 4.3) than Acoma, Laguna, or any of the Eastern Pueblos. There is a temporal difference in the data she uses, however. Data from the Hopi pueblos is from the nineteenth century, while data from the other pueblos is from 1948 or later, when pueblos had experienced extensive Euroamerican contact.

Eastern Pueblos had early and intense contact with Euroamericans beginning in the sixteenth century; Hopi was spared similar intrusions until the late nineteenth century. The lack of multistory construction, more dispersed layout, and fewer rooms per house found at Eastern Pueblos can likely be attributed to the consequences of this early Euroamerican contact.[5] These same architectural patterns begin to be seen at Western Pueblos in the late nineteenth and early twentieth centuries (Ahlstrom

Table 4.3 Rooms and Roofed Area of Pueblos of the Historic Period

	Map Date	Pop.	Total Rooms	Rooms in Room-blocks	Mean No. of Contig. Rooms	Rooms per Family	Total Roofed Area (sq. m.)	1st-floor Area (sq. m.)	Ratio 1st-floor Area to Roofed Area	Average Size (sq. m.) (Total Roofed Area/ Total Rooms)
Eastern Pueblos										
Cochiti	1952	444	225	98	4.1	1.940	5961	5961	1.00	26.7
Isleta	1948	1470	804	546	5.3	2.300	32931	32931	1.00	41.0
Jemez	1948	883	459	274	5.7	2.782	12751	12619	0.98	27.8
Nambe	1948	155	34	15	3.4	1.000	959	959	1.00	28.2
Picuris	1948	130	59	16	2.5	2.185	1444	1444	1.00	24.5
San Felipe	1948	784	276	180	4.2	1.653	12070	11396	0.94	43.7
San Ildefonso	1948	170	207	107	4.7	6.469	7499	6925	0.92	36.2
San Ildefonso	1973	413	189	120	4.3	—	—	—	—	—
San Juan	1948	768	176	159	8.8	1.143	7816	7745	0.99	44.4
Sandia	1948	139	80	36	3.2	2.105	2900	2900	1.00	36.3
Santa Ana	1948	288	136	102	5.4	1.838	5769	5718	0.99	42.4
Santa Ana	1975	498	152	82	3.7	—	—	—	—	—
Santa Clara	1948	573	144	111	6.9	1.180	4889	4622	0.94	34.0
Santo Domingo	1948	1106	500	377	6.0	2.392	21831	21245	0.97	43.7
Taos	1948	907	543	495	14.7	2.598	13428	10942	0.81	24.7
Taos	1973	1463	627	480	6.3	2.083	16777	15002	0.89	26.8
Tesuque	1948	160	116	88	7.3	4.462	4808	4245	0.88	41.4
Zia	1948	267	126	89	4.5	2.571	4469	4469	1.00	35.5
Western Pueblos										
Acoma	1948	879	387	360	13.3	1.792	10669	7967	0.75	27.6
Laguna	1948	711	189	114	6.1	1.432	7468	7431	0.99	39.5
Hopi/Western										
Shipaulovi	1882	113	131	129	65.5	5.955	2616	1491	0.56	20.0
Shongopavi	1882	216	253	248	36.1	—	5776	—	—	22.8
Sichomovi	1882	104	105	96	17.5	4.375	1215	771	0.63	11.6
Tewa Village	1882	175	158	157	26.3	4.514	2983	1725	0.57	18.9
Walpi	1882	270	363	356	45.4	6.368	7303	3905	0.53	20.1

Figures from Dohm 1990, tables 3 and 4, except column listing floor/roof ratios.

1992; Cameron 1996; Ferguson et al. 1990): decrease in multistoried construction, a more dispersed settlement plan, and—as demonstrated in this study for Orayvi— fewer rooms per house (see chapters 5 and 6).

Although there may be fewer rooms per house at pueblos that have experienced significant Euroamerican contact, room size seems to have increased, perhaps in compensation for the loss of space. Again, Dohm's (1990) study provides data from which average room size can be calculated (table 4.3). Dividing total roofed area by total number of rooms for each pueblo resulted in an approximate average room size that ranged from 11.6 sq. m. for Sichomovi (Hopi) to 44.4 sq. m. for San Juan Pueblo, an Eastern Pueblo. Mean size in Eastern Pueblos was significantly larger (34.8 sq. m., s.d. 7.4) than for the nineteenth-century Hopi pueblos (18.7 sq. m., s.d. 4.2, $t = 2.317$, $p < 0.05$ —Acoma and Laguna were not included in these calculations).

Because Dohm measured the space encompassed by an entire roomblock, calculation of average room sizes using her data must be decreased by the width of internal walls (Dohm 1990:221–22). In a study aimed at developing a new method of calculating prehistoric population at southwestern sites using ethnographic data, Gillespie (1974) also used total roomblock area and number of rooms to calculate room size. He suggested that excluding the space encompassed by internal walls (he used an unspecified correction factor) will decrease average room size between 71 and 87 percent, depending on percentage of shared walls in a roomblock. This would result in an average room size for Eastern Pueblos of between 24.7 sq. m. and 30.3 sq. m. and for the Hopi pueblos of between 13.3 sq. m. and 16.3 sq. m.

These figures indicate that the average floor area for Orayvi (15.6 sq. m.) is similar to that of other nineteenth-century Hopi pueblos but smaller than that of twentieth-century Eastern Pueblos. As the number of stories decreased and pueblos became less tightly nucleated, the number of rooms per house decreased while the size of individual rooms increased.

Room Counts and Room Use

It is likely, based on evidence presented here, that prior to European contact, both Eastern and Western Pueblos had multiple stories and a large number of rooms per house. Even though at both Eastern and Western Pueblos earlier multistoried houses may have had six to ten architectural spaces that can be called rooms, not all of these rooms may have been in active use. While determination of room use and especially contemporaneity of use are always problematic, an example from the Pecos Pueblo in north-central New Mexico provides an illustration of

this proposal. Pecos was occupied from the twelfth to the nineteenth centuries.

Kidder (1958:122–23) describes the typical habitation unit at Pecos as consisting of six or seven rooms in three or four stories, but Kidder's data suggest that not all rooms were in use at the same time. The lowest tier of rooms Kidder called "cellar" rooms (1958:122–23): "They may have first served for storage, but those we excavated practically always proved to have become dumps and to be choked, often almost to their low roofs, with household refuse." If the cellar rooms at Pecos and a conjectural fourth-floor room are discounted, the typical habitation unit at Pecos may have been three rooms: two "living rooms" and a storage or sleeping room. The "cellar rooms" were small, with low ceilings, and their size was often decreased by piles of rocks placed to buttress interior walls (Kidder 1958:93). Cellar rooms at Pecos may never have been intended as usable space but rather as a foundation for the upper rooms, placing them in a high, defensible position (Kidder 1958:124). Alternatively, they may have been used for storage areas when the house was first constructed, being abandoned as new rooms were added vertically.

As excavations at Pecos Pueblo suggest, the dark, unventilated, lower-story, interior rooms in multistoried pueblos may not usually have been part of active household space but may have functioned instead as architectural platforms, dead storage, or refuse dumps. Support for this proposition from the Orayvi data is presented in chapter 5. Archaeological assumptions about household size, organization, and use of space at large, long-lived, multistoried pueblos are directly affected by this observation.

The Pueblo Household

Archaeologists use ethnographic and historic data on household size and organization to reconstruct prehistoric households and to estimate prehistoric settlement population. Household sizes reported in ethnographic and historic accounts are highly variable, however, ranging from fewer than two to more than seven individuals (Cameron 1996). Although household size was likely affected by

Euroamerican contact, some figures may be erroneous because of the methods used to determine household size. In many studies, the total population of a pueblo is divided by the number of houses in the village. These figures are questionable, especially in the Eastern Pueblos, because population figures are often taken from lists of tribal members, many of whom no longer live in the ancestral village (Dohm 1990:216–17; Lange 1959:373; Pierson 1949:44). Because they are derived from actual numbers of residents in individual houses, the Orayvi data on household size are especially valuable.

At Orayvi, census data show several different household types, with different household sizes but with houses of similar size, as measured by room counts. Although Euroamerican contact no doubt affected Orayvi household sizes, the existence of different household types of different sizes was probably common to both historic and prehistoric pueblos. As demonstrated below with the Orayvi data, architectural constraints on the development of the extended family make it likely that a variety of household types and families also existed in the past.

The Orayvi Household

The Orayvi data, based on the 1900 U.S. census, demonstrate that variability in household structure, as well as architectural factors, affect pueblo household size. The number of persons per household at Orayvi could be determined for 110 households. The number of persons per household at Orayvi ranged from 1 to 12, with an average of 5.5 persons (s.d. 2.2).

Orayvi is at the high end of household sizes reported for the pueblos (Cameron 1996). There is evidence that population at Orayvi was growing at the end of the nineteenth century, possibly as the result of high birth rates, although some of this growth may have been through immigration. Bourke (1884:33; cited in Bradfield 1971:62) visited Orayvi in 1881 and reported a very large number of children. Bradfield (1971:62) used the 1890 census to calculate an effective birth rate for Orayvi of 18.2 per year for the years 1872 to 1890. Levy's (1992) recent examination of the 1900 U.S. census indicates that the population at Orayvi included far more children than populations

in other Hopi villages and that more children survived childhood. Both Bradfield and Levy also provide evidence of some immigration to Orayvi from other Hopi villages in the late nineteenth century.

Although many ethnographic accounts report that Hopi households were composed of matrilineal extended families, not all Hopi scholars agree. Whiteley (1988) doubts the ideal-typical model of Hopi household structure presented by Connelly (1979) and by Eggan (1950). Whiteley used Titiev's census notes to reevaluate the composition of the Orayvi household. Based on his analysis of Titiev's data, he believes that the modal household at pre-split Orayvi was not the matrilineage segment but the nuclear family (Whiteley 1988:169–70; see his table 6.2). According to Whiteley, almost half the Orayvi households may have been made up of nuclear families before the split.

Data from the 1900 U.S. census (see also table 3.5 in Levy 1992), corroborate Whiteley's findings and accord with studies by Beaglehole (1935:43–44) and Brainard (1935) of Hopi household structure during the 1930s (see also Nagata 1970). In table 4.4, household structure is divided into four types based on relationships reported on census sheets (these categories differ slightly from Whiteley's and Levy's): (1) nuclear family, consisting of household head, wife, and children; (2) matrifocal extended family, consisting of household head, wife, daughters, sons-in-law, daughter's children, and/or wife's mother, father, sisters, or young, unmarried brothers; (3) couple—household head and wife; and (4) other—all other household configurations.

Half of the 109 households for which household structure could be determined were nuclear families; fewer than 25 percent were matrifocal extended families; 8 percent were couples; and 20 percent were other household types (table 4.4). These figures are very close to those reported by Whiteley (1988:160–70) using only Titiev's census notes, and provide another indication of the similarity between the two censuses.

Matrifocal extended families at Orayvi had an average of 7.0 members, while nuclear families had only 5.4 members (t value 3.941, $p < .0007$ [table 4.4]). Matrifocal extended families were significantly larger than

Table 4.4 Variation in House Size for Households of Different Types at Orayvi, 1900

Household Type	Total Households	Mean Household Size*	Total Houses	Mean No. of Rooms	Mean House Area (sq. m.)
Nuclear family	54 (49.5%)	5.4 (s.d. = 1.7)	45	6.2 (s.d. = 3.3)	97.8 (s.d. = 45.1)
Extended family	24 (22%)	7.0 (s.d. = 2.0)	21	6.8 (s.d. = 2.8)	100.74 (s.d. = 55.1)
Couples	9 (8.3%)	2.0	5	6.5 (s.d. = 1.9)	108.4 (s.d. = 46.0)
Other household types	22 (20%)	5.2 (s.d. = 1.9)	20	6.7 (s.d. = 3.5)	90.1 (s.d. = 56.8)
Total	109	5.5 (s.d. = 2.2)	91	6.4 (s.d. = 3.3)	

* Note that the mean and standard deviation are of the distribution of sample means, not of the raw data.

nuclear families but did not have significantly larger houses, whether measured by number of rooms or total area (table 4.4). Matrifocal extended families had slightly more rooms, with an average of 6.81 rooms per house, while nuclear families had 6.1 rooms; the difference was not significant, however (t value 1.045, $p > .3083$). Matrifocal extended families also had slightly more floor area (table 4.4), with an average house size of 100.7 sq. m., while nuclear families had 98.0 sq. m., although, again, the difference was not significant (t value $-.19$, $p > .847$)

Domestic Cycles and Architectural Constraints to the Extended Family

The antiquity of the nuclear family as a predominant household type at Hopi is unknown, but it may be an ancient pattern. The clustered nature of pueblo architecture may have constrained the development of extended families, making nuclear families more common. The developmental cycle of the domestic group requires adjustment of household space to meet the needs of expanding household membership. The compact nature of pueblo architecture, however, restricts horizontal expansion, and vertical expansion has limits imposed by engineering expertise.

Titiev (1944:47) described Orayvi households as com-

posed of matrilineage segments, noting that "under favorable circumstances a household group tends to expand until the original house becomes overcrowded. When this happens a younger daughter . . . may move into new rooms contiguous to her parental home or she may build a new house adjacent or close to her mother's." Because of such assumptions about Hopi social organization, early anthropologists expected that clans would be spatially localized within pueblos. This would be the logical assumption if the lineages composing clans built houses adjacent to their parental home. Victor and Cosmos Mindeleff found that this was not the case when they began to map the Hopi villages (C. Mindeleff 1900). The Mindeleffs found that in most Hopi villages, as at Orayvi, clans were randomly distributed throughout the settlement. They theorized that with the passage of time, the original spatial organization of the pueblos had been altered (V. Mindeleff 1891:104–8; C. Mindeleff 1900:648).

During a restoration project at the Hopi village of Walpi, large blocks of rooms were claimed by clan or kiva groups (Adams 1982; Ahlstrom, Dean, and Robinson 1978), suggesting localization of clans within this First Mesa village. However, at the time of the Walpi restoration project, the village was largely abandoned. In providing information on room ownership, informants may have reflected ideal patterns of clan localization, whereas actual ownership of rooms may have differed (E. Charles Adams, personal communication, 1990).

The present study suggests that clans may never have been localized at Hopi villages. A glance at the closely packed houses on Mindeleff's map suggests that building a new house at Orayvi adjacent or close to a set of rooms in an established roomblock would have been difficult. At Orayvi, the matrilineal extended family seems to have been only a temporary configuration, and households composed of nuclear families may have been the most common type even in the past. The construction of houses in long, linear roomblocks may have meant that younger women rarely had the opportunity to relocate in spatial proximity to their mothers (C. Mindeleff 1900, plate 28; V. Mindeleff 1891:104–8; Titiev 1944:51–55, chart 7). In fact, while tracing prime and alternate segments of several lineages at Orayvi, Levy (1992:49) found that even different households of a lineage were not typically in spatial proximity, as Eggan's reconstruction might suggest, but were scattered around the village.

Emory Sekaquaptewa (personal communication, 1990; see also Levy 1992:50), a native of Ho'atvela, suggests that a neolocal residence pattern has been common at Third Mesa, representing a stage in the developmental cycle of the domestic group. He notes that a newly married couple resides with the wife's household as the husband develops relationships and work habits with her male relatives. Once he has become integrated into the affinal household and has had several children, he will build a new, independent house for his family. The process is termed *nawipti* in Hopi, meaning "going off and living on one's own."

If residence patterns changed as households progressed through the domestic developmental cycle, the community should show several different types of residence patterns at any one point in time (described for Navajo households in Henderson and Levy 1975:116–19 and Levy et al. 1989:356–57), as is the case at Orayvi. So while the matrilineage segment (extended family) may have been the ideal residence pattern, it would not necessarily have been the most common one. Most important, if most daughters moved to separate residences

after a number of years of marriage, the construction of new houses, either at the end of an existing roomblock or in a new, freestanding roomblock, would be more likely than the extension of existing units by the addition of new rooms.

Given the evidence that the nuclear family was a typical configuration at Orayvi, the construction of "outliers" (small groups of rooms built around the main pueblo roomblocks housing one or two households), may always have been common, with such units simply forming the nucleus of a new roomblock. Data obtained from maps and photographs, presented in chapter 5, support this suggestion.

The data presented here strongly suggest that the nuclear family may always have been the most common household type among the Hopi and that settlements might be expected to exhibit a number of household types. Euroamerican influences on household structure should not be completely ruled out, however. Population decline due to European diseases may have continued to affect the size and structure of the family long after Euroamerican culture had begun to intrude on the Hopi (Cameron 1996).

Summary

The Orayvi data offer an unparalleled opportunity to examine the relationship between the pueblo house and the group of individuals that use it. This chapter focuses on the size and structure of the Orayvi house and household in comparison with other ethnographic and historic pueblos. Orayvi houses had more rooms than houses at many other pueblos, especially Eastern Pueblos, containing an average of more than six rooms. Rooms were approximately the same size at Orayvi as at other nineteenth-century Hopi pueblos, but considerably smaller than at Eastern Pueblos. The number of rooms per house appears to be related to the extent of multistoried construction, which was dramatically decreased by Euroamerican contact. Comparing room size at Orayvi and at other nineteenth-century Hopi pueblos with Eastern Pueblos suggests, however, that as multistoried construction decreased, room size increased. Archaeological evidence suggests that in multistoried pueblos, not all rooms in houses were in active use. Lower-story rooms may have actually functioned as platforms for upper stories.

Ethnographically reported household size is quite variable for modern and historic pueblos, but evidence presented here suggests that this may in part be the result of variability in household structure related to the developmental cycle of the domestic group. Average size for Orayvi households seemed large but in fact showed considerable variability in size and composition. The nuclear family was the most common household type, and archi-tectural constraints to the development of the extended family may have been in operation since the appearance of massed, multistoried dwellings in the northern Southwest—after A.D. 1250.

Census data and the observations of early travelers suggest that population at Orayvi was growing at the end of the nineteenth century as a result of natural increase and, possibly, immigration (Bradfield 1971; Levy 1992; see chapter 5). Household size may have been high at Orayvi because the village was undergoing a period of growth. The Orayvi data suggest that archaeologists may need to consider dynamic aspects of population structure before applying constants to prehistoric structures.

5 / Orayvi Architectural Dynamics, 1871–1901

Photos taken between 1871 and 1901 show Orayvi in the years before the split. In analyzing these photos, I hoped to be able to characterize "ordinary" architectural dynamics—the types of building or maintenance activities Orayvi residents normally engaged in—so that I could contrast normal behavior with the way buildings were treated after the split. I found a number of patterns in the way residents built new homes and modified or abandoned old ones. Building and rebuilding were an integral part of Hopi life as residents adjusted their homes to meet domestic needs.

I also found that during the span of time 1871 to 1901, Orayvi was in the midst of two major transitions. First, I could see marked changes in building materials, methods, and architectural styles as a result of Euroamerican contact. Second, I was surprised to discover convincing evidence of significant population growth at Orayvi in the years before the split. Although this volume does not propose to explain the causes of the split, evidence of population growth presented in this chapter supports those scholars who see overpopulation as a precipitating factor (chapter 3).

Photographic Analysis, 1871–1901

Historic photographs, Mindeleff's map, Titiev's map, and the census data were all used to explore architectural dynamics at Orayvi between 1871 and 1901 (table 3.1 gives dates of the time periods used in this analysis; appendix 3 summarizes architectural change during Period 1, 1871–1901). Hillers' photographs (1871 to 1879) are the earliest available photographic documentation of Orayvi (see chapter 3), and in the main, Carpenter's photographs

(taken in 1901) provide an end point for this portion of the study; very few photographs show architectural change between 1901 and 1906. Titiev's map was used to identify the location of roomblocks observed in photographs that had been built after 1887 and to locate other roomblocks that were not visible in photographs.

Mindeleff's map provides the baseline for architectural observations, resulting in the creation of two pre-split periods: Period 1—1871/1879 to 1887 (Hillers' photographs to Mindeleff's map), and Period 2—1887 to 1901 (Mindeleff's map to Carpenter's photographs). These two time periods are of unequal duration. Period 1 (1871–87) is between eight and sixteen years long, depending upon the date of the Hillers photograph used in the analysis (see chapter 3: one of Hillers' photos dated to 1871 and the rest to 1879). Most of the rooms in this period were observed over a period of eight years (37 of 49 rooms). Because Euroamerican influence became pervasive after 1880 (chapter 3), this period should show less Euroamerican influence than the later period. Period 2 (1887–1901) is fourteen years long. Differences in the duration of these periods are considered in the following discussion.

A total of 174 of the rooms on Mindeleff's map were observed in photographs for both periods prior to 1901 (excluding three-sided cooking/storage rooms, discussed below). In addition, 36 new rooms were evident in photographs that were not present on Mindeleff's map. Other new rooms (in addition to those seen in photographs) were identified by comparing maps produced by Mindeleff (in 1887) and Titiev (for 1900) (figs. 3.1 and 3.2). Some of the same rooms were observed in photographs both before and after 1887, contributing information for

Table 5.1   Architectural Change at Orayvi, by Roomblock, Using Photograph Analysis

Roomblock	No. of Rms. Obser.	Aband.	Number of Rooms		
			Dismantled	Rebuilt	New
Period 1 (1871–1887)					
1	9				1
4	28		1	2	2
12	12				3
Total	49	0	1	2	6
% obser. rooms present, 1887			2.0	4.1	12.2
Period 2 (1888–1901)					
1	24	5		1	5
2	16	2	1	2	5
4	31	1	1	7	3
4 SW	20		4	4	3
4^1	6		3		1
7 SW	19	3	1	6	1
7 W	7	1	1		1
9	16		1	1	1
10 NE	17		1	1	2
10 S	9		2	2	1
11	7			1	1
12	13		2	2	
E/L	8				8
K/L/M	4				4
Total	197	12	17	27	36
% obser. rooms present, 1887		6.1	8.6	13.7	18.3
Total, 1871–1901	246	12	18	29	42
% obser. rooms present, 1887		4.9	7.3	11.8	17.1

both periods. As a result, when the two periods are considered separately, the total number of rooms observed (including new rooms) is 246 (table 5.1).

Because rooms in the interior of roomblocks could not be seen in photographs, the architectural change described here applied almost exclusively to exterior rooms. Photographs were typically taken of the front or east side of the roomblocks—the side on which most daily activity took place. Though the number of rooms observed in photographs represents only about 16 percent of the total number of rooms mapped by Mindeleff, it comprises more than half of the total number of east-facing exterior rooms that were potentially visible in photographs (N = 387). The rooms observed in photos were part of sixty-six houses, more than 35 percent of the houses that Titiev recorded at Orayvi in 1900.

Types of Architectural Change Observed

Architectural change observed in Orayvi photographs was the result of four types of actions: rooms were abandoned, dismantled, rebuilt, or newly constructed. Rooms

Figure 5.1 This photograph, taken by J. Hillers in 1879, shows a small plaza located in the northwest section of Orayvi. Roomblock 1 is to the left, and the north end of Roomblock 4 can be seen in the background. The foreground arrow shows Room 551 in use. This is one of the few first-story rooms at this time that had a door. The arrow at the rear of the photograph shows the "terrace" of collapsed rooms west of Roomblock 4, like those seen in figure 2.1 behind Roomblock 4. (Courtesy Smithsonian Institution, National Anthropological Archives; photo no. 56395)

that were intact but abandoned were the most difficult to recognize in photographs because such rooms may show no exterior evidence of abandonment. Abandoned rooms were identified by cracked and deteriorating walls, blocked doors, and a marked decrease in height for first-story rooms (figs. 5.1 and 5.2 show Room 551 as occupied in 1879 and abandoned in 1901). These observations are not universally indicative of abandonment, however. Blocked doors may indicate ritual storage as well as abandonment (Richard V. N. Ahlstrom, personal communication, 1989). While first-story rooms may decrease in height because the roof has been removed and the room filled with trash (Ferguson and Mills 1987:253), decrease in height could also result from the deposition of trash

and wind-blown sediments against the outside walls of the room and would not necessarily indicate abandonment (Donaldson 1893:6).

Abandoned rooms can result from several of the processes (described in chapter 2) that cause architectural change. Two interrelated causes that are most likely are structural deterioration and the developmental cycle of the domestic group. Rooms that become structurally unsound can be either abandoned or rebuilt. If a household is not growing, additional space may not be necessary and a room may be abandoned. There is no evidence that death or disease resulted in ritual abandonment of structures among the Hopi as it does among the Navajo (Jett and Spencer 1981; Regan 1922).

Figure 5.2 Roomblock 1 in a photograph taken by C. Carpenter in 1901, showing Room 551 (arrow) abandoned. Wind-blown sand has been deposited against the room, leaving only the top few feet visible and almost obscuring the door seen in figure 5.1. (Courtesy of the Field Museum of Natural History, Chicago; neg. no. 227)

Dismantled rooms formed a second type of architectural change. These are rooms that are either (1) visible in early photographs but are not on Mindeleff's map, or (2) are on Mindeleff's map but do not appear on later photographs (figs. 5.3 and 5.4). Dismantled rooms indicate both structural deterioration and new construction. Since building material was valuable and easily reused, it is likely that most abandoned rooms were eventually dismantled, especially in situations where population levels remained the same or increased. Many Orayvi photographs taken before the split show piles of masonry and stacks of roof beams that were stockpiled, ready for future use (fig. 5.5). Ownership of buildings probably extended to construction material even when a structure

was abandoned, as is the case at Zuni (B. Mills, personal communication, 1990). In most cases, then, dismantled rooms suggest new construction by the same household or a closely related household.

Some rooms were rebuilt, and this represents the third type of change identified at Orayvi. Rooms were identified as rebuilt only if major changes were noted between earlier and later photographs of the room, such as changes in the size of the room or the location of walls (figs. 5.6–5.9). The addition or removal of doors and windows suggest rebuilding, but such evidence alone was not sufficient to confirm it. In some cases, two separate rooms were combined into one during rebuilding, a practice that became much more common after 1906 (chapter 6).

Figure 5.3 Room 398 in Roomblock 4 (arrow) is an intact, apparently occupied upper-story habitation room in this photograph taken by J. Hillers in 1879. (Courtesy of the Smithsonian Institution, National Anthropological Archives; photo. no. 41831-A)

Rooms may have been rebuilt for a number of reasons: because they were structurally unsound, to change structure function, for a more exact fit with the domestic group occupying the structure, or because of changes in architectural styles. Change in room function was identified primarily by the addition (or occasional removal) of doors and by vertical location of the room. As discussed in chapter 2, habitation rooms were traditionally located in upper stories, whereas lower stories contained storage rooms, but this pattern changed with Euroamerican contact. Changes in structure function may signal changes in the size or structure of the domestic group (for example, the conversion of a habitation room to storage as household size decreases). Changes in architectural styles and the location of habitation rooms at Orayvi can be attributed primarily to Euroamerican contact (as at other southwestern pueblos: Ahlstrom et al. 1978; Ferguson and Mill 1987; Ferguson et al. 1990).

Newly built rooms are the fourth type of architectural change noted (fig. 5.10). This category included (1) rooms not seen in Hillers' photographs but recorded on Mindeleff's map, (2) rooms absent from Mindeleff's map but seen in later photographs, and (3) rooms on Titiev's map that were not on Mindeleff's map. Newly built rooms suggest the expansion of existing households or the creation of new households as part of the developmental cycle of the domestic group. Even in a static population, some households will increase in size and will need either to expand space in existing structures or to have part of the group build elsewhere. New structures may also indicate that the total population of a settlement is growing, either through immigration or internal population expansion.

Figure 5.4   In this photograph of Roomblock 4, taken by an unknown photographer about 1895, the arrow points to the space that Room 398 once occupied. The room has been completely dismantled. (Courtesy of the Southwest Museum, Los Angeles; photo no. N.24333 P6114)

Of the 246 rooms observed in photographs, 101 (41 percent) were abandoned, demolished, rebuilt, or newly built between the 1870s and 1906 (table 5.1). Two of these rooms (Room 38, floor 1 and Room 438, floor 3) underwent change both before and after 1887. In addition, at least 86 new rooms were recorded on Titiev's 1900 map that had not been on Mindeleff's 1887 map (most of these rooms could not be seen in photos).

Room Function and Architectural Change

Ethnographic data presented in chapter 2 suggest that the frequency of architectural modification is partly related to structure function, a pattern that was explored using the Orayvi data. Habitation rooms were modified more frequently than storage rooms at Orayvi; however, the pattern was complicated by a shift in the location of habitation rooms during the late nineteenth century from upper stories to lower stories (chapter 3). This shift in the location of habitation rooms eventually brought about a decrease in multistoried construction and in the number of rooms per house, a pattern that was especially pronounced after the split (chapter 6; see also chapter 4).

Identifying room function from photographs of room exteriors is difficult. Adams (1983:48) used six categories of information to identify rooms of different function at Walpi Pueblo, but most of his categories are based on architectural features that cannot be seen in the Orayvi

Figure 5.5   At the northwest end of Roomblock 4, building material from several dismantled rooms has been stacked for future use. When Orayvi's population was growing in the late 1890s and early 1900s, few rooms were abandoned for long. Other photos show that these rooms were quickly rebuilt. Roof timbers and stone for masonry walls were difficult to obtain, and both were frequently reused at Hopi villages. (Photograph by C. Carpenter, 1901; courtesy of the Field Museum of Natural History, Chicago; neg. no. 225)

photographs. Only two of the variables he suggests can be applied using exterior photographs: story and location of doors. Using these variables, especially the location of doors, two broad categories of room use were examined at Orayvi: habitation rooms and storage rooms.

Habitation rooms in Hopi pueblos were traditionally located in upper stories and had doors, while doorless lower-story rooms were used for storage (Adams 1983:53; Mindeleff 1891:103, 223). Access to hatch entrances for first-floor rooms and to upper-story rooms was via ladders or narrow staircases. The lack of first-floor doors was probably designed to protect stored goods from children and

rodents (Adams 1983:53) as well as to protect residents from raids (Whiteley 1988:29–39). Habitation began to move from upper stories to first-floor rooms in the late 1800s (with decreasing need for defense); doors and windows were added as habitation rooms were converted to storage (Ahlstrom, Dean, and Robinson 1978:58; at Zuni, Ferguson and Mills 1987:252).

At Orayvi, the change in the location of habitation rooms from upper stories to lower stories apparently began in the 1880s. The location of doors at Orayvi indicates that most east-facing, lower-story rooms still functioned as storage areas in the 1870s (table 5.2). Only two first-

Figure 5.6　This photograph, taken by G. W. James in 1896, shows Room 360 (arrow) at the southeast end of Roomblock 4. Room 360 is a lower-story, doorless room probably used for storage. The room was rebuilt in 1901 (see figures 5.7–5.9). (Photograph entitled *A Moki City*, courtesy of Dr. P. J. Lindemann and the Museum of Northern Arizona; Museum of Northern Arizona neg. no. 66.799)

floor rooms in Hillers' photographs have a door. Almost all upper-story rooms (for which the observation could be made) in Hillers' photographs had doors, suggesting that they were used primarily as habitation rooms. On Mindeleff's field maps, 26 of the 168 first-floor rooms (15 percent) appear to have doors (unfortunately, doors and windows are not always clearly distinguished on Mindeleff's field maps), suggesting that the change in the location of habitation rooms may have begun by 1887. More than half of the first-floor rooms with doors on Mindeleff's map also have hatch entries, again suggesting conversion from storage to habitation. Mindeleff recorded

only a very few upper-story rooms without doors (N = 9). By 1901, almost half of the first-floor rooms (visible in photographs) had doors, but almost all of these doors were installed in the late 1890s as part of room-remodeling projects (table 5.2). As in the earlier period, almost all upper-story rooms had doors.

Ethnographic evidence (chapter 2) suggests that habitation rooms will be modified more frequently than other types of rooms because (1) they are used more intensively, increasing deterioration, and (2) habitation rooms require a more exact fit between structure and residents and will be remodeled more often. At Orayvi, photographs show

Figure 5.7 In 1901, Charles Carpenter took this photograph of Room 360 being rebuilt (arrow). Notice the addition of doors and windows. The women kneeling at the right are probably mixing earth and water for mortar or plaster; another worker can be seen on the roof. (Courtesy of the Field Museum of Natural History, Chicago; neg. no. 223)

that of the rooms that underwent architectural change before 1887, more were in upper stories, where habitation rooms were typically located, than in first stories. All three rooms that were dismantled or rebuilt were on second or third floors (table 5.3). Furthermore, four of the six new rooms were built in upper stories. After 1887, only 40 percent of the architectural change occurred in upper-story rooms (table 5.3). However, much of the architectural activity during the later period involved the shift in function of first-story rooms from storage to habitation.

At Orayvi, sixteen of the twenty-seven rooms rebuilt after 1887 were first-floor rooms, and in most cases a door was added when the room was rebuilt, indicating a change to use for habitation. These newly remodeled

habitation rooms were balanced by the abandonment or dismantling of 14 upper-story rooms that presumably had been used for habitation (table 5.3). Although the location of habitation rooms changed, architectural change still occurred most frequently to habitation rooms. Table 5.3 suggests that in the 1890s Orayvi was just beginning to lose its upper stories, a process that became very prevalent after 1906 and resulted in a decrease in the number of rooms per house (chapter 6).

In many cases, when first-floor rooms were rebuilt as habitation rooms, they were expanded (discussed below). Although room size clearly increased at Orayvi during the late nineteenth and early twentieth centuries (chapter 4), the magnitude of the increase could not be measured.

Figure 5.8 Charles Carpenter and A. C. Vroman must have been at Orayvi at the same time. Vroman took this close-up view of Room 360 as it was being rebuilt (1901). The woman on the left may be carrying mortar. (Courtesy of the Smithsonian Institution, National Anthropological Archives; photo no. 32357-1)

Mindeleff's 1887 map provides the only accurate plan of the pueblo; hence, a longitudinal study of room size was not possible. However, a similar trend toward larger rooms was observed at other Hopi villages and at Zuni (Ahlstrom, Dean, and Robinson 1978:25; Ferguson and Mills 1987:256).

Residential Stability

In spite of the frequent modification of dwellings at Orayvi, photographs indicate that individual households made modifications only within the footprint of their house; in other words, domestic space was rarely encroached upon by another household. Rebuilt rooms are

fairly common at Orayvi before 1901; almost 15 percent of the rooms observed were rebuilt (table 5.1). As noted above, when first-floor rooms were remodeled, they were often expanded in size, occasionally by combining adjacent rooms. Combined rooms almost always belonged to the same house (table 5.4).

The prevalence of combining rooms before the introduction of Euroamerican architectural styles is unknown, but the practice may have been rare: none were recorded during Period 1 (1871/1879–1887). During Period 2 (1887–1901), in four of six cases where rooms at Orayvi were combined, both rooms belonged to the same household (table 5.4). Usually, an upper-story room would be dismantled and the first-story room below it expanded in

Figure 5.9 In this photograph, taken by G. H. Pepper in the first years of the twentieth century, an arrow points to new Room 360 after construction was completed. Notice the overhanging cornice, the door, and the windows. (Courtesy of the National Park Service Photo Archives, Western Archaeological and Conservation Center, Tucson, Arizona)

height and depth. Houses at Orayvi were generally only one room wide (chapter 4), so expanding the width of first-story rooms required using space owned by another household. In the two cases where rooms from different houses were combined, social ties facilitated acquisition of adjacent space (figs. 5.11 and 5.12). In one case, the owners of the two combined rooms were sisters; in the other case, there were clan links between the owners. In both cases, the combined rooms were on the first story, and rebuilding changed two or three storage rooms into a large habitation room. It is possible that one of the combined rooms was donated or purchased by the owner of the other and that the ease with which this transaction was accomplished was facilitated by kinship ties.

It was probably difficult to acquire rooms from another household unless there were close kinship or clan ties, although the situation may have been different for houses: one of Titiev's informants reported that *houses* at Orayvi could be either purchased or reoccupied by

another owner if vacant (Whiteley 1988:170). At Walpi, clan ownership of houses was strictly observed until the 1970s, and houses could not be bought or sold except within the clan that owned them (E. C. Adams, personal communication, 1990). At Orayvi, difficulty in acquiring space adjacent to existing houses apparently limited the expansion of rooms and may have forced some households to build outside the main roomblocks, especially when larger, Euroamerican-influenced rooms became common.

Although domestic space was rarely exchanged between houses, the movement of households between houses in the village may have been more common. Titiev (1944:51–52) compared the clan affiliation of households in 1886 (using data collected by Alexander M. Stephen; Mindeleff 1891:104–8) with his own census notes for the period around 1900. He found that in 65 percent of the households (for which comparisons could be made), the same clan name was assigned by both Stephen

Figure 5.10 Roomblock E/F, shown in this 1901 photograph by Charles Carpenter, was constructed between 1887 and 1895. Most roomblocks face southeast, but Roomblock E/F faces northwest onto the Snake Dance Plaza. The unfinished first- and second-story rooms were never completed. (Courtesy of the Field Museum of Natural History, Chicago; neg. no. 237)

in 1886 and himself in his 1933 census (Titiev 1944:53). Although Titiev felt that this was a relatively high degree of correspondence for studies fifty years apart, the comparison (1886 to 1900) represents less than a generation. It suggests that as many as 35 percent of the households had either died out or changed their place of residence within a period of about fifteen years—a fairly high proportion of household movement.

Before the split, continuity in use of space by homeowners was usual and indicates that the transferral of structures between houses was rare. Even after the split, however, rooms belonging to different houses were only occasionally combined, suggesting continuity in the use of space in spite of serious disruptions of village population structure and a great deal of movement of households between houses (chapter 6). Although the period of time covered in this portion of the study is only a little less than two generations, the observation of occupational stability is especially important for prehistoric southwestern sites, many of which were occupied for only a few generations or less (Cordell 1984:313; Dean 1969; Hantman 1983:158; Schiffer 1976:157).

Table 5.2 Doors Observed for Rooms in Photographs, 1871–1901

	1st Story	2nd Story	3rd Story	4th Story	Total
Period 1 (1871–1887)					
No Door	16 (88.8%)	1 (7.7%)			17
Door	2 (11.1%)	12 (92.3%)	16 (100.0%)	1 (100.0%)	31
Unknown*		(1)			(1)
Total	18 (100.0%)	13 (100.0%)	16 (100.0%)	1 (100.0%)	48
Period 2 (1882–1901)					
No Door	36 (50.0%)	2 (3.4%)			38
Door	2 (2.8%)	53 (90.0%)	41 (97.6%)	5 (100.0%)	101
Door added 1890s	34 (47.2%)	4 (6.8%)	1 (2.3%)		39
Unknown*	(7)	(4)	(1)		(12)
Total	72 (100.0%)	59 (100.0%)	42 (100.0%)	5 (100.0%)	178

* The Unknown row indicates rooms where not enough of the room could be seen to determine if a door was present.

Population Increase and Architectural Change

Several scholars point to population increase as an important causal factor in the Orayvi split (chapter 3), but unfortunately, most of the population estimates for the Hopi villages during the second half of the nineteenth century are not highly reliable. During this time, the villages were undergoing episodes of drought and disease that had dramatic effects on population levels. Strong evidence that Orayvi population did increase significantly during the last three decades of the nineteenth century is provided by the analysis of Orayvi photographs.

Two lines of architectural evidence suggest population increase during the late nineteenth century. First, there was an increase in the rate of architectural change —the number of rooms visible in photographs that were abandoned, dismantled, rebuilt, or newly built—during this period. Second, there were many new rooms built at Orayvi between 1871 and 1901. Some of these rooms expanded space in existing houses, but a large number of new houses were also built. Population growth appears to have been largely internal, although there may have been some immigration from other Hopi pueblos.

The proportion of abandoned, dismantled, and rebuilt rooms increased dramatically between Period 1 (1871/1879–1887) and Period 2 (1887–1901), from 7 percent to 35 percent of the total number of rooms observed (table 5.1; for Period 2, the percentage is based on existing [N = 161] rather than new rooms). Although the duration of the later period is greater than that of the earlier period (for most rooms), this should not account for so great an

Table 5.3 Architectural Change by Story, 1871–1901

	Abandoned	Dismantled	Rebuilt	New	Total
Period 1 (1873–1887)					
Third story		1 (100.0%)	1 (50.0%)	3 (50.0%)	5
Second story			1 (50.0%)	1 (16.6%)	2
First story				2 (33.3%)	2
Total	0	1 (100.0%)	2 (100.0%)	6 (100.0%)	9
Period 2 (1888–1901)					
Fourth story		1 5.9			1 (1.1%)
Third story	3 (25.0%)	3 (17.6%)	5 (18.5%)	2 (5.6%)	13 (14.1%)
Second story		7 (41.2%)	6 (22.2%)	10 (27.8%)	23 (25.0%)
First story	9 (75.0%)	6 (35.3%)	16 (59.3%)	24 (66.7%)	55 (59.8%)
Total	12 (100.0%)	17 (100.0%)	27 (100.0%)	36 (100.0%)	92 (100.0%)

increase in the rate of architectural change.[1] Furthermore, although the proportion of new rooms appears to have increased less steeply between the two periods (from 12.2 percent to 18.3 percent), the thirty-six new rooms shown on table 5.1 for Period 2 (1871/1879–1887) included only new rooms seen in photographs. Mindeleff's map suggests that many new rooms were under construction in 1887 (he shows incomplete walls, roofs under construction, etc.), and Titiev's map indicates that many other new rooms were built after 1887.

Titiev's map (fig. 3.2) shows fifty new first-floor rooms (rooms not on Mindeleff's map) in twelve detached roomblocks, some of which consist of a single room. Only twelve of these new rooms (in two roomblocks) can be seen in photographs. Titiev's map also shows fourteen other first-story rooms built within existing roomblocks;

only three of these new rooms show up in photographs. If the new rooms on Titiev's map that could not be seen in photographs (N = 49) are combined with the total number of new rooms observed in photographs (N = 36, see table 5.1), at least eighty-five new rooms were built at Orayvi during Period 2 (1887–1901). The total number of new rooms built after 1887 is undoubtedly much higher than this, as many of the new rooms on Titiev's map were probably multistoried. The eighty-five new rooms represent at least an 8 percent increase in the total number of rooms in 1887 (N = 1100), or a 22 percent increase in the total number of east-facing, exterior rooms that would have been potentially visible in 1887 (N = 387). It seems that a substantial amount of new construction occurred at Orayvi after 1887.

Both Period 1 (1871/1879–1887) and Period 2 (1887–

Table 5.4 Rooms Combined during Rebuilding, before 1901

Room Numbers	Numbers for Houses Containing Combined Rooms
527 i*	162
with 527 ii	162
422 i	129
with 423 i	130
436 i	133
with 437 ii	133
376 i	119
with 375 ii	119
357 i	115
with 351 i	114
and 350 i *new***	114
228 i	84
with 229 i	84

*i, ii denote first and second stories.
**new* indicates a new room, built after 1887.

1901) show a net increase in the total number of rooms at Orayvi (table 5.1). During Period 1, there is a net increase of five rooms (one dismantled, six new rooms) of the forty-nine rooms observed. During Period 2 (1887–1901), there is a net increase of at least fifty-six rooms (twenty-nine abandoned or dismantled, eighty-five new rooms), including those on Titiev's map. While the number of abandoned or dismantled rooms is a minimum figure, it is unlikely that an accurate total would equal the number of new rooms. These figures suggest that the population of Orayvi may have been increasing in the 1870s and that the increase continued until the 1906 split.

Two patterns of architectural growth could be identified in the placement of new rooms: (1) the expansion of existing houses through the addition of upper-story rooms or contiguous first-story rooms; and (2) the construction of new houses containing a single household, either freestanding or attached to an existing roomblock (table 5.5). New houses were identified in photographs by the construction of two or more rooms in the same location and their identification by Titiev as an independent household. Maps and photographs suggest that both the construction of new houses and the expansion of old houses had been common patterns at Orayvi since at least the 1880s.

Comparison of Hillers' photographs with Mindeleff's map (fig. 3.1) shows only the expansion of existing houses during Period 1 (1871/1879–1887) (table 5.5). Two houses added third-floor habitation rooms, and one house added a first-floor storage room. Another house underwent a major expansion, adding two upper-story rooms and a first-floor storage room. Closer examination of Mindeleff's map (fig. 3.1), however, indicates that both patterns—house expansion and new house construction—were probably present by 1887. The map shows wall segments indicating new construction in seven of the twenty-five roomblocks in the pueblo. Nine small roomblocks containing fewer than ten rooms probably represent new construction, housing one or two households. In one case, wall segments indicate that one of these small roomblocks (consisting of a single house) would later be connected with a major roomblock (Roomblocks 1 and 1¹) through the construction of an intervening house. Photographs confirm that this did occur.

Photographs show both house expansion and new house construction during Period 2 (1887–1901) (table 5.5). The thirty-six new rooms observed in photographs for this period include ten new houses (15 percent of the sixty-six houses observed in photographs). In addition to the house built between Roomblocks 1 and 1¹, another house was built at the northern end of Roomblock 1, probably connecting it with isolated Room 565. Two houses (consisting of at least five rooms in two households) were built at the northern end of Roomblock 2. These houses were apparently under construction when Mindeleff mapped Orayvi. He recorded several first-story rooms and a number of wall segments in this area. It was eventually a two-story structure. Note that much of this new construction is at the western end of the settlement, the direction in which the settlement continued to grow (see "Patterns of Settlement Growth" below). Six other new houses were observed in two freestanding roomblocks located at the southern end of the pueblo.

The remaining fifteen new rooms built during

Figure 5.11 Arrows indicate Rooms 422 (left; owned by household 129) and 423 (right; owned by household 130) at the northeast end of Roomblock 4. The photograph was taken by A. C. Vroman in 1898 when Room 423 was being reroofed. Just a few years later, these rooms were combined into one large room (fig. 5.12). (Courtesy of the Pasadena Public Library)

Period 2 (1887–1901) expanded space in existing houses (table 5.5). These rooms included eight new habitation rooms and seven new storage rooms. In one case, one of the new storage rooms was later converted to a habitation room. Thirteen of these new rooms were on the first story, expanding to some extent the ground plan of the house. Only two new rooms were in upper stories. Both expanded houses and new houses can be seen on Titiev's map (fig. 3.2).

These data suggest that the construction of new houses was prevalent at Orayvi during both Period 1 (1871/1879–1887) and Period 2 (1887–1901), although it is possible that the expansion of existing houses may

have been the most common pattern before about 1885. Hillers' photographs, although limited in number, show only the expansion of existing residences. Mindeleff's map was drawn between nine and fourteen years later, and indicates the construction of many new houses. Population growth, as suggested by the growth of households and the establishment of new households, was apparently more pronounced at Orayvi after 1885.

Explanation for Orayvi Population Growth

The large number of new rooms and new houses built at Orayvi in the late nineteenth century suggests popula-

Figure 5.12 Charles Carpenter took this photograph of Rooms 422 and 423 in 1901 after they had been combined into one large room (arrow). Clan links between the owners of these two rooms may have facilitated the transfer of rooms between households. When two rooms were combined, usually they belonged to the same household. (Courtesy of the Field Museum of Natural History, Chicago; neg. no. 208)

tion increase, but other explanations are possible. In the following discussion, population estimates for Orayvi are examined and discussed, especially those from the late nineteenth century. Alternative explanations for the new buildings, other than population increase, are then considered and largely dismissed. The source of population growth at Orayvi is determined to have been primarily internal, although some migration from other villages is likely (Bradfield 1971:62; Levy 1992). Finally, the composition of households in new roomblocks is determined to be the result of budding off newly mature families.

Population estimates for Orayvi before the late nine-teenth century may be unreliable. Several of the pre-1850 population estimates put Orayvi at more than twelve hundred people (table 5.6). As discussed in chapter 3, smallpox epidemics struck Hopi in 1853 (most severely at First Mesa) and 1866–67 (most severely at Second Mesa), as did a devastating drought in the mid-1860s (Bradfield 1971:61–62; Whiteley 1988:32, 38). These events may have lowered population at Orayvi but also caused im-migration to Orayvi from the other Mesas (Levy 1992). Dockstader (1979:525), quoting a U.S. census, reports that the population of Orayvi was reduced from eight hun-dred to two hundred people after these disasters. Other

Table 5.5 Identification of New Rooms and New Houses Observed in Photographs, by Roomblock*

Period 1 (1871–1887)

New rooms added to existing houses

Roomblock 1

Room 552n fl 1 (stor) - HHD 170

Roomblock 4

Room 433n fl 3 (hab) - HHD 132

Room 438n fl 3 (hab) - HHD 133

Roomblock 12 - HHD 23

Room 38n fl 1 (stor)

Room 37n fl 2 (hab)

Room 36n fl 3 (hab)

Total New Storage Rooms = 2

Total New Habitation Rooms = 4

Period 2 (1887–1901)

New rooms added to existing houses

Roomblock 2

Room 530n fl 1 (hab) - HHD 162

Roomblock 4

Room 401n fl 3 (hab) - HHD 125

Room 406n fl 1 (hab) - HHD 126

Room 414n fl 1 (stor) - HHD 128

Roomblock 4, sw end

Room 362n fl 1 (stor) - HHD 116

Room 357n fl 1 (hab?) - HHD 115

Room 350n fl 1 (stor/hab) - HHD 114

Roomblock 4^1

Room 220n fl 1 (hab) - HHD 80

Roomblock 7 sw end

Room 225n fl 1 (hab) - HHD 83

Roomblock 7 w. Side

Room 6xn fl 1 (unk) - HHD ?

Roomblock 9

Room 176n fl 3 (hab) - HHD 64

Roomblock 10

Room 175n fl 1 (stor) - HHD 63

Room 162n fl 1 (stor) - HHD 61

Roomblock 10 S. end

Room 132n fl 1 (hab) - HHD 51

Table 5.5 *(continued)*

Roomblock 11 NE end

Room 112n fl 1 (stor) - HHD 43

Total New Storage Rooms = 7

Total New Habitation Rooms = 8

New Houses

Roomblock 1 and 1^1 - HHD 166

Room 541n fl 2

Room 540n fl 1

Roomblock 1 - HHD 173

Room 56xn fl 2

Room 56yn fl 2

Room 56zn fl 1

Roomblock 2

Room 535n fl 1 - HHD 164

Room 534n fl 2

Room 533n fl 2 - HHD 163

Roomblock E/F

Room E/F 1 - HHD 18 or 19?

Room E/F 3

Room E/F 2 - HHD 18 or 19?

Room E/F 5

Room E/F 7?

Room E/F 8 - HHD ?

Room E/F 9

Roomblock K/L/M

(3 new residence units - HHDs 77, 78, 79)

Total New Houses = 10

* hab = habitation; stor = storage; HHD = Household number

sources do not indicate such a steep population decline (table 5.6).

Bradfield (1971:62) suggests that the population of Orayvi began to increase after 1865 and that it grew from 660 people in 1866 to 900 people in 1890. This occurred at a time when the Hopi population for the three mesas had reached a low point (Bradfield 1971:62; Levy 1992). Bradfield (1971:62–63) reports a large household size for Orayvi as evidence of internal population growth but also suggests that immigration from Songòopavi may have

Table 5.6 Population Estimates for Orayvi, 1540–1900

Date	Population Estimate *	Reference
1540	1,500–3,000	Winship 1896:518, (corrected; see Whiteley 1988:15)
1664	1,236	Scholes 1929:49
1775	800 families	Adams 1963:134–35
1780	30–40 families	Thomas 1932:233–36
1851	2,400	Whipple 1855:13
1861	800	Whiteley 1988:37
1864	600–700	Hammond 1957 1:41
1872	600	Powell 1949:482
1877	†500	Barber 1877:730
1890	†905	Donaldson 1893:44–45
1892	853	Mayhugh letters, June 9, 1892, Feb. 14, 1893
1900	**772	U.S. census

*All estimates are cited in Whiteley 1988:15–42, 81, except those with †, cited in Bradfield 1971:62.
** from Levy 1990; not included are eighty-six former residents of Orayvi who had moved to Munqapi.

accounted for as much as one-third of the increase. The 1900 U.S. census records 772 people at Orayvi; another 86 former Orayvi residents lived at Munqapi at this time (Levy 1990). The total of these two figures is very close to population estimates from Titiev's census (1944:chart 6), which reports 863 people at Orayvi.

Recent study of the 1900 census data by Levy (1992) provides evidence for both natural population increase and some immigration to Orayvi during the late nineteenth century. Levy (1992:116–19) shows that the age structures of populations on the three Hopi Mesas are quite different. There are markedly fewer people over age forty at Orayvi than at Second Mesa and somewhat fewer than at First Mesa, which suggests that during the 1852 smallpox epidemic, people left First Mesa for Second Mesa and that there were fewer people at Orayvi at this time than on either of the other two mesas. There are also more people under age twenty at Orayvi than at either First or Second Mesa, suggesting a higher rate of natural increase at Orayvi. Levy also notes that there are higher survival rates for children at Orayvi around 1900 than on the other mesas, and fewer barren women (although the figures at Orayvi are lower than those for the surrounding Navajo population). Levy also finds fewer people between thirty and thirty-nine years of age at Second Mesa, which

may be accounted for by movement of younger people from Second to Third Mesa at the time of the 1866 smallpox epidemic. Using genealogical data, Levy (1992:116) is able to identify several of these immigrant lineages at Orayvi.

Although the documentary evidence for population growth during the late nineteenth century at Orayvi is intriguing, it is not nearly as compelling as the evidence for a dramatic increase in the number of rooms and houses disclosed in this study. Alternative explanations for the explosion of new construction at Orayvi must be considered, however, before this evidence can be linked with population growth.

Instead of population growth, the construction of the many new, small roomblocks at Orayvi might represent a shift in residence from traditional multistoried dwellings to new, larger Euroamerican-style rooms. For example, as described in chapter 2, outliers were built by Zuni residents when the architectural style changed from massive, multistoried dwellings to single-storied, Euroamerican-style dwellings (Ferguson and Mills 1987:257). While similar architectural reduction did eventually occur at Orayvi (chapter 6), photographs do not indicate that large numbers of upper-story rooms were being abandoned and demolished before 1906. In fact, abandoned upper-story rooms were balanced by the conversion of lower-story rooms in the original roomblocks to use for habitation (table 5.3). At Orayvi before 1906, architectural reduction does not seem to have resulted in the movement of households to newly constructed roomblocks outside the original roomblocks.

At the fourteenth-century site of Grasshopper Pueblo, Reid and Whittlesey (1982) suggest that outliers represent newer households founded late in the occupation of the pueblo. They also suggest that outliers may only be part-time residences. Similarly, at some Hopi pueblos, residents built Euroamerican-style structures in new areas while maintaining their old houses in established roomblocks, simply because they preferred the new-style structures (E. C. Adams, personal communication, 1990). Neither of these scenarios seems to have been the case at Orayvi before 1906. Titiev's census notes record the presence of thirty-five households in the new roomblocks that do not duplicate households described elsewhere in the pueblo. If each household contained an average of 5.46 people (the Orayvi average; see chapter 4), these new roomblocks represent an increase of almost two hundred people after 1887. Finally, there is some suggestion that the construction of "outliers" may signal the presence of nonlocal households (C. Mindeleff 1900:649). At Orayvi, Titiev (n.d.) noted that at least one isolated room was owned by a woman from Hano who had married an Orayvi man; other houses were apparently owned by local women.

If changing architectural styles did not cause the building spurt at Orayvi, population growth seems the most plausible explanation. Population growth at Orayvi could have resulted from either internal growth or immigration. There are at least two possible sources of immigration. First, as discussed above, the smallpox epidemics in the 1850s and in 1866–67 were most severe at First and Second Mesa and caused emigration of Hopis to Zuni and other pueblos (Adams 1981; Adams and Hull 1981). These epidemics may also have caused migration to Orayvi, especially between 1864 and 1868 from Songòopavi (Bradfield 1971:62; Levy 1992).

Second, a contingent of fifty-two people from Songòopavi moved to Orayvi in March 1906 and may have begun to build houses (Whiteley 1988:105). However, it seems unlikely that this group built any of the new structures that have been documented here. The photographs of new rooms all date before 1906. Furthermore, Titiev's census attempted to record household locations for the period around 1900, so the new roomblocks on his map would also predate 1906. It seems likely that most of the new rooms and new roomblocks documented at Orayvi either in photographs or on Titiev's map were built before the arrival of immigrants from Songòopavi in 1906.

Titiev's census notes in many cases record the origin of household residents if they are not Orayvi natives. None of the household heads in the new roomblocks is described as non-native. This suggests no sudden influx of population at Orayvi; rather, much of the population increase was the result of internal population growth and possibly occasional immigration from other pueblos.

Data from the 1900 U.S. census permit an examination of the composition of the households that inhabit the new roomblocks at Orayvi. It is interesting to note that the households in the new roomblocks are not necessarily the youngest but are households in which the female head is about thirty years old and has had several children (appendix 1). The composition of households observed in new roomblocks appears to result from the practice of *nawipti* ("going off and living on one's own" after males become integrated into the affinal household) reported by Emory Sekaquaptewa for residents of Third Mesa (chapter 4).

Census data indicate that there were slightly more nuclear families in the new roomblocks (59 percent) as opposed to the main roomblocks (48 percent), but the difference was not significant ($\chi^2 = 4.16$, D.F. = 4, $.3 < p < .5$). The average age of the female household head in houses in the main roomblocks was 36.5, while female household heads in the new roomblocks averaged 33.5 years (the age difference was not significant; t value = $-.1391$, $p > .1811$). It does not appear that the new roomblocks housed larger households. The average household size in the old roomblocks and new roomblocks was about 5.5 people.

The new roomblocks seem to have contained new

households that split from established households in the main roomblocks. This pattern was apparently prevalent before 1900. Because Mindeleff's map (fig. 3.1) shows new roomblocks in existence and under construction in 1887, it is likely that the construction of new roomblocks for newly mature households was a common pattern before 1880, when Euroamerican contact was less frequent. Again, this pattern suggests that the marked population increase documented architecturally at Orayvi was primarily the result of internal growth rather than immigration.

Patterns of Settlement Growth

The construction of new rooms in existing houses and the construction of new houses resulted in two patterns of settlement growth at Orayvi. The first caused the slow creep of roomblocks to the south or southeast as new rooms were added to the front of houses and old rooms were abandoned at the back. As demonstrated in chapter 4, these rear rooms, especially in lower stories, may not have served as active household space anyway. Second, because of population growth, Orayvi increased in size accretionally through the addition of individual rooms or houses placed here and there throughout the settlement—sometimes attached to existing structures, sometimes freestanding. The placement of new structures was not random, however, but was conditioned by several factors: the location of ceremonial areas, topographic features, transportation routes, and possibly the location of residences of influential individuals.

Photographs and Mindeleff's map suggest that when new rooms were built in existing roomblocks, they were almost always constructed at the front, or south-/southeast-facing side of the roomblock. Houses with multiple stories are built in a stair-step fashion, trending east to west, for maximum solar efficiency, and it would be difficult and undesirable to attach new dwellings to the northwest-facing side of the roomblock. Although the rear of roomblocks was rarely shown in photos, it is apparent that rooms in these positions were often abandoned, resulting in the slow "creep" of roomblocks toward the south or southeast. It is possible that rear lower-story rooms may

once have occupied a position at the front of a roomblock, but with new construction they ended up in the back of the roomblock in a position in which they no longer functioned as useful domestic space.

This process was especially evident for the roomblocks surrounding the Main Plaza, Roomblocks 4 and 7. The Main Plaza was the most important ceremonial area in the settlement. Mindeleff (1891:76, plate XXXIX) reports that "terraces" on the west (rear) side of Roomblock 7 have been produced by filling in broken down, abandoned rooms (fig. 2.1). Photographs (including two published in Mindeleff 1891: plates 37 and 41) suggest that similar terraces may exist on the west side of Roomblock 4 (fig. 5.1). Terraces are absent on the one or two west-facing photos of other roomblocks (fig. 5.13), indicating that Roomblocks 4 and 7, surrounding the important Main Plaza, may be the oldest roomblocks in the settlement.

The "creep" of roomblocks toward the south or southeast was also observed in aerial photographs of Orayvi houses after the split (chapter 6) and would be expected at other southeast-facing, multistoried pueblos. (Mindeleff also noted "terraces" of abandoned rooms on the west side of some roomblocks at Walpi [1891:76]; see also Ascher 1968 for an example of the slow movement of structures across the landscape as the result of new construction and abandonment of old structures.)

Patterns are also apparent in the placement of new houses at Orayvi. As discussed above, Mindeleff's map (fig. 3.1) shows that the addition of new houses to the settlement frequently resulted in the construction of new, small (one- or two-house) roomblocks. New houses were sometimes attached at the ends of small roomblocks or in spaces between roomblocks, forming long, linear rows of houses. Small roomblocks recorded by Mindeleff (2^1, 4^1, 5^1, 5^{11}, 12^1, and 12^{11}; see fig. 3.1) probably represent the most recent construction at Orayvi before 1887. Expansion of existing roomblocks in 1887 is apparent in Roomblocks 1 and 1^1, 2, 6, 8^1, and 8^{11} (fig. 3.1). The newest roomblocks visible on Mindeleff's map are located around the periphery of the settlement in almost all directions, expanding the total area of the pueblo. Titiev's map (fig. 3.2) shows the construction of twelve new, small roomblocks built between 1887 and 1900.

Figure 5.13 The rear of an Orayvi roomblock in a photograph taken by Victor Mindeleff in 1887. There is no evidence of "terraces" like those observed behind Roomblocks 4 and 7 (figure 2.1). This unidentified roomblock is likely not as old as the roomblocks that surround the Main Plaza. (Courtesy of the Smithsonian Institution, National Anthropological Archives; photo no. 1852A)

Most are located at the western and southern edges of the settlement, although three are located to the east.

The locations selected for new roomblocks are partly constrained by topography and may be influenced by the location of a road. The northernmost houses on Mindeleff's map are fairly close to the mesa edge (appendix 2: aerial photograph MNA 72.530). The mesa edge also limits, less immediately, the southern periphery of the settlement, but a road that may have influenced the placement of structures is also present here.

An aerial photograph (appendix 2: SCS #RG 114 No. 846) shows the road from Kiqotsmovi reaching the top of Third Mesa at the northeastern end of the Orayvi settlement. The road curves along the easternmost tip of the mesa at some distance from Orayvi and then along the southern edge of the settlement. Photographs show that the road existed as early as 1912 (appendix 2: Stuart, distant view, MNA MS-10-3-4-01). It was probably in place much earlier, perhaps only as a path, as the route from First and Second Mesas west to Munqapi. Construction of new structures at the south end of the settlement was apparently constrained by the location of the road; none was placed south of the road. Some of the roomblocks constructed in this area appear to have been situated to overlook the Snake Dance Plaza. They are the only room-blocks at Orayvi that do not face east but west or north, toward the plaza and its several kivas. Evidence for the continuing importance of ceremonial space at Orayvi after the split is described in chapter 6.

Construction of new roomblocks at the eastern end of the settlement may have been constrained by two factors: rocky terrain and the location of the Mennonite church. Distant views of Orayvi taken from the east or southeast show uneven outcrops of bedrock east of the settlement; construction in this area may have been difficult. The Mennonite church was built at the eastern end of Orayvi in 1901–2 by the Reverend H. R. Voth, who was widely disliked at Orayvi (Whiteley 1988:85–86). The location of the church may also have restricted construction in this direction, at least toward the end of the period.

The western end of the village seems to have been the preferred location for new houses, a pattern that continued after the split (chapter 6). It may have been preferred because of even terrain or because of the road noted above. A shift in the location of ceremonial space may also have encouraged growth to the west. In 1896, the chief of Orayvi (Loololma, a Friendly) was ejected from his kiva on the Snake Dance Plaza by Hostiles who installed one of their own members as chief. Loololma established a rival Chief Kiva at Tawa'ovi (Pongovi) Kiva at the western end of the settlement. His successor, Tawaqwaptiwa, lived in a nearby roomblock and built a house for his daughter at the very west end of the settlement (Roomblock X^1). The influence of these chiefs, especially with the increasing factionalism at the end of the nineteenth century, may have prompted construction at the western end of Orayvi.

Three-Sided Cooking Rooms

Photographs of late-nineteenth-century Orayvi revealed an unusual architectural feature: small, three-sided structures that were often attached to the front of upper-story rooms (fig. 5.14). Mindeleff (1891:104) notes that cooking was frequently done in a walled and roofed recess at the end of the first terrace—presumably these three-sided structures. Mindeleff reported that the Hopi called

these cooking structures *tupu'bi*, and he translates this word as "the roofed recess at the end of the first terrace" (1891:220). Photographs and Mindeleff's field maps show tupu'bi on both first and second terraces at Orayvi. The three-sided rooms apparently were most often used for cooking *piki* (thin, waferlike bread cooked on a flat stone—Mindeleff 1891:177), although at other Hopi villages, piki rooms were detached from main roomblocks (Adams 1982:72). No detached piki rooms were observed in photographs of Orayvi. Tupu'bi at Orayvi may also have functioned as sheltered outdoor storage.

Photographs indicate that tupu'bi were very common at Orayvi during the latter part of the nineteenth century, but were being discontinued as an architectural form by the early twentieth century. Photographs taken during Period 1 show eight tupu'bi (table 5.7). By the end of the period, two were dismantled (a 25 percent decline). Forty tupu'bi were observed in photographs taken during Period 2 (table 5.7). Although nine of these had been newly built during the period, twenty had been dismantled (a 35 percent decline). Tupu'bi may have been removed because the location of cooking changed with the advent of wood-burning stoves; there may also have been a change in storage location or in the types of goods stored.

Architectural Change, 1871–1901

Historic photographs and documents of late-nineteenth-century Orayvi were examined in an effort to record "ordinary" architectural dynamics before the catastrophic events of the split. The effects of the introduction of Euroamerican technology and architectural styles, as well as a significant population increase, were also documented in the years before the split. Population increase and Euroamerican intrusion have both been implicated as causes of the split. The analysis revealed a number of patterns in the way that residents of this settlement built, modified, or rebuilt their homes. These patterns will be important for the interpretation of prehistoric pueblos.

Prior to the split, rooms used for daily living were modified or rebuilt more frequently than rooms used for storage, probably an ancient pattern and one that might

Figure 5.14　The arrow in this photograph points to a small, three-sided room called a tupu'bi. The image was taken by Reverend H. R. Voth in the late 1890s. Tupu'bi were apparently used most often for cooking *piki*, a thin, waferlike bread, but may also have functioned as a covered storage area for firewood and other materials. After the split, these special-function rooms were less and less common. (Courtesy of the Mennonite Library, North Newton, Kansas)

help archaeologists identify room function at prehistoric pueblos. Homeowners were generally restricted to making modifications within the footprint of their residence, however—an important point for archaeologists attempting to match prehistoric households with residence units at archaeological sites. A shift in the location of living rooms and a decrease in multistoried construction were the result of Euroamerican influences.

The large number of new houses built at Orayvi during the late nineteenth century suggests significant population increase. Two patterns characterized growth.

First, the placement of new rooms resulted in the "creep" of roomblocks to the southeast as rooms were added to the front of houses and abandoned at the rear. Second, the establishment of new houses resulted in the accretional growth of the settlement.

Architecture at Orayvi tended to limit intrahouse expansion. Several lines of evidence suggest that, as households matured, married daughters eventually established new houses that were usually not adjacent to their parental home. Small, new roomblocks (outliers) contained newly mature households that had apparently recently

Table 5.7 Architectural Change to Tupu'bi

	Period 1 (1871–1887)	Period 2 (1888–1901)
New Construction		9
Dismantled	2	20
Rebuilt		1
Unchanged	6	10
Total	8	40

split from the natal household. Architectural inhibitions on the growth of the extended family may be especially pronounced at Orayvi because population there was expanding. The placement of new houses appears to have been determined by the location of ceremonial areas, topographic features, access to transportation routes, and previous growth trends in the settlement. Some of these patterns continue after the split (chapter 6) and can be identified in archaeological cases (chapter 7).

Finally, an unusual architectural form is documented at Orayvi: the three-sided storage and cooking rooms. These small rooms were apparently being phased out in the late nineteenth and early twentieth centuries.

The photographs examined for this section of the Orayvi study show a settlement undergoing expansion and almost constant architectural modification. Although very few people can be seen in the photos I examined, the constantly changing buildings *themselves* express the force and energy that characterized this town in the late nineteenth century. Photographs taken after the 1906 split show a very different place.

6 / Orayvi after the Split

The exodus of families from Orayvi began on September 7, 1906, with the departure of the Hostiles but continued for decades as emigrants left for the farming village of Munqapi or Kiqotsmovi below Third Mesa (fig. 1.2; Titiev 1944; Whiteley 1988; chapter 3). Photographs show the progressive deterioration of abandoned homes and kivas as usable building material was slowly stripped away. Within two generations, many parts of this once extensive and populous community were low, silent rubble mounds. This chapter describes the patterns of architectural change that resulted from factional conflict at Orayvi.

Architectural changes already under way as a result of Euroamerican contact accelerated after the split. Upper-story rooms were dismantled while lower-story storage rooms were enlarged (sometimes by combining rooms), doors and windows were added, and storage rooms became living rooms. These changes resulted in a decrease in the number of rooms per house at Orayvi. Similar changes had probably occurred decades or even centuries earlier at Eastern Pueblos (chapter 4), causing ambiguities for archaeologists using ethnographic data to reconstruct prehistoric house size.

Although there was no evident spatial pattern to the location of Hostile and Friendly households at Orayvi before the split, a distinct pattern in the progress of structure abandonment is apparent: the eastern end of the pueblo was abandoned and largely dismantled within a few decades of the split, while the western end continued to be occupied. Hostile houses in the western end were reoccupied by the remaining Friendly households. The Friendly houses that remained occupied, and Hostile houses that were reoccupied, were principally those nearest the Main Plaza, probably the oldest part of the village. The technology of pueblo construction, with houses closely packed into roomblocks, affected patterns of abandonment at Orayvi, because abandoned structures increased maintenance costs on adjacent occupied houses. Such technological problems probably influenced decisions to relocate or even to emigrate.

Data Sources and Photographic Analysis after the Split

The period of time considered in this chapter is from 1902, just before the split, to 1948, the date of the latest aerial photograph used—a span of forty-six years. The year 1902 is used as a dividing point between the pre- and post-split periods (instead of 1906) because of available photographs. The extensive collection of images taken by Charles Carpenter in 1901 effectively ends the pre-split photographic record (chapter 3). There are few useful photographs of Orayvi buildings between 1902 and about 1911. In addition to photographs (especially aerial photographs), this chapter relies on Titiev's census and on the 1900 U.S. census, which together link individuals to houses (Levy 1992; and see chapter 3).

There are far fewer photographs of Orayvi after the split than before, partly as a result of the ban on photography at Hopi (Lyon 1988; and chapter 3). Most photographs of Orayvi after 1900 were taken by tourists rather than professional photographers. Aerial photography of Orayvi began in 1933 and provides important documentation of the progress of structure abandonment in the village.

Change to individual rooms after 1902 was identified in ground photographs in the same manner as it was for the pre-split period. A total of 112 rooms from forty-five houses was observed in photographs after the split (appendix 4). Almost all of these rooms had also been observed before 1902, so continuing change was recorded. Not all rooms that were observed before 1902 could be seen in later photographs, however. Photographs taken after 1902 were not available for some areas of the pueblo, and many rooms seen in earlier photographs had been dismantled.

Four aerial photographs were used in the analysis. The earliest was taken in 1933 (appendix 2: U AZ N-4374), a low-level oblique view that provides great detail of rooms but shows primarily the south end of the settlement. The second aerial was taken between 1933 and 1940 (appendix 2: MNA 72530), an oblique view from the north end of the pueblo. These two views, while not precisely contemporary, provide complementary views. A distant aerial taken in 1940 from the south (appendix 2: Peabody N 32078) provides detail for only a few rooms at the southwest end of the settlement. Finally, Stanley Stubbs's 1948 aerial (appendix 2: MNM 2624), from which he produced a map (fig. 27 in Stubbs 1950), is a plan view that shows the layout of the entire pueblo.

Individual rooms were difficult to identify on aerial photographs, but often houses could be identified by their position in a roomblock. Still more difficult was assessing whether intact rooms seen in aerial photographs were occupied or abandoned. In some cases, holes in roofs and other signs of decay were used as evidence of abandonment. Several first-story rooms had adjacent walled but unroofed areas and ground staining that indicated their use as animal pens. If no signs of decay or change in function was noted, the structure was assumed to be occupied. Stubbs's 1948 map (Stubbs 1950) recorded abandoned and intact rooms as well as multiple stories. Careful study of the photograph from which his map was made (appendix 2: MNM 2624; see below), however, showed several roofless rooms that Stubbs had recorded as intact.

Four post-split periods are used to examine architectural changes to rooms and houses as well as settlement-wide patterns of architectural change (table 3.1): Period 3: 1902–12; Period 4: 1913–25; Period 5: 1926–37; and

Period 6: 1938–48. These periods are of roughly equal duration and are selected both because available photographs cluster within periods and because each period shows somewhat different patterns of abandonment and dismantling of Orayvi structures.

The photographic documentation available for these periods differs. For Period 3 (1902–12) and Period 4 (1913–25), only ground photographs of individual roomblocks are available. A photograph apparently taken just two days before the split by Earl Forrest shows a ceremony on the Snake Dance Plaza but few buildings (Forrest 1961). Other photographs by Forrest date to 1908, but again, buildings are not easily seen. The earliest photographs after the split that show the condition of Orayvi houses were taken in 1911 and 1912 by Samuel E. Barrett and Stuart M. Young (a few of Young's photographs date to 1909). Period 4 (1913–25) is documented by a number of photographs taken by Wesley Bradfield in 1918 and by several unknown photographers in the early 1920s.

Period 5 (1926–37) includes both ground photographs and the two earliest aerial photographs. Most of the photographs of this period were apparently taken by tourists, although A. E. Douglass of the Laboratory of Tree-Ring Research photographed Orayvi in 1928 (during the Second Beam Expedition) and in 1934. The 1933 aerial is also credited to Douglass, although he may have merely commissioned it. The 1933–40 aerial, taken by an unknown photographer, probably dates to about 1937. Period 6 (1938–48) is documented only by the two latest aerial photographs (1940 and 1948).

There are differences in the types of coverage provided by ground and aerial photographs that affect the analysis presented in this chapter. Ground photographs provide information on changes to individual rooms, while aerial photographs can usually indicate only whether *houses* are occupied, abandoned, or dismantled. Ground photographs provide information on only a few houses, while aerial photographs have much greater coverage of the village, providing information on many houses. As a result, data on changes to individual rooms within houses are available only for the first three time periods. Furthermore, because data on changes to houses (occupied, abandoned, dismantled) for the first two periods come only from ground photographs, far fewer houses are included than in the later two periods.

Data used in the analyses presented in this chapter are compiled in appendix 1. Levy's (1992) computerized census of households (which used data from both the U.S. census and Titiev's census—see chapter 3) are included along with data on houses from photographic analysis (see chapter 3 for a discussion of the use of these censuses). These data are used to examine the effect of the split and subsequent emigration on structures. Female household heads listed in appendix 1 and their families were presumed to reside in the houses in the village where Titiev had placed them. Four columns in appendix 1 provide data on these women, including their clan, age, faction, and their location after the split (Orayvi, Ho'atvela, Paaqavi, Munqapi, or Kiqotsmovi). Because the senior woman in each household owns the house, only she was used in this portion of the study to identify household faction and destination at the split. Titiev (1944:88–89) notes that husbands and wives typically acted as a unit during the split, but even in those cases where they did not, it is the movements of the houseowner that are of most interest here.

The remaining columns of appendix 1 describe the houses and households owned by the female household heads. For each house, columns record the number of rooms per house, the number of residents (if known), and household type (see chapter 4). Five columns describe changes in individual rooms within each house before 1901 (Periods 1 and 2) for those houses that could be seen in photographs (in use, abandoned, etc.). The final three columns of appendix 1 describe changes in houses between 1902 and 1948 (Periods 3 through 6) for houses that could be seen in photographs. Dates in these last three columns indicate the latest photograph showing the house inhabited, the earliest photograph showing it abandoned, and the earliest photograph showing it dismantled. For many houses, the earliest photographs are aerials taken more than twenty-five years after the split. As discussed below, the number of rooms per house decreased during the post-split period, but if even a single room was inhabited, the house was considered to be occupied.

Social Groups and Spatial Organization

Before the effects of the split on Orayvi houses are explored, it is important to examine the spatial organization of social groups and ceremonial space at Orayvi, as both could have an effect on patterns of settlement abandonment. Two of the most important groups at Orayvi during the late nineteenth century were the clan and Hostile/Friendly factions. Neither of these social groups seem to have formed spatial enclaves within the pueblo. Furthermore, even near-neighbors did not act as a unit during the split.

Clans were not spatially segregated at Orayvi, as the Mindeleffs and other early scholars recognized (chapter 4), and regardless, Titiev had ascertained that the Orayvi split did not occur along clan lines (1944:87–89, see his table 6). In only a few cases were clans entirely Friendly or entirely Hostile, and these cases were generally the clans of leaders. Titiev (1944:89) suggests that bonds among husband, wife, and children superseded those of the clan. He found that less than one-fifth of households were divided by the split. Peter Whiteley's (1988:172) study of Paaqavi shows that this new village was initially composed of only fragments of clans and lineages.

Hostile and Friendly factions had formed in the village during the late nineteenth century, but apparently they had made no effort to segregate themselves spatially. Titiev recorded ninety-three (54 percent) Hostile households and seventy-eight (45 percent) Friendly households (appendix 1; see also Titiev 1944:89).[1] Figure 6.1 demonstrates that factions were not spatially localized. In many roomblocks, several houses of the same faction might be adjacent; in other roomblocks, Hostile and Friendly households alternate randomly. The lack of patterning in the location of clans and factions contrasts markedly with the obvious patterns in the abandonment and dismantling of structures after the split, described below.

Clans did not act as a unit during the split, and factions were not concentrated in particular areas. But did near-neighbors influence one another in decisions about emigration? In other words, were there other spa-

Figure 6.1 This version of Titiev's map shows the house location and faction affiliation—Hostile or Friendly—of female household heads in 1900. For a small number of houses, the faction of the homeowner could not be determined.

tial patterns at pre-split Orayvi that determined which households eventually settled at Munqapi, Ho'atvela, and Paaqavi? Titiev's census data allow the emigration patterns for 127 female household heads to be linked to Orayvi's town plan. The residents of the new villages formed no clear spatial segment of pre-split Orayvi (Cameron 1992, fig. 8). Absence of clear spatial patterning

is demonstrated in table 6.1, which contrasts pre-split village location for eastern and western halves of Orayvi with the location of residence after the split. Apparently, individual households at Orayvi not only acted independently of clan ties during the split but were also uninfluenced by the actions of near-neighbors.

Table 6.1 Residence Location at Orayvi and Post-Split Village Residence

Destination at Split	Location in Orayvi		
	East	West	Total
Ho'atvela	27 (58.7%)	19 (41.3%)	46
Paaqavi	7 (41.2%)	10 (58.8%)	17
Mungapi	4 (20.0%)	16 (80.0%)	20
Oraibi	18 (40.9%)	26 (59.1%)	44
Total	56 (44.1%)	71 (55.9%)	127

Ceremonial Areas

In villages throughout the world, specific spaces or structures are the scene of ceremonies and ritual activities that serve to integrate the community. These ceremonial areas often continue to be important even when the settlement has been partially or completely abandoned (chapter 2). Adler (1989) has shown, using cross-cultural data, that the need for ritual space set aside for integrative ceremonies increases with community size. Archaeologists consider kivas important ritual structures in prehistoric pueblos. Prior to A.D. 1300, Great Kivas almost certainly functioned as the focus for community-wide rituals, while smaller "kivas" may have served primarily domestic functions (Lekson 1988, 1989; but see Adler 1989). In modern and many prehistoric pueblos, plaza space was also an important locus for ceremonies that served to integrate the community (Adams 1991).

At Orayvi, the Main Plaza and the Snake Dance Plaza were the most important areas for public ceremonies, and it is obvious that these spaces continued to be important after the split. Most adults at Orayvi, male or female, belonged to one or more religious societies, each of which controlled the operation of a particular religious ceremony. A single clan controlled both the ceremony and the leadership of the society (Titiev 1944:103), although

society members were drawn from a number of clans. Ritual paraphernalia for each ceremony was housed in the "clan house," the lineage home of the male head of the clan that owned the ceremony. Kivas, the location of much of the religious activity in Hopi villages, were owned by the clans that built them (Titiev 1944:104), so particular ceremonies were associated with specific kivas. Whiteley (1988:62) notes, however, that if a kiva is not the home of a major ceremony, it may change clan ownership fairly often.

Informants reported to Mindeleff (1891:117) that, in an ideal village, kivas were located in the center of an enclosed court, with houses built on every side to protect them; terraces should be situated so that people could see dancers emerging from the kivas. This ideal situation, of course, was not entirely the case at Orayvi, or at other Hopi villages. Emory Sekaquaptewa (personal communication, 1990) suggests that a central location might not be preferred for kivas because so much of the ceremony surrounding them is secret.

Ceremonies lasted for many days, and most activities were performed inside kivas, especially during the winter. In warmer weather, dances that formed the public portion of many ceremonies were held outdoors. Titiev (1944:127, 132, 151) refers to "the plaza" (the Main Plaza) as the location of most of the outdoor dances at Orayvi. Photographs also show performances of the Snake Dance on the Snake Dance Plaza (fig. 3.2); the Blue Flute Society may also have performed there (Whiteley personal communication, 1992).

The Main Plaza is the area enclosed by Roomblocks 4, 7, and 5 (figs. 2.1 and 3.1). Roomblocks 4 and 7 may be the oldest in the village (chapter 5). The Snake Dance Plaza constitutes the southeast end of the village, an area bordered by portions of several of the older, large roomblocks and by several of the small, new roomblocks shown on Titiev's map (fig. 3.2). While the older roomblocks are east-facing like almost all others at Orayvi, the newer structures bordering the Snake Dance Plaza are not. The older roomblocks bordering the Snake Dance Plaza on the west are the southern sections of Roomblocks 4 and 7 (fig. 3.2). The south end of Roomblocks 10, 11, and 12 form a northern border for the plaza, but the houses in these roomblocks are east-facing and do not directly overlook the plaza.

Roomblocks 4¹, E/F, and K/L/M are constructed along the eastern and southern borders of the Snake Dance Plaza. Roomblock 4¹ was present when Mindeleff mapped Orayvi, but Roomblocks E/F and K/L/M were built between 1887 and 1901 (fig. 3.2). Photographs show that all three face west and north toward the Snake Dance Plaza and are the only roomblocks in the village that do not face east.² The construction of new roomblocks facing the Snake Dance Plaza, ignoring the normal eastern orientation of most Hopi structures, suggests that this plaza may have been developing as an important ceremonial area in the village during the 1890s when most of these roomblocks were constructed.

Before the split, Orayvi had thirteen kivas (Titiev 1944:245; Whiteley 1988:63), more than any other Hopi village. Numerous kivas apparently accommodated both the large population at Orayvi and the factionalism that had resulted in duplicate performance of some ceremonies (Mindeleff 1891:134–35; Eggan 1950:105; Titiev 1944:80; Whiteley 1988:69). Eight of these kivas were considered "important" because they housed the most important ceremonies. Five were "common" kivas, because they did not house important ceremonies (Titiev 1944:245). The kivas were scattered throughout the village, although five were concentrated on the Snake Dance Plaza (fig. 3.2). The latter five kivas were "important" kivas, including the "Chief Kiva" (Sakwalenvi). The three other "important" kivas were Taw Kiva (between Roomblocks 6, 7, and 10), Hawiwvi Kiva (in front of Roomblock 9), and Kwan Kiva (in front of Roomblock 12).

The Main Plaza was ceremonially the most significant area at Orayvi before the split, although the Snake Dance Plaza may have been gaining ceremonial importance. Evidence that the Main Plaza has a longer history as public space than the Snake Dance Plaza is based on the antiquity of roomblocks surrounding the Main Plaza (chapter 5) and the construction of new roomblocks facing the Snake Dance Plaza, ignoring the usual eastern orientation of other village structures. It is unlikely that factionalism was involved in the location of these new roomblocks, for they included both Hostile and Friendly houses (fig. 6.1). However, shifts in the location of kivas, especially important kivas, may have influenced the use and importance of these two public areas.

There is, unfortunately, no information about the number and location of kivas at Orayvi before 1887 or for the antiquity of the thirteen kivas that Mindeleff recorded. After this date, there is some evidence for shifts in kiva location and importance. Mindeleff (1891:135) reports that construction of new kivas was rare, yet the Kachina clan had built one within a year or two of his visit (presumably the Katsin Kiva; Titiev 1944:245). The location of this kiva within the village is uncertain; Mindeleff did not record it on his map. A photograph taken by H. R. Voth shows remodeling of the Snake Kiva during the 1890s (appendix 2: ASM 573), which may signal a change in kiva ownership (Titiev 1944:104), although this is not always the case.

Even though the ideal village organization described by Hopi informants comprised terraced roomblocks surrounding a plaza with kivas, no kivas were located on the Main Plaza; whether kivas were ever present here is unknown. Topographic conditions often explain the placement of kivas at Hopi villages (E. Charles Adams, personal communication, 1990) and may have both precluded construction of kivas on the Main Plaza and facilitated it on the Snake Dance Plaza.

The locations of kivas and public plazas may have shifted over time, but probably the Main Plaza was the most important public area long before the late nineteenth century. The location of this ceremonially significant area apparently shaped the direction of settlement growth as well as gradual settlement relocation and abandonment (discussed below). The Snake Dance Plaza may have been developing as an important ceremonial area during the late nineteenth century, but its importance apparently diminished after the split.

Architectural Trends after the Split

In the following discussion, two aspects of architectural change are examined at Orayvi after 1902. First, change to individual rooms in occupied houses is examined using data primarily from ground photographs (table 6.2). Changes observed include a decrease in the number of rooms per house, the dismantling of upper-story rooms, and the rebuilding of larger, first-story rooms. In general, these changes reflect Euroamerican influence on Hopi architectural styles. Second, patterns in the occupation, reoccupation, abandonment, and dismantling of houses are examined, using both ground and aerial photographs. Several trends develop over time: (1) continued reuse and remodeling of Hostile houses by Friendly residents who remained in Orayvi; (2) concentration of the remaining population around the Main Plaza and possibly other ceremonially significant areas of the village; and (3) dismantling of houses in areas remote from ceremonially significant locations.

Change within Houses

Architectural change within houses differed before and after the split, although the same four processes (abandonment, dismantling, rebuilding, and new construction) were observed. Before the split, the most common change was new construction; numbers of abandoned and dismantled rooms were far outweighed by the numbers of new rooms. After the split, very few new rooms were built, presumably because of population decline and because remaining households found it easier to reoccupy and rebuild abandoned houses. The effects of Euroamerican technology continue to be observed.

The primary architectural change observed within houses after the split is a decline in the number of rooms per house, especially a decline in the number of upper-story rooms. This trend away from multistoried, multi-room residences was under way in the 1890s (chapter 5), but it seems to have gained momentum in the early decades of the twentieth century. In each time period, about one-third of all observed occupied houses reveal abandoned or dismantled rooms (table 6.3). Because the same houses are observed in ground photographs for each time period, the net result is a decrease in the number of rooms per house. More than 80 percent of the rooms abandoned or dismantled in each time period were upper-story rooms

(table 6.2). Again, because the rooms observed in each time period are the same, the number of upper-story rooms in each house declined through time.

Additional evidence of a decline in the number of rooms per house is observed in aerial photographs. The 1933 aerial photograph (fig. 6.2) suggests that in some houses, perhaps many, rear rooms (rooms on the west side of the roomblock, not generally visible in ground photographs) were abandoned first, while front (east-facing) rooms remained occupied (see chapter 5). Furthermore, after the split, abandoned or dismantled rooms were not replaced. Only three newly constructed rooms were observed after 1906, a sharp contrast with previous periods, even though a smaller number of rooms was observed in photographs after the split.

Although many rooms in houses were abandoned or dismantled, and very few new rooms were built after the split, remodeling was fairly common. A total of twenty-three rooms in fourteen houses (observed in detailed photographs) were rebuilt between 1902 and 1948 (table 6.2). Most remodeled rooms were on the first story, and often two or more rooms were combined to create a larger room (fourteen rooms resulted from the twenty-three rebuilt rooms, eight combined and six not combined—table 6.4). For example, during Period 3, first- and second-story rooms were combined into one large room at two different houses (Houses 132 and 133), creating not only greater room height but larger interior dimensions. Other remodelings combined two second-story rooms from two different houses (Houses 115 and 116) and two first-story rooms within the same house (House 68). In two of the three cases (from all four time periods) where rooms from different houses were combined, one house had once belonged to a Hostile household and the other to a Friendly household or a household of unknown faction (table 6.4; in the third case, rooms belonged to households of Friendly and unknown factions). Both rebuildings occurred after 1913, suggesting that, by this time, appropriation of the space (if not the building material) once owned by Hostiles was occurring.

Table 6.2 Summary of Architectural Change for Rooms and Houses, 1902–1948

	1902–1912	1913–1925	1926–1937	1938–1948
Rooms				
Number of rooms in use				
First story	20	17	14	
Second story	19	13	5	
Third story	22	12	6	
Fourth story	2			
Total	63	42	25	
Number of rooms abandoned				
First story	6	5	4	
Second story	6	6	5	
Third story	2	6	3	
Total	14	17	12	
Number of rooms dismantled				
First story	3	7		
Second story	3	6	5	
Third story	8	9	9	
Fourth story	1	2		
Total	15	24	14	
Number of rooms rebuilt				
First story	4	7	4	
Second story	3	3		
Third story		1	1	
Total	7	11	5	
Number of rooms new				
First story	1	2		
Total	1	2		
Houses				
Number of houses in use				
Friendly	18	13	22	14
Hostile	8	8	20	10
Unknown	5	2	5	4
Total	31	23	47	28
Number of houses abandoned				
Friendly	2	5	7	2
Hostile	2	0	6	1
Unknown	0	1	0	0
Total	4	6	13	3

Table 6.2 (*continued*)

	1902–1912	1913–1925	1926–1937	1938–1948
Number of houses dismantled				
Friendly	1	4	15	21
Hostile	0	6	36	18
Unknown	0	1	4	3
Total	1	11	55	42
Total				
Total number of rooms observed	98	93	54	
Total number of houses observed	36	40	*116	*73

* Total includes houses occupied in 1940 and 1948 aerial photographs unless obviously rebuilt.

Table 6.3   Abandoned and Dismantled Rooms in Occupied Houses, by Story, Based on Ground Photographs

	1902–1912	1913–1925	1925–1937	Total
Fourth story	1			
Third story	8	4	5	17
Second story	5	2	3	10
First story	3	1	2	6
Total	17	7	10	3
Total occupied houses with aband. or dism. rooms	11	8	4	
Percent of all occupied houses	(35.0)	(34.7)	(28.5)	

Settlement-wide Patterns of Architectural Change

Settlement-wide patterns of architectural change are examined for each of the four post-split time periods (table 3.1). Trends in patterns of abandonment, occupation, and reoccupation are observable from the earliest time period and continue until 1948. Explanations for these trends are explored and then summarized in the final section of the chapter.

Period 3: 1902–1912. During this period, most of the thirty-six houses (twenty-one Friendly, ten Hostile, five unknown) visible in photographs were still occupied (appendix 1; fig. 6.3). Only five houses (14 percent) appear to have been completely abandoned; only one was dismantled. Although it might be expected that in the first few years after the split, Hostile homes would be abandoned and Friendly homes occupied, this was not always the case. Only two of the five abandoned houses had once belonged to Hostile women; the remainder had been under Friendly ownership. Furthermore, most of the homes once owned by Hostiles were occupied.

Normal domestic cycles and the reoccupation of Hostile homes by Friendlies explain the deviations from the expected pattern. Two of three abandoned Friendly houses were not visible in photographs before 1912 and may have been abandoned before 1906 as the result of normal domestic processes. In one case (House 24), the woman had one son but no daughters to inherit the

Figure 6.2. By 1933 when this aerial view was taken, many houses at Orayvi had been dismantled. At the right edge of the photo, for example, what were once houses in Roomblock 12 are just shells. At the left edge of the photo, houses surrounding the Main Plaza are still occupied. Photographer unknown, possibly commissioned by A. D. Douglass of the Laboratory of Tree-Ring Research. (Courtesy of Special Collections, University of Arizona Library, Tucson; no. N-4374).

house. She had died before 1906, and the house was probably abandoned before the split. The other house owner (House 20) had two daughters; neither appears to have resided with her after the late 1890s. If the split had not occurred, both of these houses might have been reoccupied by other Orayvi residents, perhaps clan relations of the deceased homeowners. But the population decline resulting from the split apparently insured that these houses remained unoccupied. In the final case (House 67), the household moved to Munqapi. The house was in a roomblock surrounded by Hostile households, and even though adjacent houses were rebuilt and reoccupied, ap-

parently by Friendly residents, the split may have made conditions at Orayvi unpleasant enough that use of House 67 was discontinued (although it was later reoccupied—see below).

Eight Hostile houses appear to have been in use in 1912 (appendix 1), yet examination of the 1910 U.S. census shows that none of these Hostile homeowners were resident at Orayvi in 1910. The continued use of Hostile houses after the split was apparently the result of the reoccupation of Hostile houses by Friendly families who continued to reside at Orayvi. Four of the eight Hostile houses still occupied in 1912 had been extensively rebuilt;

Table 6.4 Rooms Combined during Rebuilding, 1902–1937

Room Numbers	House Number for Combined Rooms	
1902–1912		
434 ii*	132	Hostile
with 435 i	132	
438 ii	133	Hostile
with 438 i	133	
356 ii	115	Unknown
with 362 ii	116	Friendly
186 i	68	Hostile
with 187 i	68	
1913–1925		
359 i	116	Friendly
with 360 i	116	
184 i	67	Friendly
with 183 ii	67	
and 179 i	65	Hostile
1926–1937		
517 i	160	Hostile
with 518 i	160	
400 i	125	Hostile
with 406 i new**	126	Unknown

* i and ii denote first and second stories.
**new indicates a new room built after 1901.

two others were rebuilt within the next six years. Although Whiteley (personal communication, 1989) has noted that Hostiles retained rights to their Orayvi homes and returned periodically to remove building material, photographic evidence suggests that, in some cases, houses were appropriated by Friendlies remaining at Orayvi within a few years of the split.

Two of the eight Hostile houses that appear to have been occupied but that were not rebuilt had been owned by residents who went to Paaqavi. By 1912, these individuals had been gone only three years (they had returned to Orayvi between 1906 and 1909). Both houses appear dilapidated and may have been vacant; one (House 118) was rebuilt a few years later; the other (House 85) was abandoned. In 1912, their original residents may have retained ownership from Paaqavi—ownership that was later relinquished.

Explanations for patterns of occupation and abandonment in Roomblock 9 may be also related to the Hostiles who returned to Orayvi between 1906 and 1909 (founders of Paaqavi) (fig. 6.3). Two kivas, Is Kiva and Hawiwvi Kiva, are located in front of Roomblock 9. When the Hostiles reoccupied Orayvi, they were permitted to use only Is Kiva for their ceremonies (Whiteley 1988:116). Roomblock 9 originally consisted of five houses, four Hostile and one Friendly. Between 1906 and 1912, one Hostile house and the Friendly house were abandoned, one Hostile house continued in use, and one was rebuilt (the latter not being visible in photographs).

In fact, the original owners of the Hostile houses in Roomblock 9 did not return to Orayvi in November 1906 but remained at Ho'atvela. It is possible, however, that other Hostile households who did return in 1906 (future residents of Paaqavi) reoccupied and rebuilt these houses because of their proximity to the only kiva that they were permitted to use. However, Is Kiva and several of the houses in Roomblock 9 continued in use until the 1930s (see below), suggesting use by Friendly residents who continued to reside at Orayvi. Oddly, one of the Hostile residents of Roomblock 9 was listed on the 1910 U.S. census (owner, House 65), although her house is abandoned in 1912. Whether she was living in the village or simply visiting is uncertain.

A pattern appears in the reoccupation of Orayvi houses that continues during following periods. After the split, occupation seems to have focused on ceremonially important areas of the village. Four of the eight Hostile houses that were reoccupied are located around the Main Plaza, and two face the Snake Dance Plaza (fig. 6.3). Hawiwvi Kiva and Is Kiva also seem to have been a focus for continued settlement. Two occupied Hostile houses are located in Roomblock 9 adjacent to these kivas, and two houses abandoned here during this period were reoccupied after 1913 (see below).

Some kivas were abandoned during Period 3 (1902–12) and may have influenced the abandonment, during later periods, of nearby houses. Photographs taken

Figure 6.3 This version of Titiev's map shows houses that were occupied, abandoned, or dismantled between 1902 and 1912 (Period 3). The faction of the homeowner is noted for each house. Some houses are unmarked; this indicates that they could not be seen in photographs. During Period 3, many houses were still occupied, but not all the occupied houses had been owned by Friendlies in 1900.

by Young suggest that the Snake Kiva, the Sakwalenvi Kiva, and the Antelope Kiva—all located on the Snake Dance Plaza—were abandoned by 1912. Only Maraw and Hotsitsvi Kivas remained in active use on the Snake Dance Plaza. After the split, the functions of the Chief Kiva were no longer located on the Snake Dance Plaza

but were probably moved to Tawa'ovi Kiva. The direction of causality in kiva and house abandonment is not clear. Some kivas were undoubtedly abandoned at the time of the split, but others were abandoned later as population continued to decline. A kiva located in an area surrounded by abandoned houses may have had a greater

Figure 6.4 Here Titiev's map is used to show houses that were occupied, abandoned, or had been dismantled between 1913 and 1925 (Period 4). During this period, most of the abandoned or dismantled houses were located at the east end of the town. The houses that continue to be occupied are mostly around the Main Plaza, the Snake Dance Plaza, and in front of Howiwvi and Is Kivas. This pattern continued throughout the two subsequent time periods.

likelihood of being abandoned; alternatively, the abandonment of a kiva may have precipitated abandonment of nearby houses.

Period 4: 1913–1925. During the second decade after the split, the pace of abandonment and structure dismantling increased. Of the forty houses observed in photographs,

twenty-three were still occupied: eight had originally belonged to Hostiles and thirteen to Friendlies (appendix 1; fig. 6.4). The total number of occupied Hostile houses was the same during Period 3 (1913–1926) as it had been during Period 2 (1902–1912). Of the eight Hostile houses that had been in use between 1902 and 1912 seven were still occupied and one was dismantled. One house in

Roomblock 9, facing Is Kiva (House 65), originally owned by a Hostile woman, had been abandoned between 1902 and 1912, but was reoccupied and rebuilt after 1912. It was apparently appropriated, after the second departure of Paaqavi Hostiles, by a Friendly household. In the same roomblock, a Friendly house that had been abandoned between 1906 and 1912 was also reoccupied (House 67). This family had gone to Munqapi when the split occurred and may have moved back or allowed their residence to be used by others.

Rooms were rebuilt in seven houses, generally creating larger first-story rooms. All houses with rebuilt rooms were located in either Roomblock 4 or 7 surrounding the Main Plaza or facing the Snake Dance plaza—important ceremonial areas. Two of the houses in which rooms were rebuilt had once been owned by Hostiles; the other four had been owned by Friendlies. Two rebuilding episodes combined rooms from different houses; in one instance, three rooms from two different houses were combined to create a single large room (table 6.4).

Abandoned houses were much more common than during Period 3 (1902–1912). Seventeen of the houses visible in photographs (43 percent) were abandoned or dismantled between 1913 and 1925 (appendix 1). The pace at which structures were dismantled increased, presumably to provide materials for remodeling Orayvi structures or for constructing houses in nearby villages, especially Kiqotsmovi. Two structures, originally abandoned between 1902 and 1912, were also dismantled (Houses 24 and 51). Houses that had once been owned by Hostiles were more likely to be dismantled ($N = 6$) than those once owned by Friendlies ($N = 4$); one dismantled house had been owned by a woman of unknown faction.

A new pattern in the abandonment and dismantling of houses is visible during this period. Almost all (fourteen of seventeen) of the abandoned houses were located in roomblocks on the east end of the village (Roomblocks 10, 11, and 12). The gradual Friendly exodus from Orayvi was under way by this time, as households relocated below Third Mesa to Kiqotsmovi or to Munqapi (Titiev 1944: 94, see his table 8). More than half of the abandoned structures belonged to Friendlies ($N = 10$). Only five had once been the homes of Hostiles; two had belonged to

persons of unknown faction. Most of the abandoned Hostile homes had not been visible in photographs during the previous period and may have been abandoned earlier.

Part of the reason for the abandonment of houses in eastern roomblocks more than a decade after the split may be technological. Structural problems would be created by the juxtaposition of abandoned homes and occupied homes. As discussed in chapter 2, with the numerous contiguous houses typical of Pueblo construction, an abandoned, unmaintained structure compromises the stability of adjacent structures. Walls built for interior use may become exterior walls, subject to deterioration processes they were not designed to withstand; intentional or unintentional filling of abandoned lower-story rooms can produce bulging of walls into adjacent occupied houses, and seepage of water from filled rooms can undercut walls of occupied structures (Adams 1976). Dismantlement and removal of adjacent abandoned houses might provide some relief from such structural problems, but maintenance problems may have caused the abandonment of many houses. Rebuilding and repair of structures were concentrated adjacent to public ceremonial areas, although a few occupied houses remained in otherwise dismantled distant roomblocks (see Period 5, below).

Roomblock 12 provides a good example of the potential for practical problems in abandoned and occupied houses in the same roomblock (fig. 6.5). The north end of the roomblock was occupied by Hostiles, who presumably abandoned their houses in 1906; the south end was inhabited by Friendlies. Two Friendly houses (Houses 20 and 24) may have been abandoned before the split (see Period 3 above). It is likely that only four occupied (Friendly) houses remained in the roomblock in 1912 (Houses 21, 22, 23, and 25); three were adjacent and the fourth was isolated among abandoned houses. All four houses were abandoned by 1918 (appendix 1), possibly because of problems in maintaining them. Abandoned rooms were no longer maintained, and as they began to be dismantled, shared walls were probably compromised. Such technological problems would have greatly increased necessary levels of maintenance and could have caused Orayvi residents in this roomblock to relocate. The Kwan Kiva, one of the eight "important" kivas at Orayvi,

Figure 6.5 Roomblock 12, at the southeastern end of the village, in a photograph taken by Wesley Bradfield in 1918, twelve years after the split. Kwan Kiva, in the foreground, has been abandoned. One house in the center of the photo seems to be occupied, but it is flanked by empty rooms whose wooden doors have been removed. Because of its position, isolated among abandoned houses, the occupied house, it may be surmised, probably experienced problems with the maintenance of its interior walls. (Courtesy of the Museum of New Mexico, Santa Fe; neg. no. 87311)

located adjacent to Roomblock 12, was abandoned between 1909 and 1918, which may also have influenced abandonment of adjacent houses, although whether the kiva was abandoned before or after the houses is not clear.

Another interesting pattern in the abandonment of structures during this period is the apparent dismantling of two and possibly three of the small roomblocks located around the Snake Dance Plaza that were constructed during the 1890s (Roomblocks 4^1, P^1/Q^1, and possibly E^1/F^1; appendix 1, fig. 6.4). Of this group of roomblocks, only Roomblock $K^1/L^1/M^1$ remained during Period 4 (1913–1925). As discussed above (Period 3) two kivas on the Snake Dance Plaza, one the Chief Kiva, were abandoned after the split. Although two of the five households that occupied the small roomblocks in this location were Friendly, the area surrounding the Snake Dance Plaza may have become less favorable for residence because of a shift in the location of ceremonial activities. The last Snake Dance was performed in 1918, and the Blue Flute ceremony apparently was not performed at Orayvi after about 1920 (Whiteley 1988:275–76). These may have been the only ceremonies performed on the Snake Dance Plaza. The Snake Dance Plaza seems to have been developing as an important ceremonial location prior to the split; after the split and the disruption of Orayvi's ceremonial cycle, its importance may have diminished.

Figure 6.6 Titiev's map showing houses that were occupied, abandoned, or had been dismantled between 1926 and 1937 (Period 5). This is the first period during which aerial photographs were available, and many more houses were visible than for previous periods. Most of the unoccupied houses had been largely dismantled—more than a generation had passed since the split.

Period 5: 1926–1937. This period is the third decade after the split, and although previously described patterns in the occupation and abandonment of houses continued, some changes in those patterns were observed. Most important, some houses adjacent to public ceremonial areas were abandoned (fig. 6.6). Aerial photographs show that many roomblocks in the eastern and northern end of the

village have been almost totally dismantled. Both the pace of abandonment and the pace at which structures were dismantled increased. Of the 116 houses visible in aerial and ground photographs between 1926 and 1937, 69 (60 percent) were abandoned or dismantled and 47 (40 percent) remained occupied (table 6.2, appendix 1). Of the abandoned houses, one-third had once been owned by Friendlies, two-thirds by Hostiles. Of houses that remained occupied, almost equal numbers had once been owned by Friendlies (N = 22) and Hostiles (N = 20).

Since this period is the first for which aerial photographs are available, and many more houses are visible than in the two earlier periods, some clarification of abandonment patterns can be made (figs. 6.2 and 6.6). Before 1925, as has been suggested, most houses that continued to be occupied were located around either the Main Plaza or the Snake Dance Plaza or adjacent to Hawiwvi and Is Kivas (Roomblocks 4, 7, and 9). This pattern continued after 1925: almost two-thirds (N = 25) of the occupied houses were located in these areas (fig. 6.6). However, there are no known photographs of roomblocks in the northern and western ends of the village for Periods 3 and 4 (Roomblocks 1, 2, 2¹, 5, 5¹, 6, 8, 8¹, and 12¹). Aerial photographs taken in 1933 and 1937 show several scattered houses remaining in the northwestern end of the settlement (Roomblocks 1, 2, 2¹, 5, 5¹, and 6). Very few houses were occupied in the northeastern end of the village (Roomblocks 8, 8¹, and 12¹; fig. 6.6). Roomblocks in the extreme western end of the settlement (Roomblocks Y, V, W, X, and X¹), first recorded by Titiev, seem to have been largely intact. These roomblocks could be seen only on the 1937 aerial photograph and were not visible in photographs before this period. Unfortunately, individual houses could not be identified.

Comparison of the location of occupied houses with original ownership shows that most of the occupied Friendly houses observed (70 percent) are located around the Main Plaza, the Snake Dance Plaza, or in Roomblock 9 adjacent to Hawiwvi and Is Kivas (fig. 6.6). Only 40 percent of the occupied houses once under Hostile ownership are located in these areas, however. Many of the occupied houses once owned by Hostiles are located at the western end of the settlement (Roomblocks 1, 2, 2¹, 5, and 5¹). Because detailed photographs of these areas of the village are not available for earlier periods, it is unclear when these houses were reoccupied. Because most do not appear to have been rebuilt, it is likely that they were reoccupied shortly after the split, perhaps because unoccupied houses were no longer available in the more favored areas of the village (i.e., the Main Plaza).

Titiev's 1933–34 diary (1972: fig. 20) includes a map of Orayvi showing houses occupied in 1933 and their occupants. Although this map had the potential to confirm patterns observed for Period 5 (1926–37), houses appear to have been located schematically and could not be matched with the houses identified in this study. The occupants of the houses on the 1972 map also could not be linked with households identified on the 1900 or 1910 censuses. Titiev identifies house residents mostly by Christian names rather than Hopi names, and his preface suggests that he used pseudonyms (1972:viii).

The settlement layout changed extensively during this period. The east end of the village was almost completely abandoned and was being rapidly dismantled (figs. 6.2 and 6.6); Roomblock 12 and most of Roomblock 13 were completely reduced. Roomblocks 10 and 11, also on the east side of the village, had a few intact but abandoned structures, but were mostly standing walls, especially in the 1937 aerial. Roomblocks 8 and 8¹, in the northeast end of the settlement, were largely reduced, although few photographs of these two roomblocks are available before the first aerial in 1933, and they may have been dismantled earlier.

Although a majority of the abandoned and dismantled houses were still in roomblocks at the eastern end of the village, nine houses in Roomblocks 4 and 7, surrounding the Main Plaza, were either abandoned or dismantled (fig. 6.6). The continuing decline in population began to reduce occupation even in areas of the settlement that had previously been favored. Even rebuilding slowed: only three instances of rebuilding, involving five rooms, are recorded for this period.

Abandonment of houses at the southern end of Roomblocks 10, 11, and 12, adjoining the Snake Dance Plaza, also indicates the abandonment of previously favored locations. However, the houses in this area were first seen clearly in the 1933 aerial and they may have been abandoned much earlier. Because the Snake Dance and the Blue Flute ceremony were no longer performed at Orayvi, the Snake Dance Plaza may no longer have been considered important ceremonial space, resulting in the abandonment of the southern end of Roomblocks 10, 11, and 12.

Most of the abandoned houses visible during this period were largely or completely dismantled (70 percent) (fig. 6.6, appendix 1). Hostile houses were only slightly more likely to be dismantled (71 percent) than Friendly houses (65 percent), suggesting that the use of Hostile homes by their original residents as sources of building material had probably ceased. More than a generation had passed since the split; many of the original owners of Orayvi houses may have been dead, and it is possible that their descendants did not retain rights to houses in the village. Rights to Orayvi houses by expatriate Hostiles may have been relinquished years earlier: many of the dismantled houses recorded in this period are first seen on the 1933 or 1937 aerial. Some may have been dismantled during earlier periods.

The proximity of Kiqotsmovi (New Orayvi) at the foot of Third Mesa may have increased the pace at which structures were dismantled. As this new village grew, it attracted increasing numbers of immigrants from Orayvi (Titiev 1944:94). Because the two villages are located close to one another, movement of building material from Orayvi to Kiqotsmovi would not have been difficult. The slower pace of dismantling, especially during the first period, may have been because the villages of Paaqavi and Ho'atvela are located more than seven miles from Orayvi, and movement of building material would have been more difficult. Greater access to wheeled vehicles (wagons or trucks) during the late 1920s and 1930s may also have been a factor.

Dismantling of houses at Orayvi can be contrasted with the abandonment of Walpi Pueblo, which did not involve structure dismantling. Residents of Walpi who moved to Polacca at the foot of First Mesa usually retained ownership of houses in the old village for use during ceremonies (Adams 1989a:175-76). In contrast, Orayvi Hostiles who established the villages of Ho'atvela and Paaqavi moved all ceremonial activity to these villages, severing their ties with Orayvi. A ceremonial cycle was also established at Kiqotsmovi, so that Orayvi households who relocated there presumably also shifted their ceremonial affiliation. There was no reason for departing households to attempt to maintain houses in Orayvi;

they could be dismantled and the building material used elsewhere.

There is increasing evidence during Period 5 that ceremonial locations in the village were shifting or being abandoned, although some of these changes had taken place earlier. The 1933 aerial photograph shows eight of the thirteen kivas originally reported at Orayvi. Five are still intact: Hotsitsvi and Maraw on the Snake Dance Plaza, Is Kiva and Hawiwvi in front of Roomblock 9, and Taw Kiva between Roomblocks 6, 7, 9, and 11 (fig. 6.6). Of this group, Titiev (1972, see fig. 20) reports that Taw and Is Kivas were inactive.

Three abandoned kivas (Sakwalenvi, Tsu, and Naasavi) are on the Snake Dance Plaza. A map produced by the Laboratory of Tree-Ring Research in 1928 indicates that Hano Kiva and Wiklapi Kiva were also abandoned at this time (also Titiev 1972, fig. 20). Kwan Kiva at the far eastern end of the village had been abandoned by 1918. Two other kivas at the western end of the village are indicated on Mindeleff's map (fig. 3.1) but cannot be seen in the 1933 aerial. Tawa'ovi Kiva, which may have been the Chief Kiva after the split (Titiev 1944:245), is probably located at the western end of Orayvi, adjacent to Roomblock 2, in front of the house of Tawaqwaptiwa, who was chief of Orayvi for several decades after the split (Titiev 1944:83–95; see also Titiev 1972, fig. 20). The area around Tawa'ovi Kiva may have gained ceremonial significance and influenced occupation in this area of the settlement. The road in this area may also have caused settlement there (chapter 5; Titiev 1972, fig. 20).

Period 6: 1938–1948. The aerials from 1940 (appendix 2: Spence, Peabody N32078) and 1948 (fig. 6.7) are the only available photographs of Orayvi for this period, and they largely confirm patterns of occupation and abandonment identified in the earlier periods. Stubbs's photograph (fig. 6.7) is far more useful than the Spence photograph, in which only a few houses can be identified. Of the eighty-one houses identified on Stubbs's photograph, twenty-eight (35 percent) are occupied and another nineteen (not unambiguously identified) may also be occupied; three (4 percent) are intact but abandoned; and fifty

Figure 6.7 This aerial photograph of Orayvi was taken in 1948 by the Cutter-Carr Flying Service. It was commissioned by Stanley Stubbs, who used it to produce a map of Orayvi for his 1950 study of occupied southwestern pueblos. At the left in the photograph (the southeast end of Orayvi), low mounds with faint traces of rooms are all that remain of some roomblocks. In other roomblocks, many houses are roofless and abandoned. Notice the road at the top of the photograph curving along the south end of the village. (Courtesy of the Museum of New Mexico, Santa Fe; neg. no. 2624)

(62 percent) have been largely dismantled (appendix 1, fig. 6.8). Clearly, the abandonment of Orayvi continued during this decade. Interestingly, of the twenty-eight original houses still occupied in 1948, more than one-third (N = 10) had once been occupied by Hostiles and only half by Friendlies (N = 14); the remainder were indeterminate as to faction (appendix 1).

The eastern end of the village consists only of low rubble mounds (figs. 6.7 and 6.8). The largest remaining roomblocks are 4 and 7, surrounding the Main Plaza. Two kivas remained intact on the Snake Dance Plaza, but one (Maraw Kiva) was almost isolated among ruined structures. The other (Hotsitsvi) was close to Roomblock 4. The only other intact kiva was Tawa'ovi Kiva in front of Roomblock 2. In this roomblock, only the chief's house remained occupied and it continued to be occupied until at least 1961 (appendix 1). Both Hawiwvi and Is Kiva were abandoned, although two houses in Roomblock 9 may

Figure 6.8 Titiev's map showing houses that were occupied, abandoned, or had been dismantled between 1938 and 1948 (Period 6). Of the 188 houses that Titiev recorded in 1900, only 28 are occupied (although it is possible that another 19 may have been occupied). Almost the entire eastern end of the village had been dismantled (see also figure 6.1).

still have been in use. Taw Kiva was also abandoned. Many structures in the western end of the settlement were inhabited, although individual houses cannot be identified. New houses, built farther to the west, show in Stubbs's photograph but were not included in his map.

The Architectural Effects of the Factional Split, 1902–1948

In the years after the split, Orayvi buildings underwent significant changes. Continuing trends begun before the split, houses that remained occupied lost their upper stories as lower-story rooms were remodeled into new, larger living quarters, resulting in a decrease in the number of rooms per house. Although Hostile and Friendly factions were not segregated spatially, by 1948 most of the dismantled roomblocks are located at the eastern end of the pueblo, while occupied houses are clustered at the western end. Only twelve of the original twenty-four roomblocks remain, and only twenty-eight of the original houses recorded in Titiev's census are still occupied (fig. 6.8, appendix 1). In other words, by 1948 less than one-fourth of the houses Titiev recorded at Orayvi remained occupied. One-third of the occupied houses had once been occupied by Hostiles. Structural considerations, the location of public ceremonial space, and reoccupation of Hostile houses by Friendly residents account for these patterns.

The abandonment of the eastern end of Orayvi and continued occupation of the western end was the result of a post-split realignment of the remaining Friendly residents. In the first few years following the departure of Hostiles from Orayvi, some Friendly households apparently moved into abandoned Hostile homes. Although it is possible that some Hostiles, especially those who returned to Orayvi between 1906 and 1909, retained a degree of control over their homes, many Hostile homes were rebuilt in the first decade after the split, indicating reoccupation by others, presumably remaining Friendlies.

Further evidence of reoccupation of Hostile houses by Friendlies is the fact that rebuilding occasionally combined rooms that had previously been part of different houses, suggesting that ownership of at least one of the rebuilt rooms had been suspended. Coupled with the slow exodus of Friendly households to Munqapi and Kiqotsmovi, relocation of Friendlies resulted in the abandonment of many Friendly as well as Hostile houses. There does not appear to have been any residential spatial patterning in the destination of the Hostile residents who left. Emigrants to Ho'atvela, Paaqavi, and Munqapi were apparently acting independently of near-neighbors in their decisions about relocation.

Abandonment of the eastern end of Orayvi and continued occupation or construction in the western end may be explained by several factors. First, occupation around the ceremonially important Main Plaza and abandonment of other areas was the most consistent trend observed. Second, after the split, a shift in ceremonially important locations in the settlement may have occurred: the end of the Snake Dance and Blue Flute ceremonies, the abandonment of kivas on the Snake Dance Plaza, and the apparent movement of the Chief Kiva to Tawa'ovi Kiva at the western end of the village probably influenced areas of occupation and abandonment. Third, growth at the western end of the settlement may have been a trend as early as the 1890s, possibly as a result of topographical or other conditions (chapter 5). Finally, a high-level aerial photograph dating to about 1934 (SCS #RG 114, no. 846) shows that a road led from Kiqotsmovi to the top of Third Mesa, past Orayvi and on toward Paaqavi and Ho'atvela. Occupation and growth at the western end of the settlement may have been related to use of this road.

Although the factional split at Orayvi was a unique event, its effects on the settlement were patterned in ways that may help archaeologists identify similar events at prehistoric sites. In the final chapter, these patterns are further explored and similar patterns identified in archaeological cases.

7 / Using Orayvi to Interpret the Past

Orayvi's split had lasting, visible impacts on its buildings, on the organization of the settlement, and on its future patterns of growth. Centuries from now, archaeologists will be able to distinguish traces of this factional dispute in buried wall foundations and scattered fragments of household belongings. Many other such events are recorded in the ruins of prehistoric pueblos, especially from the Pueblo III and IV periods, when the people of the northern Southwest first began to live in large, densely packed villages. The longitudinal study of Orayvi architecture can help archaeologists identify and study these events, which almost certainly were a factor in the short life span of many large, prehistoric pueblos.

The study of historic Orayvi, which begins almost forty years before the split, defined a number of *processes* that determined or influenced architectural change at the pueblo, both before and after the split. The premise of this volume is that these processes, identified at Orayvi, also operated in the past and can be used to interpret prehistoric pueblo sites. This chapter suggests how these processes can be applied to the static archaeological record and then employs them in the analysis of an archaeological case: the fourteenth-century site of Arroyo Hondo Pueblo. Although most of the processes examined operated at the household level, many have community-wide effects.

Identifying Houses in the Past

The size and configuration of houses are basic data for calculations of household size, settlement population, and household and community use of space; as a result, determination of the boundaries of houses is one of the most challenging tasks facing archaeologists who study pueblo and pueblo-like architecture (chapter 1). Archaeologists trying to determine the boundaries of domestic units are hampered by ambiguities in wall bond and abutment patterns, patterns of interconnecting doors, and assignment of room function. The Orayvi data add several lines of evidence for the archaeological determination of household boundaries. These data also challenge simple correlations between house size and household size.

Pueblos, like most vernacular structures, undergo almost constant modification, which can obscure the architectural boundaries of houses unless archaeologists learn to identify certain regular processes through which modification takes place. Both ethnographic data (chapter 2) and evidence from Orayvi (chapter 5) indicate that habitation rooms tend to be modified more frequently than other rooms. More rapid deterioration from intensive use and greater need for fit between structure and occupants partially accounts for this pattern. Frequent rebuilding might be used as one archaeological indicator of room function.

The Orayvi data suggest a need to distinguish between rebuilding and remodeling, however. For example, at prehistoric Turkey Creek Pueblo, Lowell (1986:389–95; 1991) found that storage rooms underwent remodeling more frequently than rooms of other types (she identified three functional types of rooms: storage, multiple activity, and habitation). Lowell defined remodeling as the occurrence of multiple floors, and she found that, in most cases, remodeled storage rooms continued to function as storage rooms. Complete rebuilding, as observed at Orayvi, where walls were reconstructed and roofs replaced, might reflect different processes from those indicated by a change in floor features. Rebuilding suggests either structural deterioration or changes in structure size. Floor remodeling may be the result of maintenance activities or, occasionally, change in structure function. As many ethnographic cases show (chapter 2), change in structure function is often a result of structural deterioration processes *and* decisions *not* to rebuild.

Archaeologists link house size with household size, yet the Orayvi study suggests that house size may be affected by many factors other than momentary household size. Census data from Orayvi, combined with data from Mindeleff's map, showed that both large and small households had approximately the same number of rooms and that the floor area of houses was not significantly different for households of different sizes (chapter 4). Since large extended families seem to have been only a temporary configuration at Orayvi, they may not have warranted the labor involved in new room construction.

Change in structure size also suggests to some archaeologists a change in household size (e.g., Crown and Kohler 1994). Yet at Orayvi, habitation rooms increased in size because of the adoption of new technologies—in this case, Euroamerican architectural elements. Change in architectural styles at Orayvi was the result of several aspects of Euroamerican influence: changing external social relationships that decreased the need for defense and storage rooms, as well as the availability of new materials, tools, transportation, and heating methods. The Orayvi study demonstrates the variety of influences on habitation room size that should be considered in archaeological cases where changes in size are observed. The recent study of Pot Creek Pueblo by Kulisheck and others (1994), discussed in chapter 1, is an interesting archaeological example of a prehistoric change in technology that could be misinterpreted as a change in house size and, therefore, household organization.

Another process observed at Orayvi that can help archaeologists to determine the size of prehistoric pueblo houses was evident in the decrease in the number of rooms per house after the 1906 split. The decrease in number of rooms per house was a result of two Euroamerican-influenced causes: a decrease in the number of stories in pueblos (with decreased need for defense) and

the combining of small rooms to make larger habitation rooms (made possible by new technologies). Not only were rooms combined, the decrease in stories probably eliminated some unused, rear, lower-story rooms that had been "dead" space created as the multistoried pueblo grew southeastward, adding new rooms to the front of the roomblocks (chapters 4 and 5).

Archaeologists almost always see only the ground-floor rooms of multistoried pueblos and are forced to reconstruct house size and room function from this limited view. The Orayvi study interjects a dynamic element into these calculations, suggesting that a significant portion of long-lived, multiroomed houses, especially in multistoried pueblos, was unused space. At least this space was not used for domestic or storage space. Such rooms may have changed function to serve as an elevated platform on which domestic activities could safely take place. By accounting for such architectural dynamics (for example using only upper-story, front-tier rooms in calculations of house size), archaeologists can achieve more accurate reconstructions of the size, configuration, and use of space in prehistoric domestic units.

Continuity in the use of household space is another process identified at Orayvi that can help archaeologists identify the boundaries of prehistoric houses. At Orayvi, rebuilding most often took place within the footprint of an existing house, and space was rarely appropriated from neighboring houses (chapter 5). Archaeologists defining the boundaries of domestic units at prehistoric sites might look for evidence of rebuilding episodes that are spatially confined and use this as additional evidence of house boundaries. The Orayvi study (and ethnographic evidence, chapter 2) does demonstrate, however, that a large decline in population may result in the relaxation of ownership rules and changes in house boundaries.

The architectural processes identified at Orayvi can help archaeologists identify the boundaries and dynamics of domestic units in the past. Even though the street-oriented layout of Orayvi structures makes the identification of household units easier than in some more densely packed prehistoric pueblos (Grasshopper, Turkey Creek, Mimbres sites, and even plaza-oriented sites such as Homolovi II or Arroyo Hondo), the architectural processes identified here should also help define houses at these sites.

Identifying Population Growth in the Past

The architectural remains that archaeologists see at prehistoric pueblos represent the greatest extent of the settlement, but they may not accurately reflect the settlement at any one point in its occupation. Interpretation of prehistoric pueblos, including estimates of settlement population and reconstructions of community interactions, can be seriously skewed by a lack of understanding of the dynamics by which pueblos are established, grow, and are abandoned. The Orayvi study examined a pueblo that may have been occupied for eight hundred years, which means its establishment phase (Reid 1973; see chapter 1 of this volume) is not obvious in nineteenth-century architecture. The pueblo was growing in the late 1800s, however, and the processes through which it grew can provide important information about the establishment and growth of prehistoric pueblos.

Population growth is indicated archaeologically by an increase in the number of domestic units, and the Orayvi study shows that the placement of new houses can provide significant information on the organization of households, the nature of the population increase, and trends in settlement growth. Chapter 5 demonstrates that because dwellings at Orayvi are part of contiguous structures so that houses shared walls, there were limits to the expansion of houses and, therefore, limits on household size. Spatial strictures may have limited the size of extended families and encouraged the "budding off" of nuclear families and the establishment of new houses. Such architectural restrictions on household size can certainly be projected into the Pueblo past, when many settlements were far more closely packed than Orayvi (e.g., Pueblo III and IV, and Late Mogollon and Mimbres sites). As a result, the nuclear family may be the most common household configuration at prehistoric pueblos, as it was at Orayvi.

The street-oriented layout of Orayvi, although it restricted the expansion of individual houses, did not restrict the growth of the settlement. As the pueblo grew, new houses were added to the ends of existing roomblocks or between roomblocks, or, most often, new, small, one- or two-house "outlying" roomblocks were constructed. Reid and Whittlesey (1982:696) found similar outliers at Grasshopper Pueblo and recognized that they represent the latest architectural developments at the settlement, likely occupied by newer households (although they suggest that these were part-time residences). The Orayvi study demonstrates that outliers also form a unique architectural category that indicates population growth.

Perhaps most interesting is the pattern of population growth suggested by outliers at Orayvi. Scattered one- and two-house outliers were not the result of the sudden immigration of a large group of people; they resulted from population growth by *accretion*—the occasional establishment of a new house for a new family. Accretional growth of architectural units, of course, is consistent with internal population growth, although it might also represent the periodic immigration of one or two families. At Orayvi, the residents of outliers seemed to be slightly younger households who had lived with the wife's family for a period of time and were ready to establish an independent household (chapter 5). The construction of outliers indicated that, because of population growth, habitation space in established roomblocks at Orayvi was no longer available.

If a settlement continues to grow, it is likely that outliers would become the anchor for new roomblocks and that their position as outliers will be obscured. Modern pueblos are long-lived, and many, like Orayvi, may have experienced multiple episodes of population expansion and decline. Most prehistoric pueblos had far shorter occupation spans, and episodes of population growth, indicated by the construction of outliers, should be more evident.

The construction of new structures in an established settlement, including the placement of outliers, is not random, and the Orayvi study illustrates a number of factors that may determine patterns of settlement growth. These factors very likely also influenced patterns of growth at prehistoric pueblos. At Orayvi, residents built new structures primarily to the west and south, which placed them closer to the Main Plaza, the ceremonial center of the village. Several houses were built on the edge of the Snake Dance Plaza, which became ceremonially important during the Snake Dance ceremonies every other year. Movement west and south also meant that residents were closer to transportation routes and far from the Mennonite church, which had unpleasant associations (see chapter 3). Ethnographic cases of settlement growth discussed in chapter 2 showed the importance of these factors, and others, in determining patterns of settlement growth and add additional support for their use in understanding prehistoric patterns of settlement growth.

Factionalism and Population Decline

Events like the 1906 Orayvi split, which resulted in rapid abandonment and movement of almost half of the population to nearby areas, were not uncommon prehistorically, neither in the Southwest nor elsewhere. Stanislawski (1973:382–84) suggests that factionalism may have been the single most important cause of village abandonment in Western Pueblo society (see also Titiev 1944:96 for frequency of pueblo movement). Short-distance relocation of villages is a common practice among many groups (Cameron 1991a) and seemed to be especially common among ancestral Puebloan peoples (Schlanger and Wilshusen 1993; Varien et al. 1996). Although pueblo abandonment was not always the result of factionalism, it is a likely cause of significant population loss in settlements that continue to be occupied.

The Orayvi study demonstrates several ways that significant population decline can be distinguished in prehistoric pueblos through the identification of patterns by which structures continue to be occupied or are dismantled and through patterns of trash disposal. The following discussion suggests that such abandonments should be archaeologically indicated by (1) patterns of rebuilding; (2) a lack of de facto refuse (usable but abandoned goods); and (3) extensive but *patterned* structure dismantling.

The Orayvi study revealed two related patterns of rebuilding that can indicate significant population decline. First, concentrated, spatially localized rebuilding may help delineate ceremonially important areas of prehistoric

sites (e.g., Morenon 1972, 1977). Second, concentrated rebuilding around ceremonial areas, coupled with cessation of building in outlying areas, may signal a significant decline in population. At Orayvi, the Main Plaza, the ceremonial center of the settlement, was bounded by the oldest roomblocks in the village, which remained largely intact while much of the remainder of the village was abandoned (chapter 6). The importance of ceremonial space, even in abandoned or partly abandoned settlements, was also demonstrated in ethnographic cases presented in chapter 2. Ceremonial space in partially or completely abandoned villages often continues to be an important focus of activity, and residences surrounding important ceremonial space may be the last to be abandoned.

Archaeologists have suggested the use of de facto refuse and room fill to identify abandonment sequences, calling this procedure the Room Abandonment Measure (Reid 1973, 1978; Reid and Shimada 1982; also Ciolek-Torrello 1978; Montgomery 1993; see chapter 1, this volume, for a discussion). Rooms abandoned while the site is still occupied ("early abandoned rooms") should contain little or no de facto refuse but lots of secondary refuse. Rooms abandoned at the time the settlement is abandoned should have lots of de facto refuse and little secondary refuse.

The Orayvi study adds some additional insights to the Room Abandonment Measure. Because so much of Orayvi was abandoned after the split, trash disposal in rooms and deliberate filling of rooms with trash would be most likely in those areas immediately adjacent to locations that continued to be occupied. Such patterns of trash disposal should help archaeologists to recognize significant population decline at prehistoric settlements and to identify those portions of the settlement that continued to be occupied. Indications that structures had been dismantled also suggests continued occupation of a portion of the settlement, although dismantling could also have been accomplished by residents of nearby settlements. Extensive dismantling of structures by remaining residents or residents of nearby villages would eliminate potential spaces for secondary refuse, however. As a result, large portions of the pueblo might be abandoned years before complete abandonment of the site but not become filled with secondary refuse.

De facto refuse would be expected to be depleted by residents remaining in a partially abandoned site or by residents who remain in the area, except in cases of burning or ritual room abandonment. At Turkey Creek Pueblo, for example, Lowell found that many rooms that had been abandoned early in the construction sequence (trash-filled rooms) had large numbers of vessels and other artifacts on their floors; in other words, de facto refuse was not removed after room abandonment. Some of these rooms had burned, which may account for the lack of scavenging. Lowell (1991:40) also suggests that the death of an adult in the room might have caused de facto refuse to have remained in place. Ritual abandonment and de facto refuse have also been documented for Chodistaas Pueblo, another site in east-central Arizona (Montgomery 1993).

The Orayvi study suggests that the Room Abandonment Measure may require some reconsideration in areas of a settlement that are subject to constant rebuilding, like structures around important ceremonial areas. At Orayvi, the earliest abandoned rooms will very likely be those beneath and behind Roomblocks 4 and 7 (the "terraces"; see chapter 5). These roomblocks surround the Main Plaza and are probably the oldest structures at Orayvi. Early rooms in these roomblocks have almost certainly been artificially flattened and then sealed by subsequent rebuilding. This situation approximates that of a Near Eastern *tell*, where structures are leveled and rebuilt generation after generation (see Ferguson and Mills 1987 for a Zuni example of artificially filled rooms; also Burgh 1959:198–99). Although some trash fill may be present in these rooms, it may very likely be disturbed and mixed with rubble.

At Orayvi, significant population loss was the result of factionalism. Patterns observed at Orayvi in structure rebuilding, trash disposal, and structure dismantling can be used to identify episodes of significant population decline at prehistoric pueblos. Because prehistoric pueblos tend to be shorter-lived than modern pueblos, these episodes may be easier to identify. Of course, not all such episodes can be attributed to factionalism, but, as demonstrated

in the following section, the Orayvi study does provide avenues for the identification and study of such episodes in the past.

Applying the Orayvi Study at Arroyo Hondo

In this section, the Orayvi study is used in the interpretation of settlement growth and abandonment at Arroyo Hondo Pueblo, the fourteenth-century site located near Santa Fe, New Mexico. The social dynamics of the founding of Arroyo Hondo are reconstructed and an important ceremonial area is identified through the examination of an abandonment episode. Although the significant population decline or abandonment described for the first occupation of Arroyo Hondo cannot with certainty be attributed to factionalism, the possibility warrants further study. Most important, the comparison of architectural dynamics at Arroyo Hondo with those at Orayvi demonstrates the utility of the Orayvi study for the interpretation of prehistoric pueblos.

Arroyo Hondo Pueblo

Arroyo Hondo is an adobe pueblo located near Santa Fe, New Mexico (fig. 1.1). It was occupied first during the early fourteenth century and later during the late fourteenth and early fifteenth centuries (Creamer et al. 1993). The first occupation of the site, Component 1 (A.D. 1315–35), consisted of more than one thousand one- and two-story rooms (fig. 1.5). The site may have been abandoned for several decades after the mid-1330s, although a small residual population may have remained. Component 2 (A.D. 1370–1410) was smaller, with only two hundred rooms (fig. 7.1). Although Component 1 has about the same number of rooms as Orayvi, both components at Arroyo Hondo are organized differently than Orayvi. During Component 1, rooms at Arroyo Hondo were grouped around thirteen plazas, which were either partially or completely enclosed, unlike the street-oriented layout of Orayvi (fig. 1.5). The outer row of rooms in most roomblocks was single-story, while the central portion of the roomblocks was two-story, giving the pueblo a terraced effect.

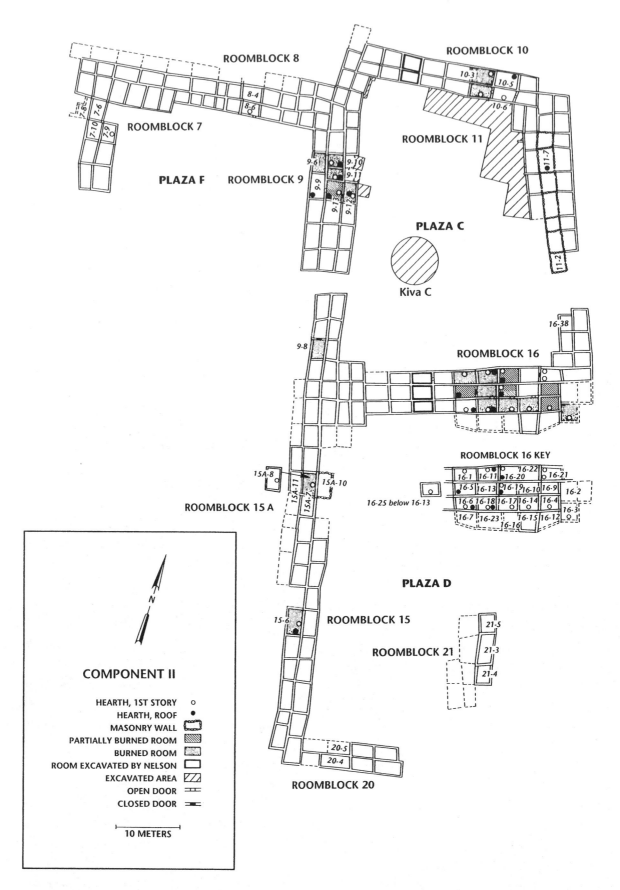

Figure 7.1 The second occupation of Arroyo Hondo (A.D. 1370–1410), Component 2, was much smaller than Component 1 (figure 1.5), having only two hundred rooms. As with Component 1, however, occupation centered on Plaza C, the only enclosed plaza in use during this occupation. (From Creamer 1993; courtesy of the School of American Research)

Tree-ring dates were insufficient to define the exact sequence in which roomblocks were constructed during Component 1,[1] but they do indicate that the entire site was built in only about fifteen years and that the earliest construction was centered on Plaza C. Roomblock 11, along the west side of Plaza C, was probably the first roomblock built. Other early roomblocks then surrounded Plaza C, which was not only the first plaza in use at the site but also the largest (fig. 1.5). Roomblock 11 and Plaza C are directly adjacent to the portion of the arroyo where a spring is located. This spring probably provided domestic water for the settlement and was no doubt the reason the settlement was first established here.

The second occupation, Component 2, was much smaller than Component 1 (fig. 7.1). Two hundred rooms were constructed directly on top of the leveled Component 1 roomblocks. Component 2 had the same plaza-oriented form as Component 1, but only a single plaza was in use at this time; again, this was Plaza C. Kiva C, in the center of Plaza C, was also the only kiva in use during Component 2.

The two components at Arroyo Hondo differed only in settlement size; Component 1 was five times bigger than Component 2. Both occupations were constructed rapidly, and each lasted for a generation or two at most. The rapid growth and sudden partial or complete abandonment of Component 1 Arroyo Hondo hints that residents of this large settlement, like those at Orayvi, may have had factional divisions that eventually ruptured the settlement.[2] The causes of Arroyo Hondo abandonments cannot be resolved here, but they offer a fruitful avenue for future research. The comparison of architectural patterns at Arroyo Hondo with processes identified at Orayvi, however, provides two important new insights: first, a new interpretation of the organization of populations in the northern Rio Grande during the fourteenth and fifteenth centuries, and second, an enhanced understanding of the significance and use of Pueblo ceremonial space.

Settlement Growth at Arroyo Hondo and Social Organization in the Northern Rio Grande

At Orayvi, settlement growth was accretional: new houses were constructed as new families became established in the village (chapter 5). Using these patterns of settlement growth identified at Orayvi for comparison, a different pattern of settlement growth can be identified at Arroyo Hondo. Building on the Orayvi study, three lines of evidence suggest that the construction of both components at Arroyo Hondo was not accretional, as at Orayvi. Instead, sections of the pueblo seem to have been built through the coordinated effort of a fairly large group of people: certainly larger than the household.

First, the form of Arroyo Hondo is an "enclosed-plaza" pattern that contrasts with the "street-oriented" layout at Orayvi (figs. 3.1 and 1.5). Orayvi's street-oriented layout allowed houses to be added to the ends of roomblocks or between roomblocks, or to form the nucleus of a new roomblock. The enclosed-plaza design at Arroyo Hondo limited this sort of expansion. Instead, at Arroyo Hondo the settlement could continue to grow by using new roomblocks to define new plaza space. This pattern of growth suggests that the people who built the site shared an understanding about the size of plaza space that would be surrounded by roomblocks, and coordinated construction of such roomblocks would be a likely approach to construction.

Like Orayvi, however, the plaza-oriented design of Arroyo Hondo did not allow the expansion of individual houses. Houses could have been expanded vertically (which has technological limits) but not horizontally. As the Orayvi study shows, this architectural pattern would limit the growth of extended families.

A second line of evidence also suggests coordinated construction rather than accretional growth. In several parts of Arroyo Hondo, at least during Component 1, wall abutments show that groups of rooms had been built in a single construction episode. For example, the rooms in the center of Roomblock 11 were apparently constructed as a unit (fig. 7.2). Two long parallel walls were constructed first and then divided by cross-walls, creating a number of cells. This building method has been called ladder-type construction (Cordell 1996). Observations of Mindeleff's original field maps show no evidence of ladder-type construction at Orayvi, where rooms appear to have been built individually (see fig. 3.1 and chapter 3).

Finally, rooms at Arroyo Hondo were generally uniform in size (fig. 7.3). Rooms during both components

0   1   2   3   4   Meters

Scale 1:20

had a mean area of about 6 sq. m. Rooms at Arroyo Hondo were far more standardized than those at Orayvi, which were much larger and more varied in size (chapter 4; Cameron in prep.).

Patterns of settlement growth observed at Orayvi demonstrate that the settlement grew through the construction of rooms and houses by individual families—the result, largely, of internal population growth. Contrasting this pattern with settlement growth observed at Arroyo Hondo demonstrates that Arroyo Hondo did not grow by accretion; instead, the construction of Arroyo Hondo seems to have been the result of a coordinated effort by a larger group of people with a predetermined, modular settlement design in mind.

Patterns of population growth observed at Orayvi showed how easily the "street-oriented" layout of Orayvi can be adjusted to an accretional increase in the numbers of households (chapter 5). New families need only add their house to the end of an existing roomblock or form the nucleus of a new roomblock. In contrast to Orayvi, the multiple enclosed plazas of Arroyo Hondo and modular construction methods suggest that large numbers of households took up residence at the site at the same time. Once defined, enclosed plazas are not easily expandable.

Comparison with Orayvi suggests, as just noted, that Arroyo Hondo was founded and grew through the coordinated action of a large number of families. This observation has important implications for understanding the dynamics of population aggregation and abandonment

Figure 7.2 Like other late prehistoric sites in the northern Rio Grande region of New Mexico, buildings at Arroyo Hondo were often constructed with a technique called "ladder construction." Two long walls were constructed first and then subdivided with cross-walls. The use of this technique suggests that construction was coordinated among a number of households and was not undertaken by individual families working alone. Roomblock 11, shown here, may have been one of the earliest built at the site and was one of the few roomblocks constructed of stone; others were of coursed adobe. (Redrafted from original by John Beal; courtesy of the School of American Research)

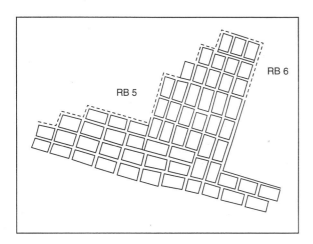

Figure 7.3 Roomblocks 5 and 6 at Arroyo Hondo show the remarkable uniformity of room size at this site. Compare this figure with Mindeleff's map of Orayvi (figure 3.1), where rooms are highly variable in size. As with the "ladder construction" technique, uniform room size suggests that residents of Arroyo Hondo coordinated their construction efforts. (Courtesy of the School of American Research)

that characterized the late thirteenth, fourteenth, and fifteenth centuries in the northern Southwest. During the late thirteenth century, the northern San Juan region was abandoned and there was a significant migration into the northern Rio Grande (Cameron 1995). Orayvi and Arroyo Hondo can help archaeologists understand the size of the social unit that operated in the northern Rio Grande and the Hopi area during the Pueblo IV period (A.D. 1300–1540).

Several archaeologists have suggested that migration into the northern Rio Grande was accomplished by small family groups. For example, Cordell (1979a, 1979b, 1989, 1995) suggests that individual immigrant families from the northern San Juan may have moved into established villages in the Rio Grande and become integrated with these ongoing communities. Kohler (1993) notes that because families in the northern San Juan region were only loosely linked into aggregated villages, they could easily decompose into smaller units if these villages dissolved. Dean's (1970) classic study of the establishment of Kiet Siel and Betatakin in the Kayenta region of northeastern Arizona showed, however, that during

the thirteenth century, population movement could be accomplished either by individual families or by a large group acting in unison. Using tree-ring dates and architectural studies, Dean found that Kiet Siel was settled by the unplanned accretion of independent household units that may have immigrated from different villages. Betatakin, on the other hand, was settled at one time by a group of substantial size that had existed elsewhere as a social unit.

Regardless of how migrants left the northern San Juan, the present study suggests that large numbers of households were acting as a coordinated social unit by the early fourteenth century in the Rio Grande. Other lines of evidence, both archaeological and ethnographic, support the proposal that the historic and prehistoric Eastern Pueblos (along the Rio Grande) had a more highly integrated social organization compared with the Hopi or other Western Pueblos (Cameron in prep.; Ware and Blinman in prep.).

Although there are clear differences in the degree of coordination that characterized construction at Orayvi and Arroyo Hondo, other explanations for these patterns must be considered. For example, accretional building at Orayvi, in contrast to the coordinated construction at Arroyo Hondo, could simply reflect differences in site longevity. Both components at Arroyo Hondo were essentially new sites; buildings were not being accommodated to existing structures. If a number of families arrived at the site at the same time, it would make sense to coordinate building activities. If the site had continued to be occupied for many generations, this "planned core" might later become obscured. In the late nineteenth century, Orayvi had been occupied for perhaps eight hundred years. Any new construction would have to adjust to existing structures and a "planned core" might no longer be visible.

A study of the architecture of modern Acoma Pueblo in west-central New Mexico suggests that the effects of coordinated construction can be observed at some modern pueblos that have been occupied for centuries. Such coordinated construction is contrasted with architecture at other modern pueblos of similar age where construction was apparently not coordinated. Earls (1988) and Robinson (1990) found striking uniformity in the construction of Acoma Pueblo, which was constructed in the mid-seventeenth century. Although a street-oriented pueblo, like Orayvi, Acoma had very standardized room sizes, similar house plans, and similarity in the numbers and sizes of vigas (Robinson 1990:104). At the Hopi pueblo of Walpi, constructed in the late seventeenth century, Robinson found that room size, house plan, and the number and size of vigas were highly variable.

Robinson (1990) suggests that the architectural differences between Acoma and Walpi are the result of differences in the degree of village integration. He offers two possible explanations for Acoma's architectural uniformity, and both explanations suggest strong coordination of construction above the level of the household. Acoma was razed by Spanish conquistadors in 1599 and was rebuilt between 1646 and 1652. The construction may have been directed by a Spanish priest, which would provide one source of leadership in the rebuilding of the pueblo. Robinson also notes, however, that Acoma has probably existed as a community for more than six hundred years, and as a result, Acoma leaders may have been able to exert more power than leaders at other pueblos, including the direction and coordination of building activities.[3]

Different degrees of architectural standardization at Acoma and Walpi suggest that site longevity is not the only explanation for the different patterns of site growth at Orayvi and Arroyo Hondo. Rather, the coordinated construction at Arroyo Hondo suggests that strongly linked social units larger than the household existed in the northern Rio Grande at this time—units of a type not present in nineteenth-century Orayvi. The differences in levels of social integration implied by architecture at Orayvi and Arroyo Hondo have been explored elsewhere and they suggest important differences in social organization between Eastern and Western Pueblos that extend perhaps several centuries into the prehistoric period (Cameron in prep.).

Settlement Abandonment and Ceremonial Space

At Orayvi, the Main Plaza is clearly the most important ceremonial area of the site, and it remained important even after the 1906 split caused a dramatic loss of popu-

lation. Using Orayvi as a model, a similar long-lived, significant ceremonial area can be identified at Arroyo Hondo: Plaza C. Plaza C was the first plaza in use during Component 1 and the only fully enclosed plaza used during Component 2 (fig. 7.1). Like the Main Plaza at Orayvi, Plaza C at Arroyo Hondo continued as a focus for settlement, even though the community suffered a significant population loss for several decades before the Component 2 occupation.

Cross-cultural data suggest that ceremonial spaces and structures may retain their functions within settlements far longer than spaces and structures of other types (chapter 2). An example of the formation of multiple plazas at a modern pueblo illustrates the likely motivation behind continuity in the use of plaza space at Orayvi and Arroyo Hondo. San Juan Pueblo (fig. 1.1), a Tewa pueblo north of Santa Fe, has four plaza areas (Ortiz 1969:20). The south plaza was once the only plaza at San Juan. As the pueblo grew, other plazas were created for dances and ceremonies. Today, public rituals are performed four times, once in each of the dance areas. However, the south plaza, the earliest plaza built, remains the most important in the village. This plaza contains the sacred center of the village—a point marked by a circle of stones (Ortiz 1969:21). For the residents of San Juan Pueblo, the entire world is defined as a series of concentric circles radiating out from this one central point in the south plaza. It is the center of their universe.

Like San Juan Pueblo, both Orayvi and Arroyo Hondo have multiple plazas, but like San Juan, one plaza seems to be the most important ceremonial space in the settlement. At Orayvi, the Main Plaza was the scene of most ceremonies, although other parts of the pueblo were occasionally used. When Orayvi was partially abandoned, residents regrouped around the Main Plaza. The reoccupation of Plaza C at Arroyo Hondo by the Component 2 population is an indication that this plaza may also have been of primary ceremonial significance. In fact, the significance of Plaza C may have transcended several decades of abandonment at Arroyo Hondo. Plaza C at Arroyo Hondo likely functioned in ways similar to the south plaza at San Juan Pueblo.

At Orayvi, we know that the same Friendly families

were present at the village both before and after the 1906 split. Continuity of populations at Arroyo Hondo between Component 1 and Component 2 (which may have been separated by more than thirty years) is uncertain but seems likely. The people who built the Component 2 structures at Arroyo Hondo were obviously aware of the Component 1 occupation: they built their rooms directly on the walls of the earlier rooms. Furthermore, the only kiva in use during Component 2 was in the center of Plaza C. For the Component 2 population, Plaza C was important ceremonial space. Although the location of the spring adjacent to Plaza C may have been one reason for resettling in this part of the site, much of the importance of this area certainly derives from its ceremonial functions during Component 1.

The long-term use of particular plazas at both Arroyo Hondo and Orayvi suggests significant continuities in architecturally defined ceremonial space that extends from the prehistoric period into the historic period. Furthermore, the similarity in patterns of rebuilding at Orayvi and Arroyo Hondo presents a strong case for the operation of similar processes of population loss that warrant further investigation.

Conclusions

This study began with a single broad goal: to use historic Orayvi to identify processes of architectural change that would help archaeologists interpret prehistoric pueblos. Because of a long-term interest in migration and settlement abandonment, I was especially interested in docu-

menting the effects of the 1906 split on Orayvi houses. The rich documentary record on Orayvi—photographs, maps, and census materials—allowed me to go much further, chronicling the interaction of buildings and residents over a period of almost eighty years.

Significant acculturation in the late nineteenth and early twentieth centuries altered Orayvi's houses, but even before this period its buildings were never static. Puebloan architecture has evolved over the past fifteen hundred years in dynamic interaction with the physical and social needs of Pueblo builders. This dynamic interaction was obvious in photographs of Orayvi as residents adjusted to a Euroamerican presence and technology and to dramatic fluctuations in population size.

Although every settlement is the result of a unique developmental history, I was able to distinguish certain social and natural processes in the architecture of Orayvi that can inform our interpretation of other pueblos and settlements. These processes include how households use, maintain, and modify their architectural space and how they handle population growth. I could also see, in historic photos, the cataclysmic effect of the split on the houses of Orayvi; yet I was able to discern patterns in the treatment of ruined and occupied buildings. Some of these patterns were echoed in archaeological remains unearthed at Arroyo Hondo. Given the brief but successful use of Orayvi data at Arroyo Hondo, the architectural processes identified at Orayvi should help untangle the architectural palimpsest recovered by archaeologists at prehistoric sites in the Southwest and elsewhere.

Appendix 1 / Summary of Household Information and Architectural Change

Key

ID#   Identification number assigned to individuals in Titiev's census (Levy n.d.).

Clan   Clan affiliation for female household heads.

HH#   A number assigned to groups of rooms identified by Titiev (Levy n.d.) as a household residence.

#Pers.   The number of persons residing in each house (from the 1900 U.S. census). · indicates that the woman and her household could not be located on the 1900 census.

#Rooms   The number of rooms comprising each house, adjusted for rooms added or removed between 1887 and 1900. · indicates that the house included new rooms indicated by Titiev on his map. As Titiev did not indicate multiple stories on his map, the total number of rooms for these houses cannot be determined.

HH Type   Household type (see chapter 4):
    Nuclear indicates nuclear family
    Exten. indicates extended family
    couple indicates married man and woman
    other indicates all other household configurations

Age   Age of the female household head as recorded in the 1900 U.S. census.

Faction   The affiliation (*Hostile* or *Friendly*) of the female household head. · indicates faction is unknown for this individual or that in 1900 she was deceased.

Post-split   The place of residence of the female household head after the split.
    Orayvi indicates that she remained at Orayvi;
    dec'd. indicates that in 1900 she was deceased.

NewH   *Yes* indicates a new house identified by Titiev;
    No indicates a house shown on Mindeleff's 1887 map.

Photo   The type of photographic coverage available for the house.
    Air indicates aerial photograph only
    Yes indicates ground photographs; may also be visible in aerial photographs
    No indicates no photographs available.

Change to Rooms between 1871 and 1901

· indicates no information

#New   The number of new rooms identified in photographs of this house between 1871 and 1901.

#Reblt.   The number of rebuilt rooms identified in photographs of this house between 1871 and 1901.

#Aband.   The number of abandoned rooms identified in photographs of this house between 1871 and 1901.

#Dism.   The number of dismantled rooms identified in photographs of this house between 1871 and 1901.

#Unchgd.   The number of rooms that appear unchanged in photographs of this house between 1871 and 1901.

Change to Houses between 1906 and 1948

· indicates no information

Inhab.   Date of latest photograph in which the house is occupied.

Aband.   Date of earliest photograph in which the house is abandoned.

Disman.   Date of earliest photograph in which the house is dismantled.

	ID#	Clan	Rmblk.	HH#	#Pers.	#Rooms	HH Type	Age	Faction	Post-split	NewH	Photo	#New	#Reblt.	#Aband.	#Dism.	#Unchgd.	Inhab.	Aband.	Dism.
1	1	Bow	A	1	•	3	•	99	•	dec'd	no	air	•	•	•	•	•	•	•	1933
2	365	Rabbit	A	2	6	3	other	20	Friendly	Munqapi	no	air	•	•	•	•	•	•	•	1933
3	5	Patki	B	5	•	3	•	98	Friendly	Orayvi	no	air	•	•	•	•	•	1933	•	1948
4	7		B	6	6	5	nuclear	38	Friendly	Orayvi	no	air	•	•	•	•	•	•	•	1933
5	9	Water Coy.	B	7	6	3	nuclear	39	Hostile	Paaqavi	no	air	•	•	•	•	•	•	•	1933
6	11	Water Coy.	B	8	5	3	nuclear	30	Friendly	Munqapi	no	air	•	•	•	•	•	•	•	1933
7	13	Parrot	B	9	4	3	nuclear	24	Hostile	dec'd	no	air	•	•	•	•	•	•	•	1933
8	15	Badger	B	10	2	5	couple	50	Hostile	Ho'atvela	no	air	•	•	•	•	•	•	•	1933
9	17	Navajo B.	B	11	•	7	•	•	Hostile	Ho'atvela	no	air	•	•	•	•	•	•	•	1933
10	19	Sand	ALPHA	12	5	•	nuclear	39	Hostile	Ho'atvela	yes	no	•	•	•	•	•	•	•	•
11	21	Spider	BETA	13	2	•	couple	28	Hostile	Paaqavi	yes	no	•	•	•	•	•	•	•	•
12	23	Kyel	AA	14	2	•	couple	24	Friendly	Orayvi	yes	no	•	•	•	•	•	•	•	•
13	25	Greasewood	AA	15	11	•	nuclear	34	Hostile	Ho'atvela	yes	no	•	•	•	•	•	•	•	•
14	27	Masau'u	AA	16	6	•	nuclear	28	Friendly	Orayvi	yes	no	•	•	•	•	•	•	•	•
15	30	Spider	EE	18	4	4	other	55	Hostile	Ho'atvela	yes	yes	4	1	2	•	•	1906	1908	1948
16	31	Lizard	EE	19	•	4	•	46	Hostile	dec'd	yes	yes	4	•	2	•	•	1906	1908	1948
17	33	Sun	C	20	9	4	exten.	33	Friendly	Orayvi	no	yes	•	•	•	2	•	•	1900	1909
18	35	Katsin	C	21	3	10	nuclear	34	Friendly	Orayvi	no	yes	•	•	•	•	3	1909	1918	1928
19	37	Patki	C	22	3	5	nuclear	32	•	dec'd	no	yes	•	•	•	1	2	1909	1918	1928
20	39	Bear	C	23	3	9	nuclear	40	Friendly	Orayvi	no	yes	•	1	•	•	2	1909	1918	1928
21	41	Lizard	C	24	•	6	•	99	Friendly	dec'd	no	yes	•	•	•	•	3	1901	1909	1918
22	43	Reed	C	25	4	7	nuclear	24	Friendly	Orayvi	no	yes	•	•	•	•	•	•	1918	1928
23	45	Gray B.	C	26	2	5	couple	49	Hostile	Paaqavi	no	air	•	•	•	•	•	•	•	1933
24	47	Gray B.	C	27	•	2	•	99	•	dec'd	no	air	•	•	•	•	•	•	•	1933
25	49	Parrot	C	28	6	3	nuclear	37	Hostile	Ho'atvela	no	air	•	•	•	•	•	•	•	1933
26	51	Lizard	C	29	8	7	nuclear	39	Hostile	Paaqavi	no	air	•	•	•	•	•	•	•	1933
27	53	Lizard	C	30	•	5	•	99	Hostile	dec'd	no	air	•	•	•	•	•	•	•	1933
28	532	Water Coy.	C	31	6	4	nuclear	26	Hostile	Ho'atvela	no	air	•	•	•	•	•	•	•	1933
29	538	Sand	C	32	8	8	exten.	34	Hostile	Ho'atvela	no	air	•	•	•	•	•	•	•	1933
30	59	Sand	C	33	6	9	nuclear	31	Hostile	Ho'atvela	no	air	•	•	•	•	•	•	•	1933
31	0	Spider	C	34	•	•	•	•	Hostile	Ho'atvela	yes	air	•	•	•	•	•	•	•	1933
32	0	Lizard	D	35	•	4	•	99	Hostile	dec'd	no	air	•	•	•	•	•	•	•	1937
33	64	Patki	D	36	4	6	other	31	Friendly	Orayvi	no	air	•	•	•	•	•	1933	•	1948
34	0	Sun	D	37	•	•	•	•	•	Orayvi	yes	air	•	•	•	•	•	1933	•	1948
35	975	Rabbit	E	38	5	18	nuclear	29	Hostile	Ho'atvela	no	air	•	•	•	•	•	1901	•	1933
36	563	Sun	E	39	8	11	exten.	27	Friendly	Orayvi	no	air	•	•	•	•	•	•	1933	1940
37	72	Water Coy.	E	40	8	7	exten.	30	Hostile	Paaqavi	no	air	•	•	•	•	•	•	1933	1940
38	74	Sun	E	41	4	6	nuclear	34	Hostile	Ho'atvela	no	air	•	•	•	•	•	•	1933	1940
39	76	Rabbit	E	42	•	6	•	99	Hostile	dec'd	no	yes	•	•	•	•	•	1901	1918	1948
40	78	Sand	E	43	9	7	exten.	39	Hostile	Ho'atvela	no	yes	1	1	•	•	2	1901	•	1918
41	80	Rabbit	E	44	5	5	other	28	Hostile	Ho'atvela	no	yes	•	•	•	•	3	1901	•	1918
42	82	Sand	F	45	•	10	•	99	Hostile	dec'd	no	air	•	•	•	•	•	•	1933	1940
43	84	Sand	F	46	•	4	•	55	Friendly	Munqapi	no	air	•	•	•	•	•	•	•	1933
44	86	Patki	F	47	2	•	couple	20	Hostile	Ho'atvela	no	air	•	•	•	•	•	•	•	1933
45	88	Greasewood	F	48	7	5	nuclear	43	Hostile	Ho'atvela	no	air	•	•	•	•	•	•	1933	1940
46	508	Greasewood	F	49	8	3	other	33	Hostile	other	no	air	•	•	•	•	•	•	•	1933
47	92	Patki	F	50	5	•	exten.	26	Hostile	dec'd	yes	air	•	•	•	•	•	•	•	1933
48	94	Eagle	G	51	8	2	nuclear	35	Hostile	Ho'atvela	no	yes	1	1	•	2	•	1901	1911	1918
49	96		G	52	•	1	•	•	Friendly	Orayvi	no	yes	•	•	•	•	1	1901	•	1918
50	98	Reed	G	53	•	3	•	20	Friendly	Orayvi	no	yes	•	•	•	•	1	1901	•	•
51	100	Greasewood	G	54	4	3	nuclear	34	Hostile	Paaqavi	no	air	•	•	•	•	•	1911	•	1918
52	102	Rabbit	G	55	•	7	•	•	Friendly	Orayvi	no	air	•	•	•	•	•	•	•	1933
53	104	Rabbit	G	56	8	9	nuclear	34	Friendly	Orayvi	no	yes	•	1	•	•	2	1912	•	1940
54	1025	Rabbit	G	57	10	6	exten.	55	Hostile	Ho'atvela	no	air	•	•	•	•	•	1933	•	1940
55	110	Piikyas	G	59	8	6	nuclear	30	Hostile	Ho'atvela	no	air	•	•	•	•	•	•	•	1933
56	112	Kyel	G	60	7	8	other	34	Friendly	Orayvi	no	air	•	•	•	•	•	•	•	1933

	ID#	Clan	Rmblk.	HH#	#Pers.	#Rooms	HH Type	Age	Faction	Post-split	NewH	Photo	#New	#Reblt.	#Aband.	#Dism.	#Unchgd.	Inhab.	Aband.	Dism.
57	114	Patki	G	61	3	17	other	60	Friendly	dec'd	no	yes	1	1	·	·	6	·	1918	1948
58	116	Rabbit	G	62	2	7	couple	52	Friendly	Orayvi	no	yes	·	·	·	·	3	·	1918	1948
59	118	Coyote	G	63	6	9	nuclear	32	Friendly	dec'd	no	yes	1	·	·	1	4	·	1918	1948
60	120	Coyote	H	64	7	5	nuclear	36	Hostile	Ho'atvela	no	yes	1	·	·	·	3	1933	·	1948
61	122	Piikyas	H	65	4	5	nuclear	25	Hostile	Ho'atvela	no	yes	·	1	·	1	1	1948	·	·
62	124	Reed	F	66	8	·	exten.	35	Hostile	Paaqavi	yes	air	·	·	·	·	·	1933	·	1948
63	126	Greasewood	H	67	·	6	·	41	Friendly	Munqapi	no	yes	·	·	·	·	3	1948	·	·
64	128	Sand	H	68	4	7	other	30	Hostile	dec'd	no	yes	·	·	·	·	4	1933	·	1948
65	130	Sand	H	69	4	6	nuclear	22	Hostile	Ho'atvela	no	yes	·	·	·	·	3	·	·	1918
66	132	Sand	I	70	4	6	exten.	39	Hostile	Ho'atvela	no	air	·	·	·	·	·	·	1933	1948
67	134	Bear	I	71	6	7	nuclear	32	Hostile	dec'd	no	air	·	·	·	·	·	·	1933	1948
68	705	Bear	I	72	3	10	nuclear	28	Hostile	Ho'atvela	no	air	·	·	·	·	·	·	1933	1948
69	138	Parrot	I	73	8	5	exten.	47	Friendly	Orayvi	no	air	·	·	·	·	·	·	1933	1948
70	0	Greasewood	I	74	·	5	·	·	Hostile	Ho'atvela	no	air	·	·	·	·	·	·	1933	1948
71	715	Greasewood	I	75	5	7	nuclear	27	Hostile	Ho'atvela	no	air	·	·	·	·	·	·	1933	1948
72	489	Greasewood	I	75	5	6	nuclear	30	Hostile	Ho'atvela	no	air	·	·	·	·	·	·	1933	1948
73	144	Coyote	I	76	·	3	·	99	·	dec'd	no	air	·	·	·	·	·	·	1933	1948
74	146		KK	77	·	1	·	·	·	Munqapi	yes	yes	1	·	·	·	·	1937	·	1940
75	148	Navajo B.	KK	78	3	3	nuclear	23	Friendly	Orayvi	yes	yes	3	·	·	·	·	1948	·	·
76	150	Coyote	KK	79	7	1	nuclear	32	Friendly	Orayvi	yes	yes	1	·	·	·	·	1948	·	·
77	152	Rabbit	J	80	·	5	·	99	Friendly	dec'd	no	yes	1	·	·	1	2	1901	·	1918
78	154	Badger	J	81	·	1	·	99	Hostile	dec'd	no	yes	·	·	·	2	·	·	·	1896
79	156	Reed	F	82	·	·	·	99	Hostile	dec'd	yes	no	·	·	·	·	·	·	·	1918
80	158	Lizard	K	83	·	4	·	35	Friendly	Munqapi	no	yes	1	·	·	·	2	1948	·	·
81	0		K	84	·	8	·	·	Friendly	Munqapi	no	yes	·	2	·	2	·	1948	·	·
82	162	Gray B.	K	85	·	9	·	99	Hostile	dec'd	no	yes	·	2	2	·	·	1901	1936	1948
83	675	Rabbit	K	86	5	7	nuclear	24	Friendly	Munqapi	no	yes	·	·	2	·	·	1948	·	·
84	166	Masau'u	K	87	6	1	other	59	Friendly	Orayvi	no	air	·	·	·	·	·	·	·	1948
85	168	Rabbit	K	88	6	16	exten.	42	Friendly	Orayvi	no	yes	·	·	·	·	3	1948	·	·
86	170	Coyote	K	89	2	10	couple	54	·	dec'd	no	yes	·	·	·	·	1	·	1920	1948
87	172	Coyote	K	90	·	10	·	29	Friendly	Orayvi	no	yes	·	·	·	·	1	1901	1933	1948
88	174	Crane	K	91	1	10	other	45	Friendly	Munqapi	no	air	·	·	·	·	·	·	1933	1948
89	0		K	92	·	1	·	·	Hostile	Paaqavi	no	air	·	·	·	·	·	·	·	1933
90	178	Lizard	K	93	6	6	other	29	Hostile	Paaqavi	no	air	·	·	·	·	·	1933	·	1948
91	180	Kyel	K	94	·	5	·	99	Friendly	dec'd	no	air	·	·	·	·	·	1948	·	·
92	182	Mille	K	95	·	8	·	25	Hostile	dec'd	no	air	·	·	·	·	·	1948	·	·
93	184	Sun	K	96	4	8	exten.	40	Hostile	dec'd	no	air	·	·	·	·	·	1948	·	·
94	186	Masau'u	K	97	6	6	exten.	50	Friendly	Orayvi	no	air	·	·	·	·	·	1933	·	1948
95	188	Piikyas	K	98	·	5	·	58	Friendly	Munqapi	no	air	·	·	·	·	·	1933	·	1948
96	190	Piikyas	K	99	5	3	exten.	48	Friendly	dec'd	no	·	·	·	·	·	·	1948	·	·
97	192	Patki	L	100	·	3	·	35	Hostile	dec'd	no	air	·	·	·	·	·	·	·	·
98	194	Badger	L	101	·	4	·	99	Hostile	dec'd	no	air	·	·	·	·	·	·	·	·
99	196	Water Coy.	L	102	·	7	·	99	Hostile	dec'd	no	air	·	·	·	·	·	·	·	·
100	198	Water Coy.	L	103	4	6	nuclear	30	Hostile	dec'd	no	air	·	·	·	·	·	·	·	·
101	0		L	104	·	6	·	·	·	·	no	air	·	·	·	·	·	·	·	·
102	200	Eagle	L	105	·	16	·	99	Hostile	dec'd	no	air	·	·	·	·	·	·	·	·
103	201	Greasewood	L	106	·	10	·	99	Friendly	dec'd	no	air	·	·	·	·	·	·	·	·
104	203	Greasewood	L	107	8	10	nuclear	38	Friendly	Orayvi	no	air	·	·	·	·	·	·	·	·
105	205	Lizard	L	108	·	9	·	99	Friendly	dec'd	no	air	·	·	·	·	·	·	·	·
106	207	Rabbit	L	109	5	·	nuclear	35	Friendly	Orayvi	yes	air	·	·	·	·	·	·	·	·
107	209	Spider	L	110	3	5	nuclear	29	Hostile	Ho'atvela	no	air	·	·	·	·	·	·	·	·
108	211	Sun	L	111	·	4	·	39	Friendly	Munqapi	no	air	·	·	·	·	·	·	·	·
109	213	Greasewood	L	112	·	3	·	99	Friendly	dec'd	no	air	·	·	·	·	·	·	·	·
110	790	Greasewood	L	113	·	5	·	21	Friendly	Orayvi	no	air	·	·	·	·	·	·	·	·
111	216	Parrot	M	114	·	10	·	99	Hostile	dec'd	no	yes	1	1	·	·	2	1921	·	1948
112	217	Parrot	M	115	·	7	·	99	·	dec'd	no	yes	1	·	·	·	2	1948	·	·

	ID#	Clan	Rmblk.	HH#	#Pers.	#Rooms	HH Type	Age	Faction	Post-split	NewH	Photo	#New	#Reblt.	#Aband.	#Dism.	#Unchgd.	Inhab.	Aband.	Dism.
113	219	Eagle	M	116	4	12	other	99	Friendly	dec'd	no	yes	1	1	·	1	3	1948	·	·
114	220		M	117	·	2	·	·	Hostile	Ho'atvela	no	yes	·	·	·	1	·	·	·	1896
115	222	Reed	M	118	4	2	nuclear	58	Hostile	Paaqavi	no	yes	·	1	·	1	·	1919	·	1921
116	224	Reed	M	119	7	6	exten.	40	Friendly	Munqapi	no	yes	·	1	·	1	1	1948	·	·
117	226	Greasewood	M	120	·	6	·	99	·	dec'd	no	yes	·	·	·	·	1	1912	·	1936
118	228	Kookop	M	121	2	9	other	55	Hostile	Ho'atvela	no	air	·	·	·	·	·	·	·	1932
119	230	Kookop	M	122	8	15	nuclear	48	Hostile	Ho'atvela	no	air	·	·	·	·	·	·	·	1932
120	232		M	123	2	6	couple	45	Friendly	Munqapi	no	air	·	·	·	·	·	·	·	1932
121	234	Masau'u	M	124	6	10	nuclear	25	Friendly	Orayvi	no	yes	·	·	·	·	1	1920	·	1932
122	236	Sun	M	125	·	8	·	99	Hostile	dec'd	no	yes	1	·	·	·	1	1948	·	·
123	238	Badger	M	126	·	10	·	30	·	dec'd	no	yes	1	·	·	·	1	1948	·	·
124	240	Masau'u	M	127	9	7	exten.	58	Friendly	dec'd	no	yes	·	·	·	·	3	1932	1948	·
125	242	Masau'u	M	128	·	15	·	99	Friendly	dec'd	no	yes	1	·	·	·	5	1948	·	·
126	244	Sun	M	129	5	6	nuclear	27	Friendly	Munqapi	no	yes	·	1	1	·	1	1933	·	1948
127	246	Bow	M	130	5	7	other	48	Friendly	Orayvi	no	yes	·	1	·	1	2	·	1928	1948
128	248	Bow	M	131	6	7	exten.	60	Friendly	Orayvi	no	yes	·	2	·	·	2	·	1928	1948
129	250	Squash	M	132	7	6	exten.	50	Hostile	Ho'atvela	no	yes	·	·	·	·	3	1948	·	·
130	252	Squash	M	133	·	6	·	19	Hostile	dec'd	no	yes	·	3	·	·	·	1948	·	·
131	254	Spider	N	134	8	5	nuclear	32	Hostile	Ho'atvela	no	air	·	·	·	·	·	1948	·	·
132	347	Reed	N	135	·	11	·	25	Hostile	Paaqavi	no	air	·	·	·	·	·	·	1937	·
133	258	Piikyas	N	136	7	9	exten.	41	Hostile	Ho'atvela	no	air	·	·	·	·	·	1948	·	·
134	260	Water Coy.	N	137	·	13	·	45	Friendly	Munqapi	no	air	·	·	·	·	·	1948	·	·
135	262	Water Coy.	N	138	4	4	nuclear	35	Hostile	Paaqavi	no	air	·	·	·	·	·	1937	·	1948
136	264	Lizard	N	139	6	5	other	42	Friendly	Munqapi	no	air	·	·	·	·	·	1937	·	1948
137	266	Lizard	N	140	·	14	·	99	Friendly	dec'd	no	air	·	·	·	·	·	·	1937	1948
138	268	Eagle	N	141	6	5	nuclear	31	Hostile	Ho'atvela	no	air	·	·	·	·	·	·	·	1937
139	270	Coyote	N	142	6	6	exten.	40	Hostile	Ho'atvela	no	air	·	·	·	·	·	·	·	1937
140	272	Eagle	N	143	·	9	·	·	Hostile	Ho'atvela	no	air	·	·	·	·	·	·	·	1937
141	274	Piikyas	N	144	4	8	nuclear	25	Friendly	Munqapi	no	air	·	·	·	·	·	·	·	1937
142	276	Parrot	N	145	3	8	nuclear	99	Hostile	dec'd	no	air	·	·	·	·	·	·	·	1937
143	278		O	146	·	3	·	·	Hostile	Ho'atvela	no	air	·	·	·	·	·	1937	1948	·
144	280	Patki	P	147	·	6	·	·	Friendly	Orayvi	no	air	·	·	·	·	·	1937	1948	·
145	282	Lizard	P	148	·	3	·	99	·	dec'd	no	air	·	·	·	·	·	1948	·	·
146	284		PP	149	·	·	·	·	Hostile	Ho'atvela	yes	yes	·	·	·	·	·	·	·	1918
147	286	Reed	PP	150	4	·	nuclear	30	Friendly	Munqapi	yes	yes	·	·	·	·	·	·	·	1918
148	288	Masau'u	RR	151	7	·	nuclear	28	Friendly	Orayvi	yes	air	·	·	·	·	·	·	·	·
149	0	Katsin	RR	152	·	·	·	·	Friendly	Orayvi	yes	air	·	·	·	·	·	·	·	·
150	291	Reed	RR	153	·	·	·	99	Hostile	dec'd	yes	air	·	·	·	·	·	·	·	·
151	293		RR	154	·	·	·	·	Hostile	Ho'atvela	yes	air	·	·	·	·	·	·	·	·
152	295	Rabbit	Q	155	5	6	exten.	50	Friendly	Orayvi	no	air	·	·	·	·	·	·	·	·
153	529	Rabbit	Q	156	5	4	nuclear	28	Hostile	Paaqavi	no	air	·	·	·	·	·	·	·	·
154	299	Coyote	Q	157	6	5	other	28	Friendly	Munqapi	no	air	·	·	·	·	·	·	·	·
155	301	Coyote	Q	158	9	6	other	50	Friendly	dec'd	no	air	·	·	·	·	·	·	·	·
156	303	Sun	Q	159	5	5	nuclear	25	Friendly	Orayvi	no	air	·	·	·	·	·	·	·	·
157	305	Lizard	R	160	·	15	·	21	Hostile	dec'd	no	yes	·	·	1	1	2	1936	·	1948
158	307	Bear	R	161	6	5	nuclear	40	Friendly	Orayvi	no	yes	·	1	·	1	1	1961	·	·
159	309	Bear	R	162	·	7	·	99	Friendly	dec'd	no	yes	2	1	·	·	2	·	1936	·
160	311	Lizard	R	163	5	3	nuclear	25	Friendly	dec'd	no	yes	1	·	·	·	·	·	·	1936
161	869	Coyote	R	164	7	4	other	19	Friendly	Orayvi	no	yes	2	·	·	·	1	·	·	1936
162	315	Bow	S	165	·	8	·	60	Hostile	dec'd	no	yes	·	·	2	·	2	·	·	1933
163	317	Spider	S	166	·	3	·	99	Hostile	dec'd	yes	yes	3	·	·	·	·	·	·	1933
164	526	Lizard	S	167	5	6	other	22	Hostile	Paaqavi	no	yes	·	·	·	·	1	1948	·	·
165	321	Reed	S	168	2	6	couple	45	Hostile	Ho'atvela	no	yes	·	1	·	·	2	1948	·	·
166	323	Masau'u	S	169	·	5	·	99	·	dec'd	no	yes	·	·	1	·	2	1948	·	·
167	325	Kookop	S	170	·	6	·	·	Hostile	Ho'atvela	no	yes	·	·	·	·	2	·	·	1933
168	327	Greasewood	S	171	·	5	·	·	Hostile	Ho'atvela	no	yes	·	·	2	·	2	·	·	1933

	ID#	Clan	Rmblk.	HH#	#Pers.	#Rooms	HH Type	Age	Faction	Post-split	NewH	Photo	#New	#Reblt.	#Aband.	#Dism.	#Unchgd.	Inhab.	Aband.	Dism.
169	328	Lizard	S	172	12	3	exten.	56	·	·	no	yes	·	·	·	·	2	·	·	1933
170	330	Reed	S	173	4	6	exten.	36	Hostile	Ho'atvela	no	yes	3	·	·	·	·	·	·	1933
171	332		U	174	·	1	·	99	·	dec'd	no	air	·	·	·	·	·	·	·	·
172	o	Masau'u	V	175	·	5	·	·	Friendly	Munqapi	no	air	·	·	·	·	·	·	·	1948
173	334	Piikyas	V	176	·	7	·	48	Friendly	Orayvi	no	air	·	·	·	·	·	·	·	1948
174	o		V	177	·	8	·	·	Hostile	Paaqavi	no	air	·	·	·	·	·	·	·	1948
175	336	Sand	V	178	5	7	other	30	Friendly	Orayvi	no	air	·	·	·	·	·	·	·	1948
176	338	Snake	X	179	4	9	other	27	Friendly	Orayvi	no	air	·	·	·	·	·	1948	·	·
177	340	Snake	X	180	·	9	·	·	Hostile	Ho'atvela	no	air	·	·	·	·	·	1937	·	1948
178	341	Lizard	X	181	7	·	other	35	Hostile	Paaqavi	yes	air	·	·	·	·	·	1937	·	·
179	1071	Masau'u	V	182	·	·	·	·	Friendly	Orayvi	yes	no	·	·	·	·	·	·	·	·
180	762	Reed	Y	183	8	·	exten.	55	Hostile	Paaqavi	yes	air	·	·	·	·	·	·	·	·
181	349	Piikyas	Z	187	6	·	nuclear	28	Friendly	Orayvi	yes	air	·	·	·	·	·	·	·	·
182	351	Reed	Z	188	·	·	·	99	Hostile	dec'd	yes	air	·	·	·	·	·	·	·	·
183	353	Piikyas	Z	189	·	·	·	29	Friendly	Orayvi	yes	air	·	·	·	·	·	·	·	·
184	355	Piikyas	Z	190	5	·	nuclear	28	Hostile	dec'd	yes	air	·	·	·	·	·	·	·	·
185	357	Rabbit	Z	191	·	·	·	·	Friendly	Orayvi	yes	no	·	·	·	·	·	·	·	·
186	o	Lizard	Z	192	·	·	·	·	·	·	·	·	·	·	·	·	·	·	·	·
187	865	Parrot	X	193	·	·	·	·	·	·	·	·	·	·	·	·	·	·	·	·

Appendix 2 / List of Photographs Collected for the Orayvi Study

The following table lists all photographs collected for the Orayvi study. The information used to identify individual photographs is that provided by the institution at which the photograph was procured, and includes some or all of the following: name of the photographer, the date of the photograph, the institution where the photo is held, and the institutional photograph number. See page 134 for a list of institutional abbreviations. In cases where the photographer was not identified, the designation *Unknown* is used; where the photographer has been only tentatively identified, a *?* follows the name; when the present study has determined that the photographer has been incorrectly identified, the name is in parentheses. Unknown dates are omitted, tentative dates are followed by a *?*, and incorrect dates are in parentheses.

Photographs are ordered in the manner that was most useful for analysis. Photographs of the Main Plaza are listed first, and are primarily photographs of Roomblock 4 and the north end of Roomblock 4. The west side of Roomblock 7 also borders the Main Plaza and is listed next. Other easily identifiable roomblocks (9, 6, 1, 2, 12, and the north ends of 10 and 11) are then listed. The Snake Dance Plaza, looking west, shows primarily the southeast end of Roomblock 4. Other roomblocks bordering the Snake Dance Plaza are the east side of Roomblock 7, and the south ends of Roomblocks 10 and 11. Roomblock E/F borders the Snake Dance Plaza to the east. Aerial photographs and distant views of Orayvi are listed next. The last section of the table includes photographs of Orayvi for which exact locations in the pueblo could not be determined, and photographs that may not be of Orayvi.

Within major subheadings, photographs are listed generally by date of photograph (earliest to latest); where photographs are not in temporal order, adjacent photographs often show complementary views that were useful for analysis. Photographs without exact dates are often placed in approximate locations in the temporal sequence, as are photographs with incorrect dates. In a number of cases, duplicate photographs were obtained from two institutions, occasionally with different attributions of photographer and date. In these cases, *same as above* is placed after the photograph number of the second photograph. Where the correct photographer or date could be identified, the name of the other photographer or date was placed in parentheses. In some cases, it was determined that the image in a photograph had been reversed. This was noted after the photograph number.

Photographer	Date	Institution	Photograph No.
Main Plaza			
John K. Hillers	1879	Smithsonian	56394
(Dellenbaugh)	(1884)	AHS	43246 (same as above, image reversed)
John K. Hillers	1879	Smithsonian	41831A
Unknown		SWM	N24333/P6114
Fewkes?		Smithsonian	88-3470
Maude		FM	2342
Maude		MNM	90946
G. W. James		Smithsonian	88-18117
G. W. James		SWM	N35053/P6158
Ben Wittick	ca. 1895	MNM	16397
A. C. Vroman	1898	PPL	Vol D1 D125
A. C. Vroman	1900	PPL	Vol 10 1040 1/2
H. R. Voth		ML	ASM #3251 Voth # 472
H. R. Voth		ML	ASM # 655 Voth # 1751
G. H. Pepper	1896–1901	NPS	Neg. 50-857 Class 970.3
G. H. Pepper	1896–1901	NPS	Neg. 50-858 Class 970.3
G. H. Pepper	1896–1901	NPS	Neg. 50-856 Class 970.3
C. Carpenter	1901	FM	218
C. Carpenter	1901	FM	241 (matches 218)
C. Carpenter	1901	FM	208
William H. Simpson	1901	MNM	37707
National Park Service		MNM	38323
Samuel Barrett		MNA	MNA 73.1522
Stuart Young	1912?	MNA	MS10-3-4-07
Stuart Young	1912	NMA	MS10-3-4-08
Wesley Bradfield	1918	MNM	87314
Wesley Bradfield	1918	MNM	87316
H. F. Robinson	1919	MNM	37112
H. F. Robinson	1919	MNM	37401
Unknown		AHS	43495
Dellenbaugh	(1884)	AHS	43245
Unknown		MNM	74865
Bortell	1920	MNM	2631
H. C. James	1920's	MNA	MNA 68.494
H. C. James	1920's	MNA	MNA 68.492
Odd Halseth		PGM	Hopi 12B

Photographer	Date	Institution	Photograph No.
Odd Halseth		PGM	Hopi 19A
Odd Halseth		PGM	23A
J. R. Willis		MNM	98191
Elizabeth Hegemann	1926	Huntington	Alb. 125 16/1
Unknown		MNM	91606
Douglass	(1902)	AHS	43696
A. E. Douglass	1928	UA Sp. Coll.	N11,201
Unknown		MNM	124403
H. Sage Goodwin	ca. 1930	MNM	119555
Gorelon L'Alleman		SWM	N35056 P6113
Imhof	1932	Maxwell	4.M.27 (same as above)
Douglass?	1934?	LTRR	Archaeo 34-13
M. Applegate	1936	MNA	RBMVE 2031
Unknown		AHS	58619

Main Plaza — North End

Photographer	Date	Institution	Photograph No.
F. H. Maude		SWM	N22273
F. H. Maude		Smithsonian	88-18111 (same as above)
H. R. Voth		ML	ASM #3061 Voth # 138
H. R. Voth		ML	ASM #887 Voth # 1290
H. R. Voth		ML	ASM #119 Voth #738
H. R. Voth		ML	ASM #193 Voth #960
H. R. Voth		ML	ASM #540 Voth #1524
James or Palmer?	1898	Smithsonian	32357A
Charles Carpenter	1901	FM	225
H. R. Voth		ML	ASM #391 Voth #1294
Samuel Barrett		MNA	MNA 73.1521
Stuart M. Young	1912?	MNA	MNA MS10-3-4-09
Lillian W. Smith	Prior to 1933	MNA	MNA 74.1582
E. Kopta		Maxwell	#18 4.885
Kopta		Maxwell	#46 4.915
Kopta		Maxwell	#44 4.913
Kopta		Maxwell	#45 4.914
Kopta		Maxwell	#17 4.884
Unknown		UA Sp. Coll.	N11,198

Photographer	Date	Institution	Photograph No.
Roomblock 7 — West Side			
Victor Mindeleff	1887	Smithsonian	1854
H. R. Voth		ML	ASM #106 Voth # 725
H. R. Voth		ML	ASM #3084 Voth #169
H. R. Voth		ML	ASM #3086 Voth #171
H. R. Voth		ML	ASM #3088 Voth #173
H. R. Voth		ML	ASM #3142 Voth #300
Monson		Huntington	#182 (241)
Dorsey	Before 1905	Smithsonian	T-789
Douglass?	1928?	LTRR	Archaeo 28-4
ROOMBLOCK 9			
George Wharton James		Smithsonian	SPC021018.00 (xerox)
Ben Wittick	ca. 1890	MNM	16083
Unknown		AHS	15769
A. C. Vroman	1900	PPL	Vol D1 D124
Charles Carpenter	1901	FM	205
Charles Carpenter	1901	FM	185
Unknown		FM	2619
H. F. Robinson	(ca. 1915)	MNM	36197
H. F. Robinson	(ca. 1919)	MNM	37094
Stuart M. Young	1912?	MNA	MNA MS10-3-4-014
(W. Bradfield?)	1918?	MNM	87313
Wesley Bradfield	1918	MNM	87318
Wesley Bradfield	1918	MNM	87307
Roomblock 6			
F. H. Maude		Seaver	2654R
H. R. Voth		ML	ASM #246 Voth #1092
Roomblock 1			
Hillers	1879	Smithsonian	56395
H. R. Voth		ML	ASM #191 Voth # 919
H. R. Voth		ML	ASM #3373 Voth #878

Photographer	Date	Institution	Photograph No.
H. R. Voth		ML	ASM #657 Voth # 1754
Charles Carpenter	1901	FM	227
Charles Carpenter	1901	FM	186

Roomblock 2

Charles Carpenter	1901	FM	210
Ben Wittick	ca. 1895	MNM	16080
Charles Carpenter	1901	FM	197
Charles Carpenter	1901	FM	235
H. R. Voth		ML	ASM #475 Voth #1441
H. R. Voth		ML	ASM #477 Voth #1443
Charles Carpenter	1901	FM	206
Charles Carpenter	1901	FM	198
M. Applegate	1936	MNA	RBMV #2030
Parker Hamilton	1961	MNA	MNA 3352
Parker Hamilton	1961	MNA	MNA 3350

Roomblocks 10 and 11

Ben Wittick	ca. 1890	MNM	16202
Ben Wittick	ca. 1895	MNM	16200
Ben Wittick	ca. 1890	MNM	16409
Ben Wittick	ca 1895	MNM	16079
A. C. Vroman		Seaver	V-1021
Monson		Huntington	#186 (1065)
Monson	1907?	MNM	74508 (same as above)

Roomblock 12

Hillers	(1879)	Smithsonian	1844
Powell	1870's	NPS	Neg.#60,145 class 970.331 (same as above)
Ben Wittick	ca 1890	MNM	16081
H. R. Voth		ML	ASM #565 Voth #1549
Charles Carpenter	1901	FM	181
Stuart Young	1909	NAU	NAU # 643-3-42
Stuart Young	1909	NAU	NAU #643-44
D. P. Johnson	1909	Nat. Arch.	95-G-84136
Wesley Bradfield	1918	MNM	87311

Photographer	Date	Institution	Photograph No.
Odd Halseth		PGM	Hopi 21A
Odd Halseth		PGM	Hopi 23B
A. E. Douglass	1928	UA Sp. Coll.	N11,197
A. E. Douglass	1934	LTRR	"Morris Photos"

Roomblock 12—Rear

Charles Carpenter	1901	FM	234

Snake Dance Plaza—Looking West

G. W. James	1896	MNA	MNA 66.799
G. W. James?	1896?	AHS	15768
J. W. Hildebrand		MNA	MS 168 71.257
F. H. Maude	ca. 1896	MNM	14424
Unknown		AHS	15767
Sumner Matteson		Smithsonian	T-1032
A. C. Vroman		Seaver	V-1643
H. R. Voth		ML	ASM #29 Voth #629
G. W. James		Huntington	Pierce Coll. #1911 (4576)
Ben Wittick	(ca. 1890)	MNM	16410
A. C. Vroman	1898	PPL	Vol D-1 D126
A. C. Vroman	1900	PPL	Vol 10 #1041
Sumner Matteson	1900	Smithsonian	42189B
Charles Carpenter	1901	FM	223
A. C. Vroman		Smithsonian	32357-I
Charles Carpenter	1901	FM	177
Charles Carpenter	1901	FM	194
Charles Carpenter	1901	FM	238
Sumner Matteson	1901	MPM	SWM-1-G-170/ 44613
Sumner Matteson	1901?	MPM	SWM-1-G-657/ 88-1
Sumner Matteson	1901	MPM	SWM-1-G-287/ 44657
Walter Runke	1902	MNA	MS 74-28
G. H. Pepper		NPS	Neg. #50-853 class #970.395
Unknown		UA Sp. Coll.	N11,200
Monson		Huntington	#164
Keystone View Co.		MNM	89371
Unknown		AHS	15759
Stuart Young	1912?	MNA	MS10-3-4-05
Stuart Young	1912?	MNA	MS10-3-4-012

Photographer	Date	Institution	Photograph No.
Unknown		Maxwell	29
Unknown		Maxwell	23
Unknown		Maxwell	43
H. F. Robinson	1919	MNM	37087
Don Williams?		AHS	43493
Wesley Bradfield	1918	MNM	87320
Wesley Bradfield	1918	MNM	87317
Wesley Bradfield	1918	MNM	87319
H. F. Robinson	1919	MNM	36195
Odd Halseth		PGM	Hopi 19B
H. C. James	1920's	MNA	68.489
H. C. James	1920's	MNA	68.493
Don Williams?		AHS	43489
Don Williams?		AHS	43494
Unknown		AHS	43492
Jack Van Ryder?	1921	AHS	41960
M. Applegate	1936	MNA	RBMVE #2029

Snake Dance Plaza—Looking North and South

Photographer	Date	Institution	Photograph No.
F. H. Maude	1896	Smithsonian	88-18113
H. F. Maude		Seaver	2682R
G. W. James		MNM	119163
Ben Wittick	1898	MNM	15991
A. C. Vroman		Seaver	V-605
A. C. Vroman	1900	PPL	Vol 10 #1052
A. C. Vroman	1900	PPL	Vol 10 #1047
H. R. Voth		ML	ASM #69 Voth #684
Munk	1902	SWM	N35146 Munk Vol VI #164
Samuel Barrett	1911?	MNA	MNA 73.1519

Roomblock 7—East Side

Photographer	Date	Institution	Photograph No.
J. W. Hildebrand		MNA	MNA 71.259
J. W. Hildebrand		MNA	MNA 71.258
F. H. Maude	1896	MNM	14422
G. W. James		Huntington	Pierce Coll. #1912 (4577)
Ben Wittick	1898	MNM	16413
Ben Wittick	1898	MNM	16427
Unknown		UA Sp. Coll.	N11,202
A. C. Vroman	1898	PPL	Vol D1 D118

Photographer	Date	Institution	Photograph No.
G. W. James		SWM	N35055/ P6110
G. L. Rose		Smithsonian	79-4285
Charles Carpenter	1901	FM	179
A. C. Vroman		Seaver	V-593
A. C. Vroman		Seaver	V-615
Edward H. Kemp	(1928)	Smithsonian	88-18122
A. C. Vroman	1898	PPL	Vol 10 #1059
Unknown	1898	LTRR	no number
Unknown		AHS	43693 (same as above)
G. W. James	1898	Smithsonian	88-18119
Stuart Young	1912	MNA	MNA MS10-3-4-011
Wesley Bradfield	1918	MNM	87309
Odd Halseth		PGM	Hopi 22B
Odd Halseth		PGM	Hopi 18B
Unknown		MNM	91605
A. E. Douglass?	1923	LTRR	Glass slide #248
A. E. Douglass?		LTRR	Nat. Geog. #4.6
A. E. Douglass?	1926	LTRR	Archaeo. 26-21
Roomblock E/F			
G. W. James	1896	SWM	N35046/ LS2506 (image reversed)
F. H. Maude	1896	MNM	14448
F. H. Maude	1896	MNM	14445
F. H. Maude	1896	MNM	T-2069
A. C. Vroman		Seaver	V-620
Ben Wittick	1898	NMN	16360
Sumner Matteson	1900	Smithsonian	88-18114
Sumner Matteson	1901	MPM	SWM-1-G-161/ 44518
Edward H. Kemp	(1928)	Smithsonian	88-18123
Charles Carpenter	1901	FM	237
Unknown		Huntington	Pierce Coll. #2022
Douglas	1902	AHS	43697
Bratley	1902	Smithsonian	53472B
Bratley	1902	Smithsonian	53472A
Forrest	1906	Huntington	Album 126 (1031)
Forrest	1908	Smithsonian	88-18115
F. Monson	1907	MNM	74522
Unknown		Huntington	Pierce Coll. #2013 (3723)
Unknown		Smithsonian	88-18112

Photographer	Date	Institution	Photograph No.
Unknown		Maxwell	9
Unknown		Maxwell	24
Unknown		Maxwell	46
Unknown		Maxwell	25
Unknown		Maxwell	20
Unknown		Maxwell	21
Aerial Photographs			
A. E. Douglass	1933	UA Sp. Coll.	N4374
Unknown		MNA	MNA 72.530
Soil Conservation Service	1934	Nat. Arch.	Navajo Proj. 846
Soil Conservation Service	1934	Nat. Arch.	Navajo Proj. 779
Spence Air Photo	1940	Peabody	Box 10-10 N32078
Cutter-Carr Flying Service	1948	MNM	2624
Arizona Dept. of Transport.	1976	ADOT	9R12 S1-1 thru S1-4
Distant Photographs			
E. O. Beaman		UA Sp Coll	no. number
F. H. Maude		Smithsonian	88-18118
F. H. Maude	1896	MNA	14423
G. W. James		SWM	N22130
F. H. Maude		SWM	N22131
Ben Wittick	ca. 1890	MNM	16078
Simeon Schwemberger		MNM	88770
G. H. Pepper		NPS	Neg. #50-854 class 970.3
Douglas	1902	AHS	43964
J. H. Bratley	ca. 1902	Smithsonian	53480
Munk		SWM	N35054/ P6119
Samuel Barrett		MNA	MNA 73.1518
Stuart M. Young	1912?	MNA	MS10-3-4-01
Unknown		Maxwell	47
Stuart M. Young	1912?	MNA	MS10-3-4-03
Wesley Bradfield	1918	MNM	77618
H. F. Robinson	1919	MNM	37400
H. F. Robinson	1919	MNM	37092
Unknown		MNM	2625
H. F. Robinson	1919	MNM	37111
L. L. Hargrave		MNA	MNA 14307
A. E. Douglass?	1923	LTRR	Archaeo 23-2

Photographer	Date	Institution	Photograph No.
Elizabeth Hegemann	1926/28?	Huntington	Album 125 D7 111
A. E. Douglass	1934	LTRR	34-10
Mallalieu	1935	AHS	73936
Mallalieu	1935	AHS	73935
Unknown		Maxwell	34

Orayvi—Location Unknown—Photographs with Kivas

Maude		Seaver	2687R
Munk?		AHS	15766 (same as above)
Charles Carpenter	1901	FM	212
Charles Carpenter	1901	FM	207
Sumner W. Matteson	1901	MPM	SWM-1-G-276/ 44621
Sumner W. Matteson	1901	MPM	SWM-1-G-20/ 112390
Sumner W. Matteson	1901	MPM	SWM-1-G-222/ 44661
Sumner W. Matteson	1901	MPM	SWM-1-G-322/ 44622
H. F. Robinson	1919	MNM	37399
Wesley Bradfield	ca. 1919	MNM	87306
H. F. Robinson	1919	MNM	37410
Unknown		AHS	43490
J. W. Hildebrand		MNA	MNA 71.256
Elizabeth Hegemann	1926	Huntington	Album 125 D17-124

Orayvi—Location Unknown although Indentification Provided

Unknown		SWM	N22128
Charles Carpenter	1901	FM	187
Ben Wittick		SWM	N22274/ P6141
Charles Carpenter	1901	FM	203
Charles Carpenter	1901	FM	220
G. H. Pepper		NPS	Neg. #50-855 class #970.3
Samuel Barrett		MNA	MNA 73.1520
Samuel Barrett		MNA	72.1484 MPL
Samuel Barrett		MNA	MNA 73.1635
Stuart Young	1912?	MNA	MNA MS10-3-4-10
Stuart Young	1909	NAU	#643-3-35
Stuart Young	1909	NAU	#643-3-38
Stuart Young	1912?	MNA	MNA MS10-3-4-13
Stuart Young	1912?	MNA	MNA MS10-3-4-04
Stuart Young	1912?	MNA	MNA MS10-3-4-06
A. E. Douglass	1928	UA Sp. Coll.	N11,199

Photographer	Date	Institution	Photograph No.
A. E. Douglass	1928	LTRR	Archaeo 28-35
Unknown	1934?	LTRR	no number
Mallalieu	1934	AHS	73934
H. C. James	1920's	MNA	MNA 68.481
H. C. James	1920's	MNA	MNA 68.486
H. C. James	1920's	MNA	MNA 68.483
H. C. James	1920's	MNA	MNA 68.482
H. C. James	1920's	MNA	MNA 68.495
H. C. James	1920's	MNA	MNA 68.484
H. C. James	1927	MNA	MNA 68.524
L. L. Hargrave	1929	MNA	MNA 14306
M. Applegate	1936	MNA	RBMVE #2026
M. Applegate	1936	MNA	RBMVE #2027

Orayvi—Location Unknown

Photographer	Date	Institution	Photograph No.
John K. Hillers	1879	Smithsonian	1850
Major Powell	1870's	NPS	Neg. # 60,143 class # 970.331
John K. Hillers		Smithsonian	1860-B-2
John K. Hillers	1879	Smithsonian	1858
Major Powell	1870's	NPS	Neg. #60.142 class #970.331
John K. Hillers	1879?	Smithsonian	Az 371
John K. Hillers	1879	Smithsonian	1860A
John K. Hillers	1879	Smithsonian	1857
John K. Hillers	1879	Smithsonian	1860-B-1
John K. Hillers	1879	Smithsonian	1848
E. O. Beaman		MNM	65223
E. O. Beaman		MNM	102136
Victor Mindeleff	1887	Smithsonian	1852-C
Victor Mindeleff	1887	Smithsonian	1852B
Victor Mindeleff	1887	Smithsonian	1856
Victor Mindeleff	1887	Smithsonian	1852A
F. Monson		Huntington	#174 (306)
F. Monson	1890	Huntington	#191
F. Monson	1890	Huntington	#181 (237)
Ben Wittick	ca. 1890	MNM	16082
Julian Scott	ca. 1890	U. Penn.	#139239
Unknown		MNA	MNA 72.2231

Photographer	Date	Institution	Photograph No.
J. W. Hildebrand		MNA	MNA 71.271
J. W. Hildebrand		MNA	MNA MS168-3-28
J. W. Hildebrand		MNA	MNA MS168-3-31
Charles Carpenter	1901	FM	228
Charles Carpenter	1901	FM	191
Charles Carpenter	1901	FM	193
Charles Carpenter	1901	FM	233
Charles Carpenter	1901	FM	182
Charles Carpenter	1901	FM	211
Charles Carpenter	1901	FM	217
Charles Carpenter	1901	FM	199
Charles Carpenter	1901	FM	184
Charles Carpenter	1901	FM	226
Charles Carpenter	1901	FM	188
Douglass	1902	AHS	43695
Frank Alrire	1911	AHS	8053
Samuel Barrett		MNA	72.1523 MPL
Samuel Barrett		MNA	MS201 MPL
H. S. Colton	1913	MNA	MNA 14295
Wesley Bradfield	1918	MNM	87315
Wesley Bradfield	1918	MNM	87310
Wesley Bradfield	1918	MNM	87308
Unknown (Bradfield?)	ca. 1919	MNM	87312
H. F. Robinson	1911	MNM	37091
Odd Halseth		PGM	Hopi 21B
Odd Halseth		PGM	Hopi 16A
Odd Halseth		PGM	Hopi 17A
O. C. Havens	1924	Smithsonian	4751
O. C. Havens	1924	Smithsonian	4731
Elizabeth Hegemann	1926	Huntington	D 7/2 114
R. L. Van Oosting	1927	SWM	N35050/ LS 3722
R. L. Van Oosting	1930	SWM	N35049/ LS1831
R. L. Van Oosting	1930	SWM	N35047/ LS1829
R. L. Van Oosting	1930	SWM	N35048/ LS1830
R. L. Van Oosting	1930	SWM	N35145/ LS1832
Unknown	1933	SWM	N35051/ LS7478
Unknown		UA Sp. Coll.	N11,186
Unknown		UA Sp. Coll.	N11,185 (image reversed?)
Unknown	1933	UA Sp. Coll.	M11,195

Photographer	Date	Institution	Photograph No.
Tad Nichols	1950's?	UA Sp. Coll.	N11,194
Unknown		Smithsonian	88-18116
Unknown		AHS	43488
Unknown		AHS	41958
Snow	1935	Maxwell	SN00011177A/ 87-44-177A
Underwood Stereo Card	1903?	AHS	74471
Keystone View Co.		MNM	89378 (same as above)
Unknown		MNM	91604
Unknown		MNM	91607
Unknown		MNM	28909
Unknown		Maxwell	48
Unknown		Maxwell	32
Unknown		Maxwell	30

Orayvi—Location Unknown—Building Houses

Victor Mindeleff	1887	Smithsonian	1846
James and Pierce	1901?	Smithsonian	88-18120

Building Houses—Not Orayvi

Curtis		U. Penn.	45531

Other Photographers—May Not Be Orayvi

John K. Hillers	1879	Smithsonian	1853
Unknown		Smithsonian	1873
Major Powell	1870's	NPS	Neg. #60,144 class #970.331
Unknown		Peabody	N32077/ H4921
Unknown	1911	AHS	8105
Neil Judd		MNA	MNA 67.835/ MS 593
H. S. Colton	1913?	MNA	MNA 14296
Unknown		LTRR	Nat. Geog. 4.7
Unknown		Smithsonian	1879-A
Unknown	1915	AHS	8124
Ben Wittick	ca. 1890	MNM	16201
Unknown		MNA	73.1483 MPL
Unknown		MNA	73.1484 MPL
Unknown		Huntington	#2016 (3725)
Casey?	1928?	Smithsonian	88-18121
Unknown		Huntington	Pierce Coll. #2019 (3728)

Institutional Abbreviations

ADOT	Arizona Department of Transportation, Photography Department, Phoenix, Arizona
AHS	Arizona Historical Society, Tucson, Arizona
FM	Field Museum of Natural History, Photography Department, Chicago, Illinois
Huntington	Huntington Library, San Marino, California
LTRR	Laboratory of Tree-Ring Research, University of Arizona, Tucson, Arizona
Maxwell	Maxwell Museum of Anthropology, Photo Archives, Albuquerque, New Mexico
ML	Mennonite Library and Archives, Information and Research Center, North Newton, Kansas
MNA	Museum of Northern Arizona, Photo Archives, Flagstaff, Arizona
MNM	Museum of New Mexico, Photo Archives, Santa Fe, New Mexico
MPM	Milwaukee Public Museum, Milwaukee, Wisconsin
Nat. Arch.	National Archives, Cartographic Branch and Still Pictures Branch, Washington, D.C.
NAU	Northern Arizona University, Cline Library Special Collections Department, Flagstaff, Arizona
Peabody	Peabody Museum of Archaeology and Ethnology, Photographic Archives, Harvard University, Cambridge, Massachusetts
PGM	Pueblo Grande Museum and Cultural Park, Phoenix, Arizona
PPL	Pasadena Public Library, Pasadena, California
Seaver	Seaver Center for Western History Research, Natural History Museum of Los Angeles County, Los Angeles, California
Smithsonian	National Anthropological Archives, National Museum of Natural History, Smithsonian Institution, Washington, D.C.
SWM	Southwest Museum, Los Angeles, California
UA Sp. Coll.	Special Collections, University of Arizona Library, University of Arizona, Tucson, Arizona
U. Penn.	University Museum, Photographic Archives, University of Pennsylvania, Philadelphia, Pennsylvania

Appendix 3 / Summary of Architectural Change to Rooms, 1871–1901

Roomblocks/Rooms	Abandoned	Demolished	Rebuilt	New
Period 1: 1871–1887				
Total No. of Rooms Observed: 49				
Rooms Unchanged: 40 (81.6%)				
Roomblock 1 and 1[1]				
552n fl. 1				x
Roomblock 4				
398 fl. 3		x		
397 fl. 3			x	
429 fl. 2			x	
433n fl. 3				x
438n fl. 3				x
Roomblock 12				
38n fl. 1				x
37n fl. 2				x
36n fl. 3				x
Total	o	1	2	6
%		2.0	4.1	12.2
Period 2 1887–1901				
Total No. of Rooms Observed: 197				
Rooms Unchanged: 105 (53.3%)				
Roomblock 1, 1[1]				
536 fl. 1	x			
537 fl. 1	x			
541n fl. 2				x
542n fl. 1				x
546 fl. 1			x	
551 fl. 1	x			
560 fl. 1	x			
561 fl. 1	x			
56xn fl. 2				x
56yn fl. 2				x
56zn fl. 1				x
Roomblock 2				
535n fl. 1				x
534n fl. 2				x

Roomblocks/Rooms	Abandoned	Demolished	Rebuilt	New
533n fl. 2				x
530n fl. 1				x
528n fl. 2				x
527 fl. 2			x	
525 fl. 1			x	
524 fl. 2		x		
517 fl. 1	x			
514 fl. 3	x			
Roomblock 4				
401n fl. 3				x
406n fl. 1				x
414n fl. 1				x
422 fl. 1			x	
420 fl. 3	x			
423 fl. 1			x	
425 fl. 4		x		
428 fl. 3			x	
432 fl. 2			x	
436 fl. 1			x	
437 fl. 2			x	
438 fl. 3			x	
Roomblock 4 sw end				
376 fl. 1			x	
375 fl. 2		x		
370 fl. 1		x		
367–369 fl. 2			x	
362n fl. 1				x
360 fl. 1			x	
361 fl. 2		x		
365 fl. 3		x		
357n fl. 1				x
351 fl. 1			x	
350n fl. 1				x
Roomblock 4[1]				
221 fl. 2		x		
222 fl. 1		x		
224 fl. 1		x		
220n fl. 1				x
Roomblock 7 sw end				
225n fl. 1				x
228 fl. 1			x	
227 fl. 2		x		
229 fl. 1			x	
231-232 fl. 3			x	
237 fl. 1	x			
238 fl. 1	x			
236 fl. 2			x	
235 fl. 3			x	
240 fl. 1			x	
242-243 fl. 3	x			

Roomblocks/Rooms	Abandoned	Demolished	Rebuilt	New
Roomblock 7 w side				
3x fl. 1	x			
6xn fl. 1				x
7x fl. 1		x		
Roomblock 9				
176n fl. 3				x
180 fl. 2			x	
181 fl. 3		x		
Roomblock 10 NE end				
175n fl. 1				x
173 fl. 3		x		
162 fl. 1			x	
162n fl. 1				x
Roomblock 10 s end				
131 fl. 1		x		
132 fl. 2		x		
132 fl. 1			x	
132n fl. 1				x
144 fl. 1			x	
Roomblock 11 NE end				
112n fl. 1				x
110 fl. 3			x	
Roomblock 12				
25 fl. 2		x		
31 fl. 1			x	
32 fl. 1		x		
38 fl. 1			x	
Roomblock E/F prime				
E/F 1n				x
E/F 2n				x
E/F 3n				x
E/F 4n				x
E/F 5n				x
E/F 7n				x
E/F 8n				x
E/F 9n				x
Roomblock K/L/M prime				
Room ?n				x
Room ?n				x
Room ?n				x
Room ?n				x
Total	12	17	27	36
% obser. 1887	6.1	8.6	13.7	(18.3)

Appendix 4 / Summary of Architectural Change to Rooms after 1906

Note: Conclusions are based on ground photos.

Hs. No.	Rm No.	1906–12	1912–25	1926–37	1937–48
162	527–531			dism. 1936	
163	532–533			dism. 1936	
164	534–535			dism. 1936	
161	525i			in use	in use
	522–523i			in use	in use
162	527i			aband.	
160	520 iii			dism. 1936	
	521 iii			dism. 1936	
	517 i			reblt. w/ 518 i	
	518 i			reblt. w/ 517 i	

Roomblock 4

Hs. No.	Rm No.	1906–12	1912–25	1926–37	1937–48
121	381–384			dism. 1932	
122	385–391			dism. 1932	
123	392–394			dism. 1932	
124	397 iii	in use	in use?	dism. 1926	
125	400 i	reblt.	in use	reblt. w/ 406 ni	
	401 niii	dism.			
	402 iii	in use	in use	in use	
126	404 iii	dism.			
	403 iii	in use	in use	aband.? 1934	
	405 ii	aband.? 1911	in use	aband.? 1932	
	406 ni	in use	in use	reblt. w/400 i	
127	410 iii	aband. 1911/ in use 1912	in use	in use	
	409 ii	in use	reblt.	in use 1932	
	408 i	in use	reblt.	in use? 1934	
128	413 iii	in use	in use	in use 1934	
	414 ii	in use	in use	in use	
	414 ni	in use	in use	aband. 1930–32	
	418 iii	in use	in use	dism.	

Hs. No.	Rm No.	1906–12	1912–25	1926–37	1937–48
	416 ii	in use	in use	aband. 1928	
	415 i	in use	in use	aband. 1928–32	
129	420 iii	in use	in use	dism. 1928–32	
	421 ii	in use?	in use?	dism. 1930	
	422–423 i	in use	in use	in use	
130	425 iii	in use	in use	aband. 1928–30	
	424 ii	in use	in use	aband.	
131	428 iii	in use	in use	aband. 1928–30	
	432 ii	in use	in use	aband.	
	429 i	aband.?		(intact)	
	430 i	in use	in use	aband.	
132	433 iii	in use	in use	in use 1934	
	434 ii	reblt. w/ 435 i	in use	in use 1934	
	435 i	reblt. w/ 434 ii	in use	in use	
133	438 iii	dism. 1911			
	438 i	reblt. w/ 438 ii	in use	in use	
	437 ii	dism. 1911			
	436 i	dism. 1911			

Roomblock 4 — West End

Hs. No.	Rm No.	1906–12	1912–25	1926–37	1937–48
119	375–376 i	in use	in use	in use	
	374 iii	dism.	reblt./ dism.	reblt. by 1936	
120	380 iii	in use		dism.	
118	367–369 ii	in use	dism.		
116	362 in	aband.	reblt.	in use	
	360 i	in use	reblt. w/ 359 i	in use	
	362 ii	reblt. w/ 356 ii	in use	in use?	
	363 iii	in use	in use	in use	
	359 i		reblt. w/ 360 i		
115	357 nni	new room	in use		
	356 ii	reblt. w/ 362 ii	in use		
	355 iii	dism.			
114	350 ii	aband.	dism.		
	352 ii	aband.	(intact)		
	350 nni		new room		

Roomblock 7 — Southeast End

Hs. No.	Rm No.	1906–12	1912–25	1926–37	1937–48
83	225 ni	in use	in use	in use	
	225 i	in use	in use	in use	
	226 ii	in use	in use	in use	
84	228–229 i	in use	in use	in use	
	230 i/ii	in use	in use	in use	
	231 iii	in use	dism.		

Hs. No.	Rm No.	1906–12	1912–25	1926–37	1937–48
85	238 i		aband.?		
	236 ii	in use	in use	dism.	
	235 ii			aband.	
	235 iii	dism.			
86	240 i	in use	reblt.		
	241 ii	in use	in use 1918/ dism. later		
	240/241 ni		new room	in use	
	242/243 iii	in use	in use 1918/ dism. later		
88	251 i	in use	dism.		
	247 iv	in use	in use 1918/ dism. later		
89	254 iv	in use	in use 1918/ dism. later		

Roomblock 9

64	178 i	in use	reblt.		
	176 ii	in use	in use		
	176 iiin	in use	dism.		
65	179 i	aband.	reblt. w/ 184 i and 183 ii		
	180 ii	aband.?	in use (reblt.?)		
67	184 i	aband.	reblt. w/ 179 i and 183 ii		
	183 ii	aband.	reblt. w/ 179 i and 184 i		
	182 iii	aband.	in use (ritual?)		
68	186 i	reblt. w/ 187 i	in use		
	189 ii	dism.			
	190 iii	dism.			
69	193 i		dism.?		
	192 ii		dism.?		
	191 iii		dism.?		

Roomblock 10

63	172 iii	in use	dism.		
62	169/170 i	in use	aband.?		
	168 ii	in use	aband.?		
	167 iii	in use	aband.?		
61	163 i	in use	aband.?		
	164 ii	in use?	aband.?		
	165 iii	in use?	aband.?		
	166 iv	dism.			
	160 iii	in use?	dism.		
56	143 ii	in use			
	143 i	in use			
	142 iii	dism.			
51	132 i	aband.	dism.		
	132 ni		dism.		

Hs. No.	Rm No.	1906–12	1912–25	1926–37	1937–48
52	133 i		dism.		
53	134 ii		dism.		
54			all rooms dism.		
Roomblock 11					
43			all rooms dism.		
44			all rooms dism.		
Roomblock 12					
20	23 i	dism. 1890's?			
	24 i	dism. 1890's?			
	25 ii	dism. 1890's			
21	31 i	in use	aband.		
	30 ii	in use	aband.?		
	29 iii	in use	aband.?		
22	32 i	in use	dism.		
	33 ii	in use	aband.	dism.	
	34 iii	in use	aband.	dism.	
23	38 i	in use	aband.		
	37 ii	in use?	aband.	dism.	
	36 iii	in use?	aband.?	dism.	
24	39 i	aband.?	dism.		
	40 ii	aband.?	dism.		
	41 iii	aband.	dism.		
25	46 i		dism.		
	45 ii		aband.	dism.	
	43 iii		aband.	dism.	

Key:
dism. = room(s) dismantled
reblt. = room(s) rebuilt
aband. = room(s) abandoned—not inhabited
in use = room(s) inhabited

Notes

Chapter 1. Archaeology and Pueblo Architecture

1. The spelling of Orayvi and other Hopi place names follows the orthography of the *Hopi Dictionary* (Hopi Dictionary Project 1998).

2. The "unit pueblo" was not found over the entire northern Southwest.

3. Great Kivas are not always incorporated into a community; sometimes they are in isolated locations, presumably in areas that could be accessed by several communities.

4. Lekson (1988, 1989) acknowledges that Great Kivas served as ritual structures from A.D. 500 through at least A.D. 1300.

5. Other instances of factionalism among Pueblo peoples have been reported. Parsons (1928) describes a factional split at Laguna Pueblo in the 1870s that resulted in the migration of a group of families to Isleta. Nagata (1977) examines factionalism at the Hopi village of Munqapi. Neither account, however, discusses the effects of factionalism on architecture.

Chapter 4. The Orayvi House and Household

1. One room number was used for each architectural space, and individual stories were indicated by roman numerals; i.e., Room 342 i and 342 ii are first and second stories. It was assumed that the same number of rooms visible in plan view was present for each lower story—a reasonable assumption, given the difficulty of building an upper-story wall without a lower-story wall to support it.

2. In some cases, Mindeleff's map appears to show an undivided room, yet two or more room numbers were assigned by the Second Beam Expedition. In these cases, additional evidence, such as the number of chimneys and the location of doors, was examined: a space with more than one chimney or door would be more likely to consist of multiple rooms rather than one.

3. The photographs were enlarged to double Mindeleff's original field scale (which was 1 inch = 20 feet) to allow rooms to be easily measured. Because of the probable distortion involved in enlarging and reducing the maps, length and width were measured only to the nearest half foot. Measurements were taken from the interior of one wall to the interior of the opposite wall. Length and width measurements for rooms were then converted to meters.

4. The number of rooms and houses is slightly lower than that used to calculate number of rooms per house because measurements could not be taken from rooms added to Mindeleff's map by Titiev; Titiev indicated only the location of these new houses and apparently made no attempt to record their size accurately. When they could be seen in photographs, the number of rooms could sometimes be counted; of course, photographs could not be used to calculate room area.

5. Multistoried construction and a nucleated layout *are* found prehistorically in the Eastern Pueblo area (e.g., Creamer et al. 1993, Kidder 1958).

Chapter 5. Orayvi Architectural Dynamics

1. Part of the increase may, however, be due to the changes resulting from the introduction of Euroamerican materials and technology.

Chapter 6. Orayvi after the Split

1. This includes households in which the female head was deceased at the time of the split but whose faction could be determined.

2. Photographs of roomblocks surrounding the Snake Dance Plaza often show ceremonial activity and for that reason were not reproduced here.

Chapter 7. Using Orayvi to Interpret the Past

1. Bond-abut patterns and other architectural evidence were used to suggest a construction sequence for Arroyo Hondo (Creamer et al. 1993).

2. The abandonment of Arroyo Hondo during both Component 1 and 2 has most frequently been attributed to poor environmental conditions and resulting population/resource imbalance (Lang and Harris 1984; Palkovich 1980; Rose et al. 1981). However, for Orayvi, as suggested by some scholars (e.g., Bradfield 1971), environmental problems resulting in subsistence stress could be an overt or covert cause of factionalism.

3. Planned, coordinated construction—on a much larger scale, of course—can be observed at Chacoan Great Houses during the tenth to the twelfth centuries. Clearly, Southwestern peoples were able to coordinate architectural efforts, when appropriate, without direction or intervention from Euroamericans.

References

Adams, E. Charles

1976 Walpi: The Archaeology of a Historic and Living Community. Paper presented at the 41st Annual Meeting of the Society for American Archaeology, St. Louis.

1979 *Walpi Archaeological Project, Phase II.* Vol. 1: *Overview and Summary.* Submitted to the Heritage and Recreation Service, Interagency Archeology Services, San Francisco.

1981 The View from the Hopi Mesas. In *The Protohistoric Period in the North American Southwest,* A.D. 1450–1700. Arizona State University Anthropological Research Papers 24. Arizona State University, Tempe.

1982 *Walpi Archaeological Project: Synthesis and Interpretation.* Museum of Northern Arizona, Flagstaff.

1983 The Architectural Analogue to Hopi Social Organization and Room Use and Implications for Prehistoric Southwestern Culture. *American Antiquity* 43:44–61.

1989a Changes in Household and Community Patterning on the Hopi Reservation and Their Reflection of Changing Economic and Social Roles. In *From Chaco to Chaco: Papers in Honor of Robert H. Lister and Florence C. Lister: 15,* edited by Meliha S. Duran and David T. Kirkpatrick. Archaeological Society of New Mexico, Albuquerque.

1989b Changing Form and Function in Western Pueblo Ceremonial Architecture from A.D. 1000 to A.D. 1500. In *The Architecture of Social Integration in Prehistoric Pueblos,* edited by W. D. Lipe and Michelle Hegmon, pp. 155–60. Occasional Papers of the Crow Canyon Archaeological Center, No. 1. Crow Canyon Archaeological Center, Cortez, Colo.

1991 *The Origin and Development of the Pueblo Katsina Cult.* University of Arizona Press, Tucson.

Adams, E. Charles, and Deborah Hull

1981 Prehistoric and Historic Occupation of the Hopi Mesas. In *Hopi Kachina: Spirit of Life.* California Academy of Sciences. University of Washington Press, Seattle.

Adler, Michael A.

1989 Ritual Facilities and Social Integration in Nonranked Societies. In *The Architecture of Social Integration in Prehistoric Pueblos,* edited by W. D. Lipe and Michelle Hegmon, pp. 35–52. Occasional Papers of the Crow Canyon Archaeological Center, No. 1. Crow Canyon Archaeological Center, Cortez, Colo.

1996 *The Prehistoric Pueblo World,* A.D. 1150–1350. University of Arizona Press, Tucson.

Agorsah, Emmanuel Kofi

1983 An Ethnoarchaeological Study of Settlement and Behavior Patterns of a West African Traditional Society: The Nchumuru of Banda-Wiae in Ghana. Ph.D. dissertation, University of California, Los Angeles.

1985 Archaeological Implications of Traditional House Construction among the Nchumuru of Northern Ghana. *Current Anthropology* 26:103–15.

Ahlstrom, Richard V. N.

1985 *The Interpretation of Archaeological Tree-Ring Dates.* Ph.D. dissertation, University Microfilms International, Ann Arbor, Mich.

1992 Casual Repeat Photography: An Illustration from Hopi History. *Journal of the Southwest* 34 (2): 166–86.

Ahlstrom, Richard V. N., Jeffrey S. Dean, and W. J. Robinson

1978 *Tree-Ring Studies of Walpi Pueblo.* Laboratory of Tree-Ring Research, University of Arizona, Tucson.

Ascher, Robert

1968 Time's Arrow and the Archaeology of a Contemporary Community. In *Settlement Archaeology,* edited by K. C. Chang, pp. 43–52. National Press Books, Palo Alto, Calif.

Bannister, Bryant, William J. Robinson, and Richard L. Warren

1967 *Tree-Ring Dates from Arizona J, Hopi Mesas Area.* Laboratory of Tree-Ring Research, University of Arizona, Tucson.

Beaglehole, Ernest

1937 *Notes on Hopi Economic Life.* Yale University Publications in Anthropology 15. New Haven, Conn.

Beaglehole, Pearl

1935 Census Data from Two Hopi Villages. *American Anthropologist* 37 (1, pt. 1): 41–54.

Bernardini, Wesley

1996 Transitions in Social Organization: A Predictive Model from Southwestern Archaeology. *Journal of Anthropological Archaeology* 15:372–402.

146 / References

Blanton, Richard E.
   1994   *Houses and Households: A Comparative Study.* Plenum Press, New York.
Bloom, Lansing B., ed.
   1938   Bourke on the Southwest, 13. *New Mexico Historical Review* 13:192–238.
Bonine, Michael E.
   1979   The Morphogenesis of Iranian Cities. *Annals of the Association of American Geographers* 69:209–24.
Bourke, John G.
   1884   *The Snake Dance of the Moquis of Arizona; Being a Narrative of a Journey from Santa Fe, New Mexico, to the Villages of the Moqui Indians of Arizona.* Charles Scribner's Sons, New York.
Bradfield, Maitland
   1971   *Changing Patterns of Hopi Agriculture.* Royal Anthropological Institute Occasional Paper No. 30. Royal Anthropological Institute of Great Britain and Ireland, London.
Brainard, Margaret
   1935   The Hopi Indian Family: A Study of the Changes Represented in Its Present Structure and Functions. Ph.D. dissertation, University of Chicago.
Brew, J. O.
   1946   *The Archaeology of Alkali Ridge, Southeastern Utah.* Papers of the Peabody Museum of American Archaeology and Ethnology No. 21. Harvard University, Cambridge, Mass.
   1979   Hopi Prehistory and History to 1850. In *Handbook of North American Indians,* vol. 9: *The Southwest,* edited by Alfonso Ortiz, pp. 514–23. Smithsonian Institution, Washington, D.C.
Brumfiel, Elizabeth M.
   1994   Factional Competition and Political Development in the New World: An Introduction. In *Factional Competition and Political Development in the New World,* edited by Elizabeth M. Brumfiel and John W. Fox, pp. 1–13. Cambridge University Press, Cambridge, Eng.
Brumfiel, Elizabeth M., and John W. Fox
   1994   *Factional Competition and Political Development in the New World,* edited by Elizabeth M. Brumfiel and John W. Fox. Cambridge University Press, Cambridge, Eng.
Bunting, Bainbridge
   1976   *Early Architecture in New Mexico.* University of New Mexico Press, Albuquerque.
Burgh, Robert F.
   1959   Ceramic Profiles in the Western Mound at Awatovi, Northeastern Arizona. *American Antiquity* 25 (2): 184–202.
Cameron, Catherine M.
   1991a   Structure Abandonment in Villages. In *Archaeological Method and Theory,* vol. 3, edited by Michael B. Schiffer, pp. 155–94. University of Arizona Press, Tucson.
   1991b   Architectural Change at a Southwestern Pueblo. Ph.D. dissertation, University Microfilms International, Ann Arbor, Mich.
   1992   An Analysis of Residential Patterns and the Oraibi Split. *Journal of Anthropological Archaeology* 11:173–86.
   1993   Photographic Analysis: A Study of Architectural Change at Oraibi Pueblo. *Expedition* 35 (1): 23–33.
   1995   Migration and the Movement of Southwestern Peoples. *Journal of Field Archaeology* 14 (2): 104–24.
   1996   Observations on the Pueblo House and Household. In *People Who Lived in Big Houses: Archaeological Perspectives on Large Domestic Structures,* edited by Gary Coupland and E. B. Banning, pp. 71–88. Monographs in World Archaeology, No. 27. Prehistory Press, Madison, Wis.
   in prep.   Room Size and Social Organization. Submitted to the *Journal of Anthropological Archaeology.*
Carneiro, Robert L.
   1967   On the Relationship between Size of Population and Complexity of Social Organization. *Southwestern Journal of Anthropology* 23:234–43.
Carter, T. H., and Pagliero R.
   1966   Notes on Mudbrick Preservation. *Sumer* 22:65–76.
Ciolek-Torrello, Richard
   1978   A Statistical Analysis of Activity Organization: Grasshopper Pueblo, Arizona. Ph.D. dissertation, Department of Anthropology, University of Arizona, Tucson.
   1985   A Typology of Room Function at Grasshopper Pueblo, Arizona. *Journal of Field Archaeology* 12:41–63.
Ciolek-Torrello, Richard, and J. Jefferson Reid
   1974   Change in House Size at Grasshopper. *The Kiva* 40 (1–2): 39–48.
Clemmer, Richard O.
   1978   *Continuities of Hopi Culture Change.* Acoma Books, Ramona, Calif.
Connelly, John C.
   1979   Hopi Social Organization. In *Handbook of North American Indians,* vol. 9: *The Southwest,* edited by Alfonso Ortiz, pp. 539–53. Smithsonian Institution, Washington, D.C.
Cordell, Linda S.
   1979a   *Cultural Resources Overview of the Middle Rio Grande Valley, New Mexico.* U.S. Government Printing Office, Washington, D.C.
   1979b   Prehistory: Eastern Anasazi. In *Handbook of North American Indians,* vol. 9: *The Southwest,* edited by Alfonso Ortiz, pp. 131–51. Smithsonian Institution, Washington, D.C.
   1984   *Prehistory of the Southwest.* Academic Press, Orlando.
   1989   Northern and Central Rio Grande. In *Dynamics of Southwest Prehistory,* edited by Linda S. Cordell and George J. Gumerman, pp. 293–336. Smithsonian Institution Press, Washington, D.C.

1995 Tracing Migration Pathways from the Receiving End. *Journal of Anthropological Archaeology* 14:203–11.

1996 Big Sites, Big Questions: Pueblos in Transition. In *The Prehistoric Pueblo World*, A.D. 1150–1350, edited by Michael A. Adler, pp. 228–40. University of Arizona Press, 1996.

Creamer, Winifred, with Catherine M. Cameron and John D. Beal

1993 *The Architecture of Arroyo Hondo Pueblo, New Mexico.* School of Arroyo Hondo Archaeological Series, vol. 7, American Research Press, Santa Fe, N.Mex.

Crosby, Anthony

1983 Common Sources of Deterioration. In *Adobe: Practical and Technical Aspects of Adobe Conservation*, edited by James W. Garrison and Elizabeth F. Ruffner. Heritage Foundation of Arizona.

Crown, Patricia L.

1991 Evaluating the Construction Sequence and Population of Pot Creek Pueblo, Northern New Mexico. *American Antiquity* 56:291–314.

Crown, Patricia L., and Timothy A. Kohler

1994 Community Dynamics, Site Structure, and Aggregation in the Northern Rio Grande. In *The Ancient Southwestern Community: Models and Methods for the Study of Prehistoric Social Organization*, edited by W. H. Wills and Robert D. Leonard, pp. 103–18. University of New Mexico Press, Albuquerque.

Cully, Anne C., et al.

1982 Agriculture in the Bis sa'ani Community. In *Bis sa'ani: A Late Bonito Phase Community on Escavada Wash, Northwest New Mexico*, edited by Cory D. Breternitz, David E. Doyel, and Michael Marshall, pp. 115–64. Navajo Nation Papers in Anthropology No. 14. Navajo Nation Cultural Resources Management Program, Window Rock, Arizona.

David, Nicholas

1971 The Fulani Compound and the Archaeologist. *World Archaeology* 3:111–31.

Deal, Michael

1985 Household Pottery Disposal in the Maya Highlands: An Ethnoarchaeological Interpretation. *Journal of Anthropological Archaeology* 4:243–91.

Dean, Jeffery S.

1969 *Chronological Analysis of Tsegi Phase Sites in Northeastern Arizona.* Papers of the Laboratory of Tree-Ring Research, No. 3. University of Arizona, Tucson.

1970 Aspects of Tsegi Phase Social Organization: A Trial Reconstruction. In *Reconstructing Prehistoric Pueblo Societies*, edited by William A. Longacre, pp. 140–74. University of New Mexico Press, Albuquerque.

1978 Independent Dating in Archaeological Analysis. In *Advances in Archaeological Method and Theory*, vol. 1, edited by Michael B. Schiffer, pp. 223–55. Academic Press, New York.

Dewar, John

1989 Old Oraibi, 1934, Hopi Portfolio. *Journal of the Southwest* 31:534–47.

Dockstader, Frederick J.

1954 *The Kachina and the White Man: A Study of the Influences of White Culture on the Hopi Kachina Cult.* Cranbrook Institute of Science Bulletin 35. Bloomfield Hills, Michigan.

1979 Hopi History, 1850–1940. In *Handbook of North American Indians*, vol. 9: *The Southwest*, edited by Alfonso Ortiz. Smithsonian Institution, Washington, D.C.

Dohm, Karen

1990 Effect of Population Nucleation on House Size for Pueblos in the American Southwest. *Journal of Anthropological Archaeology* 9:201–39.

1996 Rooftop Zuni: Extending Household Territory beyond Apartment Walls. In *People Who Lived in Big Houses: Archaeological Perspectives on Large Domestic Structures*, edited by Gary Coupland and E. B. Banning, pp. 89–106. Prehistory Press, Madison, Wis.

Donaldson, Thomas C.

1893 Extra Census Bulletin: Moqui Pueblo Indians of Arizona and Pueblo Indians of New Mexico. *Eleventh Census of the United States (1890).* U.S. Census Office, Washington, D.C.

Douglass, Andrew E.

1929 The Secret of the Southwest Solved by Talkative Tree Rings. *National Geographic Society Magazine* 56 (6): 736–70. Washington, D.C.

n.d. Letters on file, Laboratory of Tree-Ring Research, University of Arizona, Tucson.

Dozier, Edward P.

1954 The Hopi-Tewa of Arizona. *University of California Publications in American Archaeology and Ethnology* 44 (3): 259–376. Berkeley.

Earls, Amy C.

1988 History of Room Use in Area H of Acoma Pueblo, Cibola County, New Mexico. Mariah Associates, Austin, Tex.

Eggan, Frederick R.

1950 *Social Organization of the Western Pueblos.* University of Chicago Press, Chicago.

Ellis, Florence M.

1974 *The Hopi: Their History and Use of Lands.* Garland Publishing, New York.

Ferguson, T. J.

1996 *Historic Zuni Architecture and Society: An Archaeological Application of Space Syntax.* University of Arizona Anthropological Papers, no. 60. University of Arizona Press, Tucson.

Ferguson, T. J., and Barbara J. Mills

1987 Settlement and Growth of Zuni Pueblo: An Architectural History. *The Kiva* 52:243–66.

Ferguson, T. J., Barbara J. Mills, and Calbert Seciwa

1990   Contemporary Zuni Architecture and Society. In *Pueblo Style and Regional Architecture*, edited by Nicholas C. Markovich, Wolfgang F. E. Preiser, and Fred G. Sturm, pp. 103–21. Van Nostrand Reinhold, New York.

Fewkes, J. Walter

1906   The Sun's Influence on the Form of Hopi Pueblos. *American Anthropologist* n.s. 8.

Firor, James

1988   Agents of Deterioration. In Ruins Stabilization Report, Technical Series No. 53, Ruins Stabilization: A Handbook. MS on file, National Park Service, Southwest Region, Santa Fe, N.Mex.

Fitch, J. M., and D. P. Branch

1960   Primitive Architecture and Climate. *Scientific American*, 203:134–44.

Fleming, Paula, and Judith Luskey

1986   *North American Indians in Early Photography*. Harper and Row, New York.

Forrest, Earle R.

1961   *The Snake Dance of the Hopi Indians*. Westernlore Press, Los Angeles.

Fowler, Don D.

1989   *The Western Photographs of John K. Hillers, Myself in the Water*. Smithsonian Institution Press, Washington, D.C.

Fraser, Douglas

1968   Village Planning in the Primitive World. In *Planning and Cities*, edited by G. R. Collins. George Braziller, New York.

Gillespie, William B.

1974   Estimating Population Sizes of Southwestern Pueblo Sites from Dimensions of Habitation Space: A Review of Techniques and an Outline of a New Method. MS in possession of the author.

Goody, Jack, ed.

1958   *The Developmental Cycle in Domestic Groups*. Cambridge University Press, Cambridge, Eng.

Guidoni, Enrico

1975   *Primitive Architecture*. Harry N. Abrams, New York.

Gullini, G.

1968   Contributions to the Study of the Preservation of Mud-Brick Structures. *Mesopotamia* 3/4:443–73.

Hack, John Tilton

1942   *The Changing Physical Environment of the Hopi Indians of Arizona*. Peabody Museum of American Archaeology and Ethnology, 35 (1): Awatovi Expedition.

Hall, G., S. McBride, and A. Riddel

1973   Architectural Study. *Anatolian Studies* 23:245–69.

Hammond, George P., and Agapito Rey

1966   *The Rediscovery of New Mexico*. University of New Mexico Press, Albuquerque.

Hantman, Jeffery

1983   Social Networks and Stylistic Distributions in the Prehis-

toric Plateau Southwest. Ph.D. dissertation, Arizona State University, Tempe.

Hargrave, Lyndon L.

1932   Oraibi: A Brief History of the Oldest Inhabited Town in the United States. Museum of Northern Arizona, *Museum Notes* 4 (7): 1–8.

Hassan, Ferki A.

1978   Demographic Archaeology. In *Advances in Archaeological Method and Theory*, vol. 1, edited by Michael B. Schiffer, pp. 49–103. Academic Press, New York.

1981   *Demographic Archaeology*. Academic Press, New York.

Hayden, Julian

1945   Salt Erosion. *American Antiquity* 4:373–78.

Hayes, Alden C.

1981   A Survey of Chaco Canyon Archaeology. In *Archaeological Surveys of Chaco Canyon, New Mexico*, edited by Alden C. Hayes, David M.Brugge, and W. James Judge. Publications in Archaeology, 18A: Chaco Canyon Studies. Washington, D.C.

Hegmon, Michelle, and W. D. Lipe

1989   Introduction. In *The Architecture of Social Integration in Prehistoric Pueblos*, edited by W. D. Lipe and Michelle Hegmon, pp. 1–3. Occasional Papers of the Crow Canyon Archaeological Center, No. 1. Crow Canyon Archaeological Center, Cortez, Colo.

Henderson, Eric B., and Jerrold E. Levy

1975   *Survey of Navajo Community Studies, 1936–1974*. Lake Powell Research Project Bulletin No. 6. Institute of Physics and Geophysics, University of California, Los Angeles.

Hieb, Louis A.

1990   The Metaphors of Hopi Architectural Experience in Comparative Perspective. In *Pueblo Style and Regional Architecture*, edited by Nicholas C. Markovich, Wolfgang F. E. Preiser, and Fred G. Sturm, pp. 122–32. Van Nostrand Reinhold, New York.

Hill, James N.

1970   *Broken K Pueblo: Prehistoric Social Organization in the American Southwest*. University of Arizona Anthropological Papers No. 18. University of Arizona Press, Tucson.

Hill, W. W.

1982   *An Ethnography of Santa Clara Pueblo, New Mexico*, edited and annotated by Charles H. Lange. University of New Mexico, Albuquerque.

Hillier, Bill, and Julienne Hanson

1984   *The Social Logic of Space*. Cambridge University Press, Cambridge, Eng.

Hopi Dictionary Project, Bureau of Applied Research in Anthropology, University of Arizona

1998   *Hopi Dictionary/Hopìikwa Lavàytutuveni: A Hopi-English Dictionary of the Third Mesa Dialect*. University of Arizona Press, Tucson.

Horne, Lee

1980 Dryland Settlement Location: Social and Natural Factors in the Distribution of Settlements in Turan. *Expedition* 22 (4): 11–17.

1983 Recycling an Iranian Village: Ethnoarchaeology in Baghestan. *Archaeology* 36 (4): 16–21.

1994 *Village Spaces: Settlement and Society in Northeastern Iran.* Smithsonian Institution Press, Washington, D.C.

Jacobs, Linda

1979 Tell-i Nun: Archaeological Implications of a Village in Transition. In *Ethnoarchaeology: Implications of Ethnography for Archaeology*, edited by Carol Kramer. Columbia University Press, New York.

Jett, Stephen C., and Virginia E. Spencer

1981 *Navajo Architecture.* University of Arizona Press, Tucson.

Jorgensen, Julia

1975 A Room Use Analysis of Table Rock Pueblo, Arizona. *Journal of Anthropological Research* 31:149–61.

Judd, Neil M.

1959 *Pueblo del Arroyo, Chaco Canyon, New Mexico.* Smithsonian Miscellaneous Collections 138, no. 1. Smithsonian Institution, Washington, D.C.

Kent, Susan

1990a The Relationship between Mobility Strategies and Site Structure. In *The Interpretation of Archaeological Spatial Patterns*, edited by E. Kroll and D. Price. Plenum Press, New York.

1990b *Domestic Architecture and the Use of Space.* Cambridge University Press, Cambridge, Eng.

Kidder, Alfred Vincent

1958 *Pecos, New Mexico: Archaeological Notes.* Papers of the Peabody Foundation for Archaeology 5. Phillips Academy, Andover, Mass.

Knowles, Ralph

1974 *Energy and Form: An Ecological Approach to Urban Growth.* M.I.T. Press, Cambridge, Mass.

Kohler, Timothy A.

1993 News from the Northern American Southwest: Prehistory on the Edge of Chaos. *Journal of Archaeological Research* 1 (4): 267–321.

Kramer, Carol

1982 *Village Ethnoarchaeology.* Academic Press, New York.

Kroeber, Alfred L.

1917 Zuni Kin and Clan. *Anthropological Papers of the American Museum of Natural History* 18 (2): 39–204.

Kulisheck, Jeremy, Michael Adler, and John Hufnagle

1994 Diversity and Continuity in Classic and Protohistoric Villages in the Taos District, Northern New Mexico. Paper presented at the 59th Annual Meeting of the Society for American Archaeology, Anaheim, Calif.

Laboratory of Tree-Ring Research, University of Arizona

n.d. Maps of Orayvi, on file.

Laird, W. David

1977 *Hopi Bibliography.* University of Arizona Press, Tucson.

Lange, Charles H.

1959 *Cochiti: A New Mexico Pueblo, Past and Present.* University of Texas Press, Austin.

Lange, Frederick, et al.

1986 *Yellowjacket: A Four Corners Anasazi Ceremonial Center.* Johnson Books, Boulder, Colo.

Lawrence, Denise L., and Setha M. Low

1990 The Built Environment and Spatial Form. *Annual Review of Anthropology* 19:453–505.

Lekson, Stephen H.

1986 *Great Pueblo Architecture of Chaco Canyon, New Mexico.* University of New Mexico Press, Albuquerque.

1988 The Idea of the Kiva in Anasazi Archaeology. *The Kiva* 53:213–34.

1989 Kivas? In *The Architecture of Social Integration in Prehistoric Pueblos*, edited by W. D. Lipe and Michelle Hegmon, pp. 161–68. Occasional Papers of the Crow Canyon Archaeological Center, No. 1. Crow Canyon Archaeological Center, Cortez, Colo.

1991 Settlement Patterns and the Chaco Region. In *Chaco & Hohokam: Prehistoric Regional Systems in the American Southwest.* School of American Research Press, Santa Fe, N.Mex.

in press Great Towns in the Southwest. In *Great Towns, Regional Polities.* University of New Mexico Press, Albuquerque.

Lekson, Stephen H., ed.

1983 The Architecture and Dendrochronology of Chetro Ketl. *Reports of the Chaco Center*, No. 6. Division of Cultural Research, National Park Service, Albuquerque, N.Mex.

Lekson, Stephen H., and Catherine Cameron

1995 Abandonment of Chaco Canyon, the Mesa Verde Migrations, and Reorganization of the Anasazi World. *Journal of Anthropological Archaeology* 14:184–202.

Lekson, Stephen H., et al.

1988 The Chaco Canyon Community. *Scientific American* 259 (1): 100–109.

Levy, Jerrold E.

1990 The Demographic Consequences of Social Stratification in an "Egalitarian" Society. Paper presented at the 89th Annual Meeting of the American Anthropological Association, New Orleans.

1992 *Orayvi Revisited: Social Stratification in an "Egalitarian" Society.* School of American Research, Santa Fe, N.Mex.

Levy, Jerrold E., Eric B. Henderson, and Tracy J. Andrews

1989 The Effects of Regional Variation and Temporal Change on Matrilineal Elements of Navajo Social Organization. *Journal of Anthropological Research* 45 (4): 351–77.

Lightfoot, Ricky R.

1994 *The Duckfoot Site*, vol. 2: *Archaeology of the House and Household.* Occasional Paper No. 4. Crow Canyon Archaeological Center, Cortez, Colo.

Lipe, W. D., and Michelle Hegmon

1989a *The Architecture of Social Integration in Prehistoric*

Pueblos. Occasional Papers of the Crow Canyon Archaeological Center, no. 1. Crow Canyon Archaeological
Center, Cortez, Colo.

1989b   Historical Perspectives on Architecture and Social Inte-
gration in the Prehistoric Pueblos. In *The Architecture
of Social Integration in Prehistoric Pueblos*, edited by
W. D. Lipe and Michelle Hegmon, pp. 15–34. Occasional
Papers of the Crow Canyon Archaeological Center, No. 1.
Crow Canyon Archaeological Center, Cortez, Colo.

Longacre, William A.

1968   Some Aspects of Prehistoric Society in East-Central
Arizona. In *New Perspectives in Archaeology*, edited by
Sally R. Binford and Lewis R. Binford, pp. 89–102. Aldine
Publishing, Chicago.

1970   *Archaeology as Anthropology: A Case Study*. University of
Arizona Anthropological Papers 17. University of Arizona
Press, Tucson.

1975   Population Dynamics at Grasshopper Pueblo. In Population Studies in Archaeology and Biological Anthropological Anthropology: A Symposium, edited by Alan C.
Swedlund. *American Antiquity* 40 (2): 71–74.

1976   Population Dynamics at Grasshopper Pueblo, Arizona. In
Demographic Anthropology, edited by Ezra Zubrow, pp.
169–84. University of New Mexico Press, Albuquerque.

Lowell, Julie Carol

1986   The Structure and Function of the Prehistoric Household
in the Pueblo Southwest: A Case Study from Turkey
Creek Pueblo. Ph.D. dissertation, University of Arizona,
Department of Anthropology, Tucson.

1988   The Social Use of Space at Turkey Creek Pueblo: An
Architectural Analysis. *The Kiva* 53 (2): 85–100.

1991   *Prehistoric Households at Turkey Creek Pueblo, Arizona*.
Anthropological Papers of the University of Arizona,
No. 54. University of Arizona Press, Tucson.

Lyon, Luke

1988   *History of Prohibition of Photography of Southwestern
Indian Ceremonies*. Papers of the Archaeological Society
of New Mexico, 14. Ancient City Press, Santa Fe, N.Mex.

Markovich, Nicholas C., Wolfgang F. E. Preiser, and Fred G.
Sturm, eds.

1990   *Pueblo Style and Regional Architecture*. Van Nostrand
Reinhold, New York.

Mayhugh, John S.

1892–94   Letters. Record Group 75, National Archives, Washington, D.C.

McGuire, Randall, and Michael B. Schiffer

1983   A Theory of Architectural Design. *Journal of Anthropological Archaeology* 2:277–303.

McIntosh, Roderick J.

1974   Archaeology and Mud Wall Decay in a West African
Village. *World Archaeology* 6:154–71.

1976   Square Huts in Round Concepts. *Archaeology* 29:92–101.

1977   The Excavation of Mud Structures: An Experiment from
West Africa. *World Archaeology* 9:185–99.

Mindeleff, Cosmos

1900   Localization of Tusayan Clans. *Bureau of Ethnology
Nineteenth Annual Report*, 635–53.

Mindeleff, Victor

1891   A Study of Pueblo Architecture: Tusayan and Cibola. In
*Eighth Annual Report of the Bureau of American Ethnol-
ogy 1886–'87*, pp. 13–228. Governnment Printing Office,
Washington, D.C.

n.d.   Field Maps of Oraibi. On file, National Anthropological
Archives, Smithsonian Institution, Washington, D.C.

Montgomery, Barbara K.

1993   Ceramic Analysis as a Tool for Discovering Processes of
Pueblo Abandonment. In *Abandonment of Settlements
and Regions: Ethnoarchaeological and Archaeological
Approaches*, edited by Catherine M. Cameron and
Steve A. Tomka, pp. 157–64. Cambridge University Press,
Cambridge, Eng.

Montgomery, Ross G., Watson Smith, and John O. Brew

1949   *Franciscan Awatovi: The Excavation and Conjectural
Reconstruction of a 17th Century Spanish Mission Establishment at a Hopi Indian Town in Northeastern Arizona*.
Papers of the Peabody Museum of American Archaeology
and Ethnology, Harvard University, 36. Cambridge, Mass.

Morenon, E. Pierre

1972   Intra-Site Spatial Change in the American Southwest: An
Alternative View. Paper presented at the Annual Meetings
of the American Anthropological Association, Toronto.

1977   Architectural Attributes and Intra-Site Variability: A Case
Study. Ph.D. dissertation, Southern Methodist University,
Dallas, Tex.

Morgan, Lewis H.

1881   *Houses and House-Life of the American Aborigines*. Contributions to North American Ethnology 4. Government
Printing Office, Washington, D.C.

Morris, Don P.

1986   *Archaeological Investigations at Antelope House*. National
Park Service, Department of the Interior, Washington,
D.C.

Nabokov, Peter

1986   *Architecture of Acoma Pueblo: The 1934 Historic American
Buildings Survey Project*. Ancient City Press, Santa Fe,
N.Mex.

1989   Introduction. *A Study of Pueblo Architecture in Tusayan
and Cibola*. Smithsonian Institution Press, Washington,
D.C.

Nabokov, Peter, and Robert Easton

1989   *Native American Architecture*. Oxford University Press,
New York.

Nagata, Shuichi

1970   *Modern Transformations of Moenkopi Pueblo*. University
of Illinois Press, Urbana.

1977   Opposition and Freedom in Moenkopi Factionalism. In
*A House Divided? Anthropological Studies of Faction-
alism*, edited by M. Silverman and R. F. Salisbury, pp.

146–70. Social and Economic Paper, no. 9. Institute of Social and Economic Research, Memorial University of Newfoundland, Saint John's, Newfoundland.

Netting, Robert McC., Richard R. Wilk, and Eric J. Arnould, eds.

1984   *Households*. University of California Press, Los Angeles.

Ortiz, Alfonso

1969   *The Tewa World*. University of Chicago Press, Chicago.

Park, Thomas K.

1988   Indigenous Responses to Economic Development in Mauritania. *Urban Anthropology* 17 (1): 53–74.

Parsons, Elsie C.

1922   Oraibi in 1920. In Contributions to Hopi History, edited by Elsie C. Parsons, pp. 283–98, *American Anthropologist* 24 (3): 253–98.

1923   *Laguna Genealogies*. Anthropological Papers of the American Museum of Natural History 19 (5). American Museum of Natural History, New York.

1925   *The Pueblo of Jemez*. Yale University Press, New Haven, Conn.

1928   The Laguna Migration to Isleta. *American Anthropologist* 30:602–13.

1929   *The Social Organization of the Tewa of New Mexico*. Memoirs of the American Anthropological Association 36.

Pierson, Lloyd M.

1949   The Prehistoric Population of Chaco Canyon, New Mexico: A Study in Methods and Techniques of Prehistoric Population Estimation. M.A. thesis, University of New Mexico, Albuquerque.

Plog, Fred T.

1974   *The Study of Prehistoric Change*. Academic Press, New York.

Powell, John Wesley

1875   The Hopi Villages: The Ancient Province of Tusayan. *Scribner's Monthly* 11 (2): 193–213.

Prudden, T. Mitchell

1914   The Circular Kivas of Small Ruins in the San Juan Watershed. *American Anthropologist* 16 (1): 33–58.

1918   *A Further Study of the Prehistoric Small House Ruins in the San Juan Watershed*. Memoirs of the American Anthropological Association 5 (1).

Prussin, Labelle

1969   *Architecture in Northern Ghana: A Study of Forms and Functions*. University of California Press, Berkeley.

Rapoport, Amos

1969   *House Form and Culture*. Prentice Hall, Englewood Cliffs, N.J.

1982   *The Meaning of the Built Environment*. Reprint, University of Arizona Press, Tucson, 1990.

1990   Systems of Activities and Systems of Settings. In *Domestic Architecture and the Use of Space*, edited by Susan Kent, pp. 9–20. Cambridge University Press, Cambridge, Eng.

Regan, Albert B.

1922   *The "Flu" among the Navajo*. Transactions of the Kansas Academy of Science 30, pt. 2. Topeka, Kan.

Reid, J. Jefferson

1973   *Growth and Response to Stress at Grasshopper Pueblo, Arizona*. Ph.D. dissertation, University of Arizona, University Microfilms, Ann Arbor, Mich.

1978   Response to Stress at Grasshopper Pueblo, Arizona. In *Discovering Past Behavior: Experiments in the Archaeology of the American Southwest*, edited by P. Grebinger, pp. 195–213. Gordon & Breach, New York.

Reid, J. Jefferson, and Izumi Shimada

1982   Pueblo Growth at Grasshopper: Methods and Models. In *Multidisciplinary Research at Grasshopper Pueblo, Arizona*, edited by William A. Longacre, Sally J. Holbrook, and Michael W. Graves, pp. 12–18. University of Arizona, Anthropological Papers, 40.

Reid, J. Jefferson, and Stephanie M. Whittlesey

1982   Households at Grasshopper Pueblo. *American Behavioral Scientist* 25 (6): 687–703.

Reynolds, William E.

1981   The Ethnoarchaeology of Pueblo Architecture. Ph.D. dissertation, Department of Anthropology, Arizona State University, Tempe.

Rinaldo, John B.

1964   Architectural Details, Carter Ranch Pueblo. In Chapters in the Prehistory of Eastern Arizona 2, by Paul S. Martin et al. *Fieldiana: Anthropology* 55:15–58.

Robinson, William J.

1990   Tree-Ring Studies of the Pueblo de Acoma. *Historical Archaeology* 24.

Rock, James T.

1974   The Use of Social Models in Archaeological Interpretation. *The Kiva* 40 (1–2): 81–92.

Rohn, Arthur H.

1965   Postulation of Socio-Economic Groups from Archaeological Evidence. *Society for American Archaeology Memoirs* 19:65–69.

1971   *Mug House*. National Park Service Archeological Research Series, No. 7-D. Washington, D.C.

1977   *Cultural Change and Continuity on Chapin Mesa*. Regents Press of Kansas, Lawrence.

Roney, John R.

1992   Prehistoric Roads and Regional Integration in the Chacoan System. In *Anasazi Regional Organization and the Chaco System*, edited by David E. Doyel, pp. 123–32. Maxwell Museum of Anthropology, Anthropological Papers, No. 5. University of New Mexico, Albuquerque.

Rose, Martin R., Jeffrey S. Dean, and William J. Robinson

1981   *The Past Climate of Arroyo Hondo, New Mexico, Reconstructed from Tree Rings*. School of American Research Press, Santa Fe, N.Mex.

Roys, Lawrence
   1936   Lowry Ruin as an Introduction to the Study of Southwest-
          ern Masonry. In Lowry Ruin in Southwestern Colorado,
          by Paul S. Martin, pp. 115–42. *Field Museum of Natural
          History, Anthropological Series* 23 (1).
Saile, David G.
   1977a Architecture in Prehispanic Pueblo Archaeology: Ex-
          amples from Chaco Canyon. *World Archaeology* 9 (2):
          157–73.
   1977b Making a House: Building Rituals and Spatial Concepts
          in the Pueblo Indian World. *Architectural Association
          Quarterly* 9 (2/3): 72–81.
   1990   Understanding the Development of Pueblo Architecture.
          In *Pueblo Style and Regional Architecture*, edited by
          Nicholas C. Markovich, Wolfgang F. E. Preiser, and
          Fred G. Sturm, pp. 49–63. Van Nostrand Reinhold,
          New York.
Scarborough, Robert, and Izumi Shimada
   1974   Geological Analysis of Wall Composition at Grasshopper
          with Behavioral Implications. *The Kiva* 40 (1–2): 49–66.
Schiffer, Michael B.
   1976   *Behavioral Archaeology*. Academic Press, New York.
   1987   *Formation Processes of the Archaeological Record*.
          University of New Mexico Press, Albuquerque.
   1989   Formation Processes of Broken K Pueblo: Some Hypothe-
          ses. In *Quantifying Diversity in Archaeology*, edited by
          Robert D. Leonard and George T. Jones. Cambridge
          University Press, Cambridge, Eng.
Schiffer, Michael B., et al.
   1987   Deterioration of Adobe Structures: A Case Study from
          San Pedro de Atacama, Northern Chile. In *Natural For-
          mation Processes and the Archaeological Record*, edited by
          D. T. Nash and M. D. Petraglia. BAR International Series
          352. Oxford, Eng.
Schlanger, Sarah H.
   1985   *Prehistoric Population Dynamics in the Dolores Area,
          Southwestern Colorado*. Ph.D. dissertation. University
          Microfilms International, Ann Arbor, Mich.
   1987   Population Measurement, Size, and Change, A.D. 600–
          1175. In *Dolores Archaeological Program: Supporting
          Studies; Settlement and Environment*, compiled by
          Kenneth Lee Peterson and Janet D. Orcutt, pp. 569–
          616. Bureau of Reclamation, Engineering and Research
          Center, Denver, Colo.
Schlanger, Sarah H., and Richard H. Wilshusen
   1993   Local Abandonments and Regional Conditions in
          the North American Southwest. In *Abandonment of
          Settlements and Regions: Ethnoarchaeological and
          Archaeological Approaches*, edited by Catherine M.
          Cameron and Steve A. Tomka, pp. 85–98. Cambridge
          University Press, Cambridge, Eng.
Schumm, S. A., and R. J. Chorley
   1964   The Fall of Threatening Rock. *American Journal of
          Science* 262 (9): 1041–54.

Schwerdtfeger, Friedrich W.
   1982   *Traditional Housing in African Cities: A Comparative
          Study of Houses in Zaria, Ibadan, and Marrakech*. John
          Wiley, New York.
Scully, Vincent
   1972   *Pueblo. Mountain, Village, Dance*. Viking, New York.
Seeden, Helga
   1982   Ethnoarchaeological Reconstruction of Halafian Occu-
          pational Units at Shamus-el-Din Tannira. *Berytus* 30:
          55–95.
   1985   Aspects of Prehistory in the Present World: Observations
          Gathered in Syrian Villages from 1980–1985. *World
          Archaeology* 17:289–303.
Serageldin, Mona
   1982   Planning for a New Nubia, 1960–1980. In *The Changing
          Rural Habitat*, edited by Brian Brace Taylor. Aga Khan
          Award for Architecture, Singapore.
Shapiro, Jason S.
   1997   Fingerprints on the Landscape: Space Syntax Analysis
          and Cultural Evolution in the Northern Rio Grande.
          Ph.D. dissertation, Department of Anthropology,
          Pennsylvania State University.
Simmons, Leo W., ed.
   1942   *Sun Chief: The Autobiography of a Hopi Indian*. Yale
          University Press, New Haven, Conn.
Simmons, Marc
   1979   History of Pueblo-Spanish Relations to 1821. In *Handbook
          of North American Indians*, vol. 9: *The Southwest*, edited
          by Alfonso Ortiz, pp. 178–93. Smithsonian Institution,
          Washington, D.C.
Stanislawski, Michael B.
   1973   Ethnoarchaeology and Settlement Archaeology. *Ethno-
          history* 20:375–92.
Steadman, Sharon R.
   1996   Recent Research in the Archaeology of Architecture: Be-
          yond the Foundations. *Journal of Archaeological Research*
          4 (1): 51–93.
Stein, John R., and Stephen H. Lekson
   1992   Anasazi Ritual Landscapes. In *Anasazi Regional Orga-
          nization and the Chaco System*, edited by David E.
          Doyel, pp. 87–100. Maxwell Museum of Anthropology,
          Anthropological Papers, No. 5. University of New Mexico,
          Albuquerque.
Strum, Fred G.
   1990   Aesthetics of the Southwest. In *Pueblo Style and Regional
          Architecture*, edited by Nicholas C. Markovich, Wolfgang
          F. E. Preiser, and Fred G. Sturm, pp. 11–22. Van Nostrand
          Reinhold, New York.
Stubbs, Stanley
   1950   *Bird's-Eye View of the Pueblos*. University of Oklahoma
          Press, Norman.
Stubbs, Stanley, and W. S. Stallings
   1953   *The Excavation of Pindi Pueblo, New Mexico*. Mono-

graphs of the School for American Research, 18. University of New Mexico Press, Albuquerque.

Sullivan, Alan P., III

1974   Problems in the Estimation of Original Room Function: A Tentative Solution from the Grasshopper Ruin. *The Kiva* 40 (1–2): 93–100.

Swentzell, Rina

1976   An Architectural History of Santa Clara Pueblo. M.A. thesis, University of New Mexico, Albuquerque.

1988   Bupingeh: The Pueblo Plaza, in *El Palacio*, Winter.

1990   Pueblo Space, Form, and Mythology. In *Pueblo Style and Regional Architecture*, edited by Nicholas C. Markovich, Wolfgang F. E. Preiser, and Fred G. Sturm, pp. 23–30. Van Nostrand Reinhold, New York.

1991   *Understated Sacredness*. In the Colores Series, a KNME-TV production. Albuquerque, N.Mex.

Titiev, Mischa

1944   *Old Oraibi: A Study of the Hopi Indians of Third Mesa*. Peabody Museum of American Archaeology and Ethnology Papers 22, no. 1. Harvard University Press, Cambridge, Mass.

1972   *The Hopi Indians of Old Oraibi: Change and Continuity*. University of Michigan Press, Ann Arbor.

n.d.   Household Census of Oraibi Done in 1933–34. Transcription and computerized database in possession of Dr. Jerrold Levy, Department of Anthropology, University of Arizona, Tucson.

U.S. Census of Population

1900   Population Census Schedules: Moqui Indian Reservation. National Archives of the United States. Microfilm Roll T623, Tape 48. Washington, D.C.

Varien, Mark D., and Ricky R. Lightfoot

1989   Ritual and Nonritual Activities in Mesa Verde Region Pit Structures. In *The Architecture of Social Integration in Prehistoric Pueblos*, edited by W. D. Lipe and Michelle Hegmon, pp. 73–88. Occasional Papers of the Crow Canyon Archaeological Center, No. 1. Crow Canyon Archaeological Center, Cortez, Colo.

Varien, Mark D., et al.

1996   *Southwestern Colorado and Southeastern Utah Settlement Patterns:* A.D. *1100–1300*. University of Arizona Press, Tucson.

Vivian, Gordon, and Tom W. Mathews

1965   *Kin Kletso: A Pueblo III Community in Chaco Canyon, New Mexico*. Southwest Parks and Monuments Association, Technical Series 6 (1).

Ware, John, and Eric Blinman

in prep.   Archaeology, Historical Ethnography, and Pueblo Social History. MS in possession of the authors.

Watson, Patty Jo.

1979   *Archaeological Ethnography in Western Iran*. Viking Pub-

lications in Anthropology No. 57. University of Arizona Press, Tucson.

Webb, William, and Robert A. Weinstein

1973   *Dwellers at the Source: Southwestern Indian Photographs of A. C. Vroman, 1895–1904*. Grossman, New York.

White, Leslie A.

1962   *The Pueblo of Sia, New Mexico*. Bureau of American Ethnology Bulletin no. 184. Smithsonian Institution, Washington, D.C.

Whiteley, Peter M.

1985   Unpacking Hopi "Clans": Another Vintage Model Out of Africa? *Journal of Anthropological Research* 41:359–74.

1986   Unpacking Hopi "Clans" II: Further Questions about Hopi Descent Groups. *Journal of Anthropological Research* 41:69–79.

1988   *Deliberate Acts: Changing Hopi Culture through the Oraibi Split*. University of Arizona Press, Tucson.

1994   Review of *Orayvi Revisited: Social Stratification in an "Egalitarian" Society*, by Jerrold E. Levy. *Anthropos* 89: 286–87.

Wilcox, David R.

1975   A Strategy for Perceiving Social Groups in Puebloan Sites. In Chapters in the Prehistory of Eastern Arizona 4. *Fieldiana: Anthropology* 65:120–59.

1982   A Set-Theory Approach to Sampling Pueblos: The Implications of Room-Set Additions at Grasshopper Pueblo. In *Multidisciplinary Research at Grasshopper Pueblo, Arizona*, edited by William A. Longacre, Sally Holbrook, and Michael W. Graves, pp. 19–27. University of Arizona Anthropological Papers 40. University of Arizona Press, Tucson.

Wilk, Richard R., and William L. Rathje

1982   Household Archaeology. *American Behavioral Scientist* 25:617–39.

Wilshusen, Richard H.

1989   Unstuffing the Estufa: Ritual Floor Features in Anasazi Pit Structures. In *The Architecture of Social Integration in Prehistoric Pueblos*, edited by W. D. Lipe and Michelle Hegmon, pp. 89–112. Occasional Papers of the Crow Canyon Archaeological Center, No. 1. Crow Canyon Archaeological Center, Cortez, Colo.

1991   Early Villages in the American Southwest: Cross-Cultural and Archaeological Perspectives. Ph.D. dissertation, University of Colorado, Boulder.

Winship, George Parker

1896   The Coronado Expedition, 1540–1542. *Bureau of American Ethnology Annual Report*, 14, for the years 1892–1893.

Wyckoff, Lydia L.

1985   *Designs and Factions*. University of New Mexico Press, Albuquerque.

Index

abandonment, 3, 27, 33, 111, 143n; of houses, 94–95, 97–100; of kivas, 92–94, 96; at Orayvi, 90–91; partial, 4, 38; of rooms, 15, 59, 69–70, 106–7; scavenging and, 30–31; social organization and, 31–32

aboveground structures, 7

Acoma, 10, 24, 32, 36, 48, 50, 111–12

Adams, E. Charles, 17–18, 48

aerial photographs, 44, 82, 83, 91(fig.), 97, 99–100, 102, 129(table)

agriculture, 37–38

Ahlstrom, Richard V. N., 44

Alkali Ridge, 7

Anglos. *See* Euroamericans

Antelope Kiva, 93

archaeomagnetism, 16

architecture, 12, 17; development of, 7–10; Euroamerican influences on, 48, 50, 51, 57, 61, 66, 76, 104; Orayvi, 6–7, 79–81, 87–102, 113, 115–19, 135–41(table); population and, 69–70; Puebloan, 4–5, 7–10, 21, 22–27; and social change, 31–33; technological changes and, 36–37

Arroyo Hondo Pueblo, 7, 10, 11(fig.), 16, 104, 113, 143nn; plaza use at, 18, 23; settlement growth at, 109–12; structure of, 107–9

Asvan (Turkey), 32

Bannister, Bryant, 41

Baptists, 36

Barrett, Samuel E., 83

Beaman, E. O., 44

Betatakin, 15, 17

Black Mesa, 36

Blue Flute Ceremony, 96, 98, 102

Bradfield, Wesley, 74, 83

building materials: scavenging, 29, 63(fig.), 99

buildings, 10, 60; construction of, 22–25; decay of, 27–29; maintenance and remodeling of, 29–31, 57; pueblo, 4–5; use-life of, 25–27. *See also* roomblocks; rooms

built environment, 10

Bureau of American Ethnology, 19, 38–39, 44

Carnegie Institution, 38, 39

Carpenter, Charles, 44, 57, 60, 65, 66, 68, 73(fig.), 82

catastrophic events, 29

cellar rooms, 52

censuses: of Orayvi, 20, 39, 41, 43, 47, 73, 76

ceramics, 4, 17

ceremonial areas, 17–18, 32; building around, 105–6, 112; at Orayvi, 86–87, 92–94

ceremonial cycle, 96, 98–99, 102

ceremonies, 17–18, 43–44, 86

Chaco Canyon, 7–8, 27–28

Chaco Phenomenon, 7–8, 143n

Chetro Ketl, 28

Chief Kiva, 79, 87, 93, 99

Chodistaas, 107

Civil War, 36

clan houses, 86

clans, 84; and households, 67–68; and Orayvi split, 84–85; and settlement organization, 31–32; and social organization, 47–48; spatial organization of, 54–55

coal, 36

Colton, Harold S., 41

construction, 14, 24; coordinated, 111–12; and use-life, 27–28. *See also* rebuilding

construction sequences, 13, 17

Coronado, Francisco Vásquez de, 4

cottonwood beams, 41

Creamer, Winifred, 16

Crown, Patricia, 14–16

cultural landscape, 10

Cyprus, 32

Dean, Jeffrey, 15, 17

decay: of structures, 27–29. *See also* deterioration

dendrochronology, 13; at Orayvi, 39–41; settlement history and, 15–16

deposition processes, 17

deterioration, 30, 95–96. *See also* decay

developmental cycle, 31, 90

Dohm, Karen, 50, 52

domestic group: developmental cycle of, 31, 90

doors, doorways, 13, 25, 59; at Orayvi, 63–64, 65(fig.), 69(table), 82, 143n

Douglass, Andrew F., 39–41, 44, 83

droughts, 35–36, 38
Duckfoot site, 13–14

earthquakes, 29
Eastern Pueblos, 24, 48, 50, 52, 55–56, 82. *See also by name*
economics, 38
education, 37
Eggan, Fred, 47
emigration. *See* migration
environment, 10, 28–29, 37–38
Euroamericans, 19, 32, 36–38; architectural influences of, 48, 50–51, 57, 61, 66, 76, 88, 104
extramural space, 18

factionalism, 143n; in Orayvi, 3, 18–19, 35, 37–38, 42–43, 79, 82; and settlement formation and abandonment, 31–32
families, 3, 14, 53; extended, 7, 31, 81; and houses, 12–13; nuclear, 53, 55; at Orayvi, 19, 20, 53–54; and Orayvi split, 94–95
farmland, 38
Fennemore, James, 44
Field Museum of Natural History, 44
First Beam Expedition, 40
First Mesa, 30, 32, 35–36, 73, 76, 78
floor artifacts, 13
Forrest, Earl, 83
Four Corners region, 10
Friendlies, 3, 37–38, 43, 79, 82, 84, 87; houses of, 90–91, 94–95, 98–99, 102; remodeling by, 88, 91–92
Fulani, 30

gender, 25
Ghana, 32
Gila Pueblo, 40
Gillespie, 52
Grasshopper Pueblo, 13, 15–18, 76, 104–5
Great Houses, 7–8, 10, 23, 143nn
Great Kivas, 7, 17, 86, 143nn

habitation rooms: at Hopi, 63–65
habitation units, 17
hamlets, 7
Hano, 35, 76
Hano Kiva, 99
Hargrave, Lyndon, 39, 41
Harrison, Benjamin, 37
Hassanabad (Iran), 30
hatchways, 13
Hawiwvi Kiva, 44, 87, 92, 98–99
Hegmon, Michelle, 17
Hill, James, 48–49
Hillers, John, 44, 57, 59, 71–72
historical data, 21
Ho'atvela, 37, 84–85, 92, 99, 102

Homolovi II, 104
Hopi, 10, 19, 30–31, 50; ceremonial areas at, 86–87; room use at, 63–66; social organization of, 47–48; Spanish period and, 35–36; wall construction at, 24–25
Hopi agency, 36
Hopi mesas, 6(fig.)
Horne, Lee, 32
Hostiles, 3, 37–38, 42, 79, 87; emigration of, 82, 84, 99; houses of, 88, 91–92, 94–95, 98, 102
Hotsitsvi Kiva, 93, 99, 100
households, 12, 31, 43, 56, 84, 104, 143n; clan affiliation and, 67–68; definition of, 6, 13–14; Hopi, 47–48; Orayvi, 53–54, 76–77, 115–19; Pueblo, 52–53; rebuilding within, 66, 104
houses, 6, 14, 21, 24, 47, 84, 143n; abandonment of, 90–91, 97–100; archaeological definition of, 12–13; architectural changes in, 88–90; and kivas, 93–96; multistoried, 50–52; new construction of, 79–80; at Orayvi, 23(fig.), 55–56, 71, 74(table); in prehistoric pueblos, 103–5; remodeling, 101–2; sizes of, 48–49

immigration. *See* migration
inheritance, 31
insects, 29
Iran, 30, 33
Is Kiva, 44, 92, 95, 98–100

James, G. W., 64
James House, Quincy, 41
Jemez, 49

kachina religion, 17–18
Kampmeier, Herman, 43
Katsin Kiva, 87
Keam, Thomas, 36
Keams Canyon, 36
Kidder, A. V., 13, 52
Kiet Siel, 15, 17
Kiqotsmovi, 38, 78, 82, 84, 95, 99, 102
kivas, 10, 17, 25, 32; Hopi, 23, 86; at Orayvi, 45, 87, 92–93, 95–96, 99. *See also* Great Kivas
Kividhes (Cyprus), 32
Kohler, Timothy, 14
Kroeber, Alfred, 33
Kwan Kiva, 44, 87, 95–96, 99

Laboratory of Tree-Ring Research, 40–41, 83, 99
ladder construction, 110
Laguna Pueblo, 32, 50
land, 33, 38; rights, 33
leadership, 38
Lekson, Stephen, 17
Levy, Jerrold, 75; social stratification research of, 19, 38, 42–43
Lightfoot, Ricky, 13–14
lineages: Hopi, 47–48

Lipe, William, 17
Little Colorado region, 18
Longacre, William, 17
Loololma, 37, 79
Lowell, Julie, 13
Lowry Ruin, 25

Main Plaza (Orayvi), 45, 77, 82, 86–87, 92, 107, 112; photos of, 22(fig.), 44, 122–23(table); population concentration at, 88, 94(fig.), 95, 98, 100, 105–6
maintenance: of buildings, 29–30. *See also* masonry structures
maps: of Orayvi, 19, 20, 38–40(fig.), 42(fig.), 45, 49, 55, 57, 64, 70, 85, 93(fig.), 94(fig.), 97(fig.), 101(fig.)
Maraw Kiva, 93, 99
masonry structures, 27; construction and maintenance of, 22, 24–25; environmental deterioration of, 28–29
matrifocal extended families, 53–54
matrilineal extended families, 53
Maya highlands, 31, 33
Mennonite church, 79, 106
Mesa Verde, 17, 27
Mexican-American War, 4
migration, 10, 99, 111; to and from Hopi, 35–36, 76; to Orayvi, 53, 73–75; after split, 82, 102
Mindeleff, Cosmos, 21, 38–39, 54
Mindeleff, Victor, 30, 48, 54, 67, 78; maps of Orayvi by, 19, 20–21, 38, 40(fig.), 45, 49, 57, 64, 70; on pueblo construction, 23–25; "A Study of Pueblo Architecture: Tusayan and Cibola," 39
missions, 35–36
Morgan, Lewis Henry, 10, 12
Mormons, 36
Morovians, 36
mortar: mud, 24, 28
mud plaster, 30
Mug House, 17
multistoried structures, 14, 48, 107; architectural changes in, 63–65, 70(table), 75–76, 82; and house size, 50–52; prehistoric, 7, 8–11(fig.); and room size, 55–56
Munqapi, 38, 75, 78, 82, 84–85, 91, 95, 102, 143n
Museum of Northern Arizona, 41

Naasavi Kiva, 99
National Geographic, 38–39
natural processes, 5
Navajos, 36, 38
nawipti, 76
Nelson, Margaret, 33
New Archaeology, 17
New Orayvi. *See* Kiqotsmovi
nuclear families, 53, 55

oral tradition, 3
Orayvi, 10, 24, 30, 107, 112; anthropological research at, 19–20,

39–43; architectural change at, 63–66, 70–72, 79–81, 87–102; architecture of, 6–7, 12, 45–46; ceremonial areas, 86–87, 92–94; clans at, 54, 84–85; factionalism at, 18–19; household information at, 115–19; households at, 47, 52–53, 104; house sizes at, 49–50; Main Plaza at, 22(fig.), 112; new roomblocks at, 77–79; photographic analysis of, 57–62, 82–84; photographs of, 121–34; population of, 19–20, 69–77; population concentration at, 105–6; rebuilding at, 33, 66–68, 104; room function at, 62–66; room information from, 135–41(table); room size at, 55–56; settlement growth at, 77–79, 106, 109–10; Spanish period at, 35–36; split of, 3, 4, 18–19, 37–38, 82, 84
Orayvi Valley: entrenchment in, 37–38
Ortiz, Alfonso, 23
ownership, 32; clan, 54–55; of structures, 60, 67, 92, 97–98

Paaqavi, 37, 84–85, 92, 95, 99
Pecos, 13, 52
Pepper, Barbara, 43
photographs, 19; analysis of, 44–46, 143n; architectural change in, 58–62; of Orayvi, 20, 43–44, 57–58, 82–84, 121–34. *See also* aerial photographs
piki houses, 36, 79, 80(fig.)
pit structures, 7
planning, 24, 143n
plants, 29
Plaza C (Arroyo Hondo), 109, 112
plazas, 18, 22(fig.), 23; at Arroyo Hondo, 7, 10, 107, 109, 112; community-wide ceremonies and, 17–18. *See also* Main Plaza; Snake Dance Plaza
Polacca, 32, 33, 99
population, 7, 8; and architectural change, 31–32; factional split and, 19–20; of Orayvi, 6, 38, 53, 69–77; in prehistoric pueblos, 105–6; reconstructing, 14–15; and settlement patterns, 17, 18
Pot Creek Pueblo, 14–16
Powell, John Wesley, 44
prehistoric pueblos, 3–5, 12; houses in, 103–5; multistoried, 8–11(fig.); pattern of, 23–24; population reconstruction, 14–15, 105–6; settlement histories of, 15–17, 18
property. *See* ownership
prophecies, 38
Pueblo I period, 7, 13–14, 17
Pueblo II period, 7–8
Pueblo III period, 8, 10, 12, 18
Pueblo IV period, 8, 10, 12
Pueblo Bonito, 7, 9(fig.), 29
Pueblo people, 3; households of, 52–53; house sizes of, 48–49; and prehistoric ruins, 4–5
Pueblo Revolt, 35
pueblos, 4; architecture of, 12, 22–27; multistoried, 8–11(fig.); settlement histories of, 15–16. *See also* prehistoric pueblos; *by name*

railroad, 19
rainwater, 28, 30

rebuilding, 33, 63–66, 88, 91–92, 101–4. *See also* construction

recycling, 24

refuse. *See* trash deposition

Reid, J. Jefferson, 15, 76, 105

religion, 33. *See also* ceremonies; kachina religion

religious societies, 86

remodeling. *See* rebuilding

residence: and Orayvi split, 85–86

residential units, 14

residents: census information on, 43, 98. *See also* censuses

resources: access to, 38

Rio Grande, 10, 18, 111

Rio Grande Pueblos, 35, 36, 48, 50, 110. *See also* by name

rituals: abandonment, 107; construction, 24. *See also* ceremonial cycle; ceremonies

roads: and Great Houses, 7–8

rodents, 29

roof beams, 29

roofs, 18, 25, 28–30

Room Abandonment Measure, 16–17, 106–7

roomblocks, 23–24, 97, 109; abandonment of, 98–99, 106–7; at Duckfoot site, 13–14; new construction of, 77–80; at Orayvi, 38, 41, 70–71, 75–77, 86–87, 92, 95–96, 124–26, 143n; photographs of, 22(fig.), 44–45, 59(fig.), 60(fig.), 61(fig.), 62(fig.), 68(fig.), 72(fig.), 124–26(table), 127–29(table); and Second Beam Expedition, 39–40

room features, 13

rooms, 15, 27, 77; abandonment of, 106–7; architectural changes in, 58–59, 88–90; at Arroyo Hondo, 109–10; clan ownership of, 54–55; filling abandoned, 28–29; functions of, 24, 30, 62–68, 82; households and, 13–14; in houses, 24, 88; at Orayvi, 71–72, 74(table), 143nn; photographic analysis of, 57–62; sizes of, 13, 49–52, 55–56, 65–66, 88

room suites, 13

Sakwalenvi Kiva, 87, 99

Salmon Ruin, 18

San Juan Pueblo, 23, 52, 112

San Juan region, 111

Santa Clara, 23, 48–49

scavenging: and building deterioration, 30–31; of building materials, 29, 63(fig.), 99

schools, 36–37

Second Beam Expedition, 38–41, 83, 143n

Second Mesa, 30, 36, 73, 75–76, 78

Sekaquaptewa, Emory, 43, 86

settlement formation: and social factors, 31–34

settlement histories: of pueblos, 15–18

settlement patterns, at Arroyo Hondo, 109–12; growth, 12; at Orayvi, 77–79, 98, 106

settlement plans, 23–24

Sia, 49

Sichomovi, 52

smallpox epidemics, 35–36, 73, 75–76

Smithsonian Institution, 39, 44

Snake Dance, 38, 43, 96, 98, 102

Snake Dance Plaza (Orayvi), 86–87, 92–93, 96, 99, 106; photos of, 44–45, 79, 83, 126–27, 143n; population concentration at, 94–95, 98, 100

Snake Kiva, 87, 93

social integration, 17, 18, 31, 112

social organization, 43; and architecture, 10, 12, 17, 31–33; community level, 17–18; Hopi, 47–48

social processes, 5

social services, 33

social stratification: Levy on, 19–20, 38, 42–43

Songòopavi, 36, 74–76

Spanish period, 3, 4, 35–36

Stanislawski, Michelle, 31–32

Stephen, Alexander M., 67–68

stone quarrying, 24

storage structures, 7

structures: decay of, 27–29; use-life of, 25–27. *See also* buildings

Stubbs, Stanley, 38, 83, 99

"Study of Pueblo Architecture: Tusayan and Cibola" (V. Mindeleff), 39

suprahousehold groups, 17

Swentzell, Rina, 23

Talayesva, Don (Sun Chief), 41

Tawa'ovi (Pongovi) Kiva, 79, 93, 99–100

Tawaqwaptiwa, 3, 41, 79, 99

Taw Kiva, 87, 99, 101

technology: and architectural change, 36–37

terraces, 77

Tewa world, 23

Third Mesa, 3, 30, 35, 37, 75

three-sided cooking rooms, 79, 80(fig.), 81

timber, 25

Titiev, Mischa, 19–20, 38–40, 46, 54, 57; census by, 41–42, 76, 143n; clan information, 67, 84; Hopi social organization, 47, 53; maps by, 67, 70–71, 85, 93(fig.), 94(fig.), 97(fig.), 98, 101(fig.); room construction, 77–78

towns: Puebloan, 8, 10

trading post, 36

transportation: and architectural change, 36–37

trash deposition: in abandoned rooms, 29, 107; and settlement history, 16–17

tree-ring dates, 4, 109

Tsu Kiva, 99

tupu'bi, 79, 80(fig.), 81

Turkey, 32

Turkey Creek Pueblo, 13, 16–17, 103–4, 107

United States, 4, 36–37

U.S. Census, 38–39, 43

U.S. Indian Agency, 36
unit pueblos, 7, 8(fig.), 143n
University of Arizona Laboratory of Tree-Ring Research, 40
use-life: of structures, 25–27, 31

villages, 106; lateral movement of, 31–33, 77, 80
Voth, H. R., 79–80, 87
Vroman, A. C., 43, 66, 72

wagons, 36
wall bond/abutment studies, 13, 16
wall openings, 13
walls, 24–25; maintenance of, 29–30; structural decay of, 27–29
Walpi, 24, 28, 32, 45, 48, 112; abandonment of, 33, 99; clans and, 54–55, 67; roof construction at, 25, 77; room functions at, 62–63

Western Pueblos, 48, 50–51, 106. *See also by name*
Whiteley, Peter, 38, 48, 53, 84, 92
Whittlesey, Stephanie, 76, 105
Wiklapi Kiva, 99
Wilshusen, Richard, 7
windows, 25, 82
world view, 12, 23

Yellowjacket site, 8(fig.)
Yokioma, 3
Young, Stuart M., 83

Zuni, 18, 30–33, 39, 45, 48; abandoned rooms at, 28, 107; construction at, 24–25; and Hopi, 35–36, 76

About the Author

Catherine M. Cameron is an assistant professor of anthropology at the University of Colorado in Boulder. She has worked in southwestern archaeology for the past two decades. During the late 1970s and early 1980s, she was part of the National Park Service's research project in Chaco Canyon, where she directed analysis of chipped-stone tools. In the 1980s, she directed chipped-stone analysis for the Black Mesa Project in northeastern Arizona. From 1992 to 1995, she was a staff member on the President's Advisory Council on Historic Preservation. Cameron's research interests focus on prehistoric population movement, vernacular architecture, regional abandonment, and the development of social complexity. Currently, she is investigating the far northwestern frontier of the Chacoan Regional System at the Bluff Great House in southeastern Utah. Cameron also maintains a strong interest in archaeological ethics and public archaeology. Cameron's publications include *The Abandonment of Settlements and Regions: Ethnoarchaeological and Archaeological Approaches*, edited with Steve A. Tomka; an issue of the *Journal of Anthropological Archaeology* (vol. 14, no. 2, 1995: "Migration and the Movement of Southwestern People," ed. Cameron) that brings together a range of analyses of the late-thirteenth-century movement of people from the Four Corners region to the Rio Grande; a 1996 paper, "Observations on the Pueblo House and Household," in *People Who Lived in Big Houses* (1996), edited by Gary Coupland and E. B. Banning; and an issue of the journal *Nonrenewable Resources* (vol. 6, no. 2, 1997) that looks at destruction and preservation of archaeological sites worldwide.